A SPORTING HISTORY OF
THE AMERICAN CENTURY

BY ROBERT LIPSYTE AND PETER LEVINE

Turner Publishing, Inc.
ATLANTA

Library of Congress Cataloging-in-Publication Data
Lipsyte, Robert.
Idols of the game: a sporting history of the American century /
by Robert Lipsyte and Peter Levine. — 1st ed.
p.   cm.
ISBN 1-57036-154-1 (alk. paper)
1. Athletes—United States—Biography. 2. Sports—United States—Sociological aspects.
I. Levine, Peter.   II. Title.
GV697.A1L567   1995
796'.092'2—dc20
[B]   95-18929
CIP

Published by Turner Publishing, Inc.
A Subsidiary of Turner Broadcasting System, Inc.
1050 Techwood Drive, N.W.
Atlanta, Georgia 30318

Distributed by Andrews and McMeel
A Universal Press Syndicate Company
4900 Main Street
Kansas City, Missouri 64112

First Edition
10 9 8 7 6 5 4 3 2 1

Printed in the U.S.A.

FOR THE TRUEST IDOLS OF ALL OUR GAMES:
THE PARENTS, COACHES, AND ATHLETES WHO TEACH
OUR CHILDREN THAT WINNING IS NOTHING
WITHOUT THE JOY, THE HEALTH, AND THE INSPIRATION
THAT LIE IN THE HEART OF SPORT.

TABLE OF CONTENTS

INTRODUCTION

THIS JOURNEY BEGINS WITH THE OPENING OF AN ELEVATOR DOOR. A STOOPED, old man shuffles forward. His eyes are dull and downcast in a puffy face. He is uncertain of his footing. His hands, dangling at his sides, are trembling. He seems lost in his clothes. He shuffles out to the hallway.

The small group waiting to greet him gasp; this is not the shuffle they remember, the fancy footwork that confused George Foreman and Smokin' Joe Frazier. Those steps choreographed a dazzling dance through the sixties and seventies that carried this man, Muhammad Ali, into the hearts and minds of his generation.

In the group is historian Peter Levine, who feels sad for the former champion whom he has never met but admired for thirty years; this man, who in the midst of assassinations and social upheaval inspired a generation of young people out to change the world, or at least stop a war.

Ali's eyes flick up at the group and a light goes on. His head rises slowly from the collar of his white dress shirt. His massive chest and shoulders swell; they seem to fill the black suit jacket. Ali is growing larger, younger before their eyes.

They move into a hallway outside an auditorium at Miami University in Ohio. They are at an academic conference to discuss Ali's life and impact, and although he was invited, no one was absolutely sure Ali would show up.

Enter Levine's friend, Robert Lipsyte, the sportswriter, who has covered Ali for thirty years. He hugs the champ, then introduces him to Levine. "A great historian," says Lipsyte. He recalls a joke from the old days and adds, "the next white hope."

A smile drains the champ's puffiness. "Looks to me," says Ali, "like the great white dope."

Levine and the group explode with relief and laughter. This is the Ali that lives in their minds, and he responds to their memories. Ali is suddenly the robust 6-feet, 3-inches of his prime as he shouts, "Let's go, here I am, still pretty...." He leads them into the auditorium as if he were swaggering into the arena for a heavyweight title fight.

The crowd leaps to its feet, roaring. Another standing ovation for The Greatest.

Throughout that day and the next, Ali listened to lectures recalling his history, upbringing, religion, politics, and his times. He smiled, nodded, and occasionally nodded off. Once or twice he raised a mock threatening fist at an imagined insult. Fashioning the ultimate critique, he snored loudly. Whatever he did was considered brilliant commentary; the professors and townsfolk were thrilled to be in his presence, waiting patiently for autographs and to pose for snapshots. Ali, in turn, was endlessly generous, signing anything offered with a careful if shaky hand, reminding nervous shutterbugs to take off their lens caps, chatting in a hoarse and whispery voice.

Ali basked in the attention yet took it for granted because he was comfortable in his role as idol; he meant something special to these people because they had found, in his life, clues to understanding their own. Nevertheless, it was obvious that Ali was frequently bored or surprised by the information and analysis coming from the stage. It seemed as though he often knew less than those assembled—or cared less than they did— about everything else that had been going on socially, culturally, and politically during those frequently turbulent years in which he won and lost the title three times and became the most famous face on the planet.

Like most of the people at the conference, Levine and Lipsyte spent considerable time monitoring Ali's reactions and talking about him, their conversation continuing long after the conference was over. They gossiped about his wives and girlfriends, his toughest fights, speculated on his current physical condition, and tried to solve the mystery of how a simple man with simple goals became such a complex of symbol—fueling our imaginations and filling our personal and cultural needs even before his own beliefs and principles matured and solidified.

We compared him to other athletic heroes and wondered what it was that lifted one above all others, out of the game itself and into the larger social arena. It all evoked memories of childhood when, in different New York neighborhoods, we had argued over whether Mickey Mantle of the Yankees, Willie Mays of the Giants, or Duke Snider of the Dodgers was the best centerfielder. It's an argument that rages still among those of a certain age. Yet there is no question that of the three, Mantle has become the most enduring symbol of that era. How did that happen? Did we choose him or was he given to us? And why?

Our attempts to answer such questions, part dormitory bull-session and part talk-radio yammer, became warm-ups for this book. We came to think that while our idols may be entertaining and provocative in their own right, while they are indeed often fascinating individuals with rich personal stories, all tend to become less important as people than as symbols. They tell us about ourselves—in this case about the promise and problems of American life in the twentieth century.

Look at the very different way we treated our original "Babes" Ruth and Didrikson for a glimpse of gender politics. Or the different ways Americans of different classes and races responded to the poundings John L. Sullivan, Jack Johnson, and Joe Louis handed out to their victims.

See Arnold Schwarzenegger pump iron for the President's Council on Physical Fitness and Sport one moment, then *terminate* a generation of movie stunt actors the next.

Watch Michael Jordan slam-dunk hamburgers for McDonald's at

$900,000 per thirty-second spot on Super Bowl Sunday while young boys who want to "be like Mike" rob and kill for his Nike Air Jordans.

Each of our idols is unique, yet all experienced life in ways that illuminate the history and culture of their times. Although not all came up swinging or dribbling from the slums, their stories suggest how sport can empower not only individuals, but entire classes, races, and generations of people—even those, perhaps especially those, who have been denied the full opportunities of American life.

From John L. Sullivan's last bare-knuckle brawl through Muhammad Ali's first title fight, to Martina Navratilova's final, emotional appearances on the tennis tour, these idols' stories weave vivid threads through the tapestry of America's transformation from producer to consumer culture. Their careers reveal the development of American sport as part of a leisure and communications revolution that began at the turn of the century and continues as we move into the next millennium. Because their lives helped, in part, to shape our values, habits, and, arguably, the content of our character, no full understanding of America is possible without an understanding of its sports idols.

And there is, obviously, no one right "take" on them. Our idols can have different meanings for different groups of people, even serve contradictory social and political agendas. Independent of their own intentions and beliefs—sometimes even counter to those intentions and beliefs—idols can be co-opted to represent both the dominant culture and the concerns and interests of outsiders.

At the heart of this relationship is a certain presumption made by Americans. We have come to believe that sport exerts a positive force on the national psyche; that competitive games are not only physically and emotionally healthful for individuals, they form the crucible of our country's soul and the theater of its energy and power.

In the sports arena, we believe our children will learn courage and self-control, and our most beautiful and gifted young people will be transformed into role models of the work ethic, of masculinity, femininity, good character, style, and success. Our idols will show us the way, and through their lives we will come to understand how Americans have both criticized and celebrated the culture that created them.

But we also need to appreciate the sheer joy they give us, the reason they are celebrated in the first place. When we remember the blur of Jim Thorpe breaking tackles on a romp downfield, Jackie Robinson barrelling home, Billie Jean King racing to net, or the breathtaking ballet of Michael Jordan rising above the rim, we are thrilled anew by the transcendent beauty, even the spiritual fulfillment, that is possible through sport.

This, too, is no simple pleasure; sometimes our fascination with idols can warn us of empty places in our culture and our soul.

The sixteen idols chronicled here are, obviously, our choices. There are only three women. America has lionized the male athlete to the female athlete's disadvantage; since there is a definite misogynist streak in the sensibility of the big-time locker room and its boys-will-be-boys rationale. Five of the sixteen are African-Americans, one is part–Native American. This represents a large percentage of non-whites, which is appropriate given that the book spans the twentieth century and black domination of the major spectator sports is fairly recent. Of the twelve white athletes here, seven are what might be termed "ethnics"—recent immigrants or first or second generation Americans—another clue to the importance of sports as a fast track to becoming an American.

You probably have your own roster of idols or at least think we should drop a couple of ours and add a few of yours. No argument there. But we do think this cast of characters is equal to the great tale about to unfold in the pages that follow of America seeking to find itself.

We begin with the *Great White Hopes*—John L. Sullivan, Jack Johnson, and Jim Thorpe. All lived in a time when Irish immigrants, Black freedmen, and unassimilated Native Americans were considered a threat to the sons of the White Anglo-Saxon Protestant founders who were being "over-civilized," perhaps even feminized, by the close of the frontier. Sports became the artificial arena in which to encourage the bursting spirit of a new nation flexing its muscles at home and abroad. It was also a way of taming its new citizens.

The stereotype of the American "sitcom family" may have been created during *The Golden Age*. There was the coach, like Knute Rockne, who became our father who knows best, and there were the lusty if some-times dim males with their appetites, and the females who would feed them, physically and emotionally. As sports was being professionalized, balls were put in the hands of boys and snatched from girls. It was fine to aspire to be a Babe Ruth—an athlete was a super-male—but don't be like his namesake, Babe Didrikson, in those days when a great female athlete was seen as something less than a total woman.

The greatest sustained period of crisis in the American century—from the Great Depression through World War II produced two of our most mythologized idols: Joe Louis and Jackie Robinson—*Credits to the Race*. Louis's rise to heavyweight champion and black icon made America confront racial discrimination even as it promoted the fighter as a hero against racist Nazi aggression. Louis helped open the door for Robinson, and major league baseball's first black player in the twenti-eth century himself became a trailblazing symbol of possibility and pride to African-Americans.

In *Fairways to the Future*, we follow the promise of post–World War II America on those sunny afternoons in the fifties when everything seemed possible, and Mickey Mantle, Arnold Palmer, and Vince Lombardi enabled us to roam centerfield, the golf course, and the grid-iron vicariously—three patches of green lawn that symbolized the pros-perity of a country seemingly without limits.

It is in *The Whole World is Watching* that we begin to see some of those limits. Muhammad Ali and Billie Jean King struggled through the turbulent sixties, a time in which sport as well as the larger culture con-fronted the inequities of race, sex, and class. For the authors it's no wonder, after attending the conference in Ohio, that Ali is the subject of the longest chapter.

In *Postmodern Idols*, more complex characters emerge. Michael Jordan is a commercial hero to those who sell sneakers, a moral hero to those who see his baseball dreams as a meaningful challenge, and an amoral hero to those who maintain that he stands for nothing but himself. Arnold Schwarzenegger and Martina Navratilova, each immigrants who changed themselves and their chosen sport, bring the story of the century full circle: in finding the meaning of America for themselves they renewed it for others, as newcomers so often do.

This story is a continuum; it does not end on the last page, not as long as we find in sports this beautiful, false, ephemeral, ennobling, corrupting, inspirational world. It is a sweaty Oz and it is bone real. Its idols, at their best, give us the heart to go the distance, to be the best that we can.

For our idols are us, the reflection of America's dream of itself.

PART I

GREAT WHITE HOPES

CHAPTER ONE

JOHN L.
SULLIVAN

IT WAS HELL AT HIGH NOON. UNDER A BLISTERING MISSISSIPPI SUN, TWO OF THE toughest men in America, John L. Sullivan and Jake Kilrain, stood toe to toe and slugged it out with bare hands for the heavyweight championship of the world. The match had started briskly enough, the old gunfighter Bat Masterson shouting "Time," the two boxers striking brief poses before lunging at each other. Sullivan, the champion, supposedly washed up, debauched beyond repair, missed with a left, and the challenger, a clean-living family man, grabbed him around the neck and rolled him over his hip to the ring floor. A crowd of five thousand politicians and pickpockets, lowlifes and literateurs, roared, exchanged money, and stomped in the boot-sucking mud.

In the fifth round, the challenger drew first blood with a jab to the champion's nose. Furious, Sullivan unleashed his deadly right and knocked Kilrain down. He took over now, stalking the challenger and sneering, "Fight like a man," words and tones Muhammad Ali would use almost a century later. The challenger wisely danced away. He decided to wait until the champion made a mistake; like most everyone

else, he had underestimated the older man's strength and will to win.

Some rounds lasted as long as fifteen minutes, some only a few seconds as Kilrain, weakening, dropped to one knee to end a round. By the forty-fifth round, both men were staggering through pools of their own blood, sweat, and vomit. Their cornermen slapped them alert, held bottles of water and whiskey to their lips, and closed their cuts with mud and ointments. They fought for 2 hours, 16 minutes, and 13 seconds in a haze of heat that rose above 100 degrees. In a noisy storm of bloodlust, the twin engines of American sport—money and macho—kept them going.

By the seventy-fifth round the champion, the Great John L., incredibly fresh and dominating, was hammering Kilrain at will. It would be the last round: the challenger couldn't—wouldn't—come out for the seventy-sixth. His second threw in the sponge: it was over.

Brutal, thrilling, and illegal, that last bare-knuckle prize fight on July 8, 1889, was also a turning point in the history of American sport. It was the beginning of the modern age of sports spectaculars in which a single event starring larger-than-life athletes could stir people and capture the spirit of its time. It was only a prize fight, and yet it came to symbolize an era. Two sons of Irish immigrants hitting each other struck a national nerve because their fight had broader implications; it was about ethnicity, race, masculinity, commercialism, and survival of the fittest.

The next day's *New York Times'* headline, "The Bigger Brute Won," may have been condescending, but it was also on the front page. And within weeks, America was singing about the fight.

> His colors are the Stars and Stripes
> He also wears the green,
> And he's the grandest slugger that
> The ring has ever seen.
> No fighter in the world can beat
> Our true American,
> The champion of all champions
> Is John L. Sullivan!

John L. Sullivan was America's first great sports idol. The image of his power symbolized what we thought we were all about on the eve of the twentieth century—a newcomer nation with the boundless strength and determination necessary to hammer our way to the top.

Sullivan was by turns a braggart, drunkard, racist, and wife-beater. But his mighty right fist, as one sportswriter of his time wrote, was "like the clapper of some great bell that ... boomed the brazen message of America's glory as a fighting nation from one end of the earth to the other."

Like the Great John L., America was going to be heavyweight champion of the world, and no henpecked do-gooders, no women whining for the right to vote, no unwashed immigrants, were going to slow us down. That's what the politicians, journalists, and businessmen said, and it got them elected, sold their papers, made them rich.

John Lawrence Sullivan believed it all, too. He was born on October 12, 1858, two weeks before the birth of his future friend Theodore Roosevelt, the twenty-sixth president, and one year before a young British naturalist named Charles Darwin published *On the Origins of Species*.

Talking about tortoises, Darwin outlined his theory of evolution by natural selection. It didn't take long for writers, politicians, and businessmen both in England and the United States to embellish it for their own purposes. Life among human beings, they insisted, was a struggle in which only the strongest of the species survived and passed on their dominant traits to the next generation—a useful rationalization to explain their exploitation of blacks, immigrants, and working people like the Sullivans.

The misuse of Darwinism cut both ways. The Great John. L., who claimed he could "lick any son of a bitch alive," who trumpeted a clarion cry of renewal, who became a symbol of masculinity and white Anglo-Saxon American might, also empowered the visions and dreams of the very immigrants who seemed to threaten it.

John L. Sullivan was born into a time of "no dogs or Irish allowed" signs and low paying, backbreaking jobs. If he had merely worked hard like his dad, Mike, a hod-carrier from County Kerry, Ireland, he would have lived and died in the Boston neighborhood of Roxbury, finding comfort in a saloon world of drinking and sports where bare-knuckle boxing was the ultimate test of one's manhood.

Off limits to "decent" women who were supposed to be home raising the brood, it was a world of loud camaraderie and violent confrontation where a man's physical strength symbolized independence and worth. This was celebrated as real masculinity, not the oppressive, white-collar, middle-class version imposed by the captains of industry and middle managers who were in charge. As historian Elliott Gorn has pointed out, the Victorian-American definition of masculinity included "taking responsibility, controlling one's impulses, and resisting temptation."

It was in the saloons and music halls of the Irish ghettoes that working-class men could find relief from the conventions of sensibility and decorum that excluded them from jobs and schools and were used to justify discrimination. Here they found laughter, understanding, male togetherness, and a pecking order that excluded nagging women and pencil-necked bosses.

A man who could stand up to a punch in a bare-knuckle brawl was a real man, no matter how lowly his job or dim his prospects. Fighting was an American tradition, after all; when frontier men had a dispute, the first question was, "You want a fair one or a rough and tumble?" A fair fight meant no eye-gouging, no face-biting, and a third party to enforce the rules. In backwoods-anything-goes-fights, the mythology maintained, no one could beat the young Abe Lincoln.

Saloon keepers staged fights and became fight promoters with the financial support of the penny press, who covered the fights. They were always on the lookout for a promising young heavyweight, a good-looking banger who could deck a man with a single punch. The fact that fighting for money was illegal in many states—including Sullivan's home state of Massachusetts—only added to its appeal.

John L. fit the bill. He had spirit. He was bold and ambitious. He had a temper he loved to back up with his fists and was practically unbeatable in schoolyard brawls. When he went to work at age sixteen, he weighed

200 pounds and stood 5-feet, 11-inches tall. He was a big man for those days and was tough. He apprenticed as a plumber, tinsmith, and mason. He wouldn't take guff. He fought his way off every job.

Like so many Boston Irish kids growing up in the 1860s and 1870s, his heroes were baseball players like the Boston Red Stockings' ace pitcher Albert G. Spalding, who hurled his team to four consecutive championships in baseball's first professional league, the National Association of Professional Baseball Players. While the young Sullivan was earning up to twenty-five dollars a game as a first baseman and left-fielder for local semipro teams, Spalding was off to Chicago to captain the White Stockings, start his sporting-goods empire and, with the motto "Everything is possible to him who dares," help shape baseball into America's national pastime.

Sullivan later boasted that he turned down a contract from the Cincinnati Red Stockings, baseball's first professional team, in 1879. By that time he had decided to get paid for what he did for free and become a professional boxer. In a notice in the *Boston Daily Globe*, Sullivan challenged Jack Hogan of Providence for $250 a side.

That fight never happened, but in February 1880 Sullivan boxed in an exhibition that "made" his career. His opponent was Mike Donovan, eleven years older and forty pounds lighter, who was far more experienced—a boxer of finesse and teacher of pugilism who would someday be Teddy Roosevelt's personal sparring partner.

But on that wintry day, Donovan was the twenty-one-year-old John L.'s punching bag, his craftiness nullified by the novice's sheer speed and power. Sullivan missed more punches than he landed, but those that connected felt like a "sledgehammer," according to Donovan. By the fourth round, the last one, Donovan's nose was crushed, his right wrist broken, and thumb sprained. Donovan later said, "I had just fought the coming champion of the prize-ring."

Donovan returned to New York full of praise for the so-called Highland Strong Boy. The hype was spread in bars and gyms. The newspapers picked it up. By May, the *National Police Gazette* referred to Sullivan, who had yet to fight a pro match, as "the great pugilist of

Boston." A month later John L. challenged anyone in America, with or without gloves, for $500. That led to several bouts which he won easily, and a challenge to "any man breathing" for any amount between $1,000 and $10,000. Obviously, John L. now had big-time backers.

The legend had begun. The first great sporting hero was coming into national focus. Just in time.

Davy Crockett was long dead and the Alamo he died in would become a museum signifying America's lost manhood. According to the 1890 census, the western frontier no longer officially existed. Westward expansion was blocked by the Pacific Ocean. According to a young American historian named Frederick Jackson Turner, there was no more free, uninhabited land (the census taker had never counted Indians as inhabitants with title to the soil), a place between "savagery and civilization" in which mere men could transform themselves into the stalwart, strong Americans who would keep democracy alive and lead the country to global greatness. No longer was there a place where new immigrants, crowded into eastern American cities, could seek their own American dreams.

Politicians, preachers, and journalists also wondered out loud about the fate of the nation. Where would our masculine role models come from now that the frontier was gone? The land had been tamed and the Indian subdued; the "savages" who had tested the courage of settlers and soldiers were now a sullen, beaten pack relegated to hardscrabble reservations. What to do now with more than twenty million immigrants from southern and eastern Europe and Asia who poured into America between 1880 and 1924? Where were the new arenas to train and test the heroes America would need for the twentieth century, the American century?

Male heroes. White heroes. Local heroes.

It wasn't strictly an American problem. After all, Baron de Coubertin did resurrect the Olympic Games in 1896 as a way of getting French youth back into shape after losing the Franco-Prussian War.

But America's image of itself was based on the muscle and know-how of bold, lusty white men who had invaded and tamed a wilderness with gun and plow. The most enduring images of the late nineteenth century, the paintings of Frederic Remington, are of a mythical West of noble white cowboys and war-painted hostiles. Lost from memory were all the women on those prairie schooners and out in the fields, and the black slaves and Asian workers who provided so much of the nineteenth century's muscle.

Remington must have believed his own paintings, offering this solution to those who worried about the virility, dominance, and racial purity of white Anglo-Saxon Protestant America: "Jews, Injuns, Chinamen, Italians, Huns—the rubbish of the Earth, I hate—I've got some Winchesters and when the massacring begins, I can get my share of 'em, and what's more I will… "

The "rubbish" crowded into the cities they were building and began to demand—sometimes with strike and bomb—decent working conditions and a livable wage. The enhanced quality of life they were creating for the Remingtons was perceived as creating a threat to American manhood. Without sweaty, dangerous work, middle- and upper-class white men were becoming, according to end-of-the-century commentators, effeminate, nervous, slovenly, and slothful, dragged down by "overcivilization" and "conspicuous consumption."

Those who could afford it dabbled in the Japanese tradition of the Samurai warrior, went on safari with Teddy Roosevelt, and built "camps" on lakes in upper Michigan and around the Adirondacks that exist to this day as deluxe resorts. On more modest levels closer to home, they practiced the "strenuous life" by joining Boone and Crockett clubs to hunt and fish on weekends.

On a political level, there was an aggressive foreign policy that led to war with Spain and meddling in the internal affairs of countries as near as Cuba and as far away as China.

But it was sport that became the intense experience of choice; this new frontier, "the safety-valve of an overworked Nation," as one writer exclaimed, "artificial adventure, artificial colonizing, artificial war," as another put it, that would produce a "better formed race," America's new generations of "muscular Christians."

Teddy Roosevelt's praise of the "strenuous life," the work of social reformers to turn immigrants into Americans by teaching them baseball and basketball, and the efforts of a new breed of sports capitalist who promoted watching and playing games as a respectable choice in a developing culture of leisure, all contributed to an athletic explosion. There was professional baseball, college football, the birth of the country club, a bicycling craze, and a renewed interest in boxing.

No wonder John L. Sullivan became such an important symbol. He personalized the new sports boom as surely as later idols Babe Ruth, Billie Jean King, and Michael Jordan would become handy slap-on icons for the baggage of their times. But John L. came first. The way in which he was merchandised and lionized became the model for all who would follow. And we are still trying to pour our heroes into molds to suit our needs.

Of course, it didn't just happen. Sullivan's rise to international celebrity through an underworld sport was primarily the work of saloon keepers and newspaper editors with their eyes on the main chance and their fingers on the pulse of a new urban America.

When twenty-two-year-old John L. swaggered into Harry Hill's New York City saloon in 1881 to take on all comers for $50 a man in four-round matches under the Marquis of Queensberry rules—which basically called for padded gloves and timed rounds—he must have felt right at home. Hill's saloon was bigger than the Roxbury pubs of John L.'s youth, yet it offered its male patrons the same opportunity to toast, boast, wager on dog-fights, rat-baiting and boxing matches, ogle show girls, and pick up prostitutes. It was a watering hole for the sporting set of hustlers, gamblers, and wealthy swells, who to this day seem to take their greatest pleasures in slumming.

On a good night at Hill's, one might run into the great impresario P. T. Barnum, the inventor Thomas A. Edison, the writer Oscar Wilde, and the judges, police chiefs, and hoodlum bosses who made sure there were no raids or robberies.

Among those who frequented Hill's was Richard Kyle Fox, an Irishman who owned the *National Police Gazette*, one of America's most popular newspapers, a combination *National Enquirer* and *Sporting News*. The *Gazette* sold one hundred fifty thousand copies a week, its shocking pink pages filled with pictures of undressed women, train wrecks, hangings, and titillating stories of murder and illicit sex.

Fox was a tabloid journalism visionary. He thought that sport—particularly boxing—would appeal to his working-class audience and build circulation. He spent weeks "steaming up" a championship fight between Paddy Ryan and Joe Goss with records, statistics, training camp gossip, and profiles. It was innovative—and a smash. The *Gazette*'s coverage of the fight, complete with inside stories and sketches, sold over 400,000 copies nationally and changed journalism. Joseph Pulitzer and William Randolph Hearst were quick to make the sports page an essential section of their big city dailies, and with that steady coverage and tacit approval, sport itself became an integral and accepted part of urban leisure.

In the interest of selling newspapers, Fox became boxing's most important promoter. His support of the Marquis of Queensberry rules was part of his effort to bring a measure of control and respectability to the sport even as his newspaper emphasized its blood and gore.

Many people believed at the time—and still do—that the Queensberry rules actually made boxing more dangerous. The padded gloves protected fragile hand bones but didn't do much for a brain rattled inside the skull by a hard punch. With gloves on, fighters were likelier to throw more punches, harder punches, and such go-for-broke knockout punches as the hook and uppercut. Bare-knuckle fighters, who relied as much on wrestling holds as boxing techniques, often "pulled" their punches, especially in the later rounds when their hands hurt.

The three-minute rounds with one-minute rest periods only seem humane; this format actually took control of the fight away from the fighters and gave it to the referee, who was often in cahoots with the promoters who wanted shorter fights that could be packaged for indoor arenas.

In the bare-knuckle days, a fighter could drop to one knee to end the round or dance around an opponent for as long as his legs held out.

A fight would last until one man quit. With standardized-gloved fights of four or six or ten rounds, there was greater pressure to launch a brutal attack.

The hype hasn't changed since David whipped Goliath; whatever the rules, it's been the personalities of the fighters—even if only symbolic—that have sold the fight. Black-white matchups dominated the middle of the twentieth century, and as African-Americans came to dominate boxing, there would be battles between "good" and "evil," as clumsily hyped as wrestling matches. Nothing new there. Fox's *National Police Gazette* relentlessly promoted Sullivan as a raging beast who had to be beaten for the moral good of the country. The hype sold tickets.

It was Fox who arranged John L.'s first bare-knuckle championship fight against Paddy Ryan in 1882, selling the fight in his paper months before it took place and putting up $2,500 to back Ryan in the illegal match. Sullivan won the championship.

"When Sullivan struck me," Paddy exclaimed (or at least the *Gazette* reported he exclaimed, in its eight-page special illustrated edition), "I thought a telegraph pole had been shoved against me endways."

It was the start of a decade of hoopla orchestrated by Fox and thoroughly enjoyed by the "Boston Strong Boy." Sullivan's reign as heavyweight king was as much vaudeville and circus as it was fistiana. In fact, he sometimes barnstormed with acrobats and clowns and once toured the nation in "Honest Hearts and Willing Hands," a plodding melodrama written especially for him.

By the time he left the ring in 1892, Sullivan claimed to have made more than a million dollars—Michael Jordan money for the time. It was the railroad that made it all possible.

Binding America together with iron tracks, the railroad carried Sullivan, in one 238-day swing, through 24 states and 5 territories. He boxed 195 four-round exhibitions under Queensberry rules and rarely missed a chance to raise a glass in a whistle-stop tavern and bellow, "I can lick any man in the house," a local version of his trademark cry.

More than 100,000 people, mostly boys and men, came face-to-face with the champion during that tour; they could now boast that they had "met" the toughest man alive. For that tour alone, Sullivan earned more than $80,000, far more than any other professional athlete of the time and three times the annual salary of the President of the United States, Chester Alan Arthur. But who remembers him?

Although Sullivan made his fortune in carefully controlled exhibitions with timed rounds and padded gloves, it was his reputation as a brutal, bare-knuckle championship brawler that brought out the crowds. He defended his title twice in 1883 in Madison Square Garden fights promoted by Fox and hyped by the sporting press. Both fights were illegal, of course, and the second fight, against the Englishman Charlie Mitchell, was actually stopped by the New York police, either because they hadn't been properly paid off, or perhaps because they had been—to save the champ. Sullivan was fat, he may have been drunk, and for the first time in his career he was knocked down. Also for the first time, the crowd booed the Great John L.

America's idol of masculinity, like so many sports heroes to follow, had begun to believe his own press clippings: that he was invincible, a raging beast beyond everyday morality. Sullivan married Annie Bailey in 1883; she filed for divorce two years later accusing Sullivan of drunken rages, infidelities, and abuse. It was probably all true. Both sides brought their own character witnesses to court and, as still often happens, the rich jock celebrity won. Although they remained legally bound for the next quarter century, they never lived together again.

Sullivan was an alcoholic, alternating between periods of debauchery and sobriety. His weight fluctuated by as much as fifty pounds. His assembly-line sexual escapades would be a preview of Babe Ruth, Wilt Chamberlain, and Magic Johnson.

Thus, no one was surprised when, in 1888, the Boston Strong Boy, only thirty years old, suffered a total physical breakdown. He was in the hospital for weeks—his career and his life in jeopardy. Fox used Sullivan's collapse to further smear the champion's reputation and trumpet his own candidate for the title, Jake Kilrain, who was, according to the *Gazette*, everything that Sullivan was not: sober, respectable, reliable, a family man. He had become a fighter, the story went, not because he was a bully like Sullivan, but because he had been picked on as a clumsy kid and needed to learn to defend himself.

Fox fashioned a silver-and-gold studded championship belt and declared Kilrain the true heavyweight king. Newspapers lined up behind Sullivan or Kilrain and circulation soared. The *Gazette* ran a poem:

> A conq'ror brave and tried and true,
> whose record bears no stain,
> Our hearts and hands we give to you,
> our champion, Jake Kilrain.

But you can never count a real champion out. In what became a stirring saga of revival and manhood redeemed, John L. hauled his soggy bulk out of the hospital and staggered off to the upstate New York retreat of William Muldoon, a well-known wrestler, strong-man, and health guru. It was there that the intrepid reporter, Mrs. Elizabeth Cochrane Seaman, who wrote under the byline Nellie Bly, found them for one of her *New York World* exclusives.

John L. was at his charming best. He told Nellie Bly about being awakened at five o'clock every morning by Mrs. Muldoon's "singing cow," and he let her feel his muscle ("a rock," wrote Nellie Bly). Nellie found the Great John L. "half-bashful ... boyish ... dark, bright eyes ... soft, small hands..."

She was surprised to find beautiful wildflowers on the table, which he picked during his daily twelve-mile run-walks. And he admitted to her that although Muldoon's regime was "the worst thing going," it was leading him down the path of righteousness toward the title.

For all her chirpiness as a pioneer celebrity interviewer, Bly was a shrewd observer. She wrote: "Almost as soon as a boy learns to walk he learns to jump into position of defense and double up his fists."

The thirty-year-old man-boy she found on the farm may have seemed a contradiction to Fox's beast, but both versions were true. Like the modern athlete he preceded, Sullivan's arrogant air of entitlement and sometimes brutal quest for pleasure was only one side of his personality— he was still the Roxbury boy who could be easily flattered and intimidated by "class." And his willingness to suffer and sacrifice to get back into shape, his will to win, his hunger for the spotlight, would be replayed over and over by champions to come in every sport.

His trainer Muldoon's take that spring day in 1889 was simple, practical, and mythic. He told Bly: "It was a case of a fallen giant, so I thought to get him away from all bad influences and to get him in good trim."

And he did. The John L. Sullivan who fought under the blistering sun on that Mississippi field was in the best shape of his life. While the pine tar bubbled out of the grandstand planks and heat blisters popped up on the boxers' backs, he hammered Kilrain into a boxing footnote.

As a bare-knuckle prizefight, the match was illegal. Arrest warrants had been issued for both fighters. But in the routinely hypocritical ways of Victoriana, mayors and sheriffs could be paid off to turn a blind eye to vice and bluster routinely until the deed was done.

The fight had been scheduled for New Orleans, a fast-rising "sin city," but the governor of Louisiana swore he would stop it with the militia. Other governors offered troops, and between the politics and betting odds, the fight received international attention—Sullivan's name was appearing on the front pages as often as the sports pages.

Fox and the promoters arranged for railroad cars filled with fans to leave New Orleans at night, destination unknown. The secret site was the estate of a Richburg, Mississippi, lumber baron whose field was only a half-mile from the rail line.

The crowd tumbled out of the railroad cars at sunrise. The fight began around ten o'clock.

In Kilrain's corner were Mike Donovan, the famous boxing teacher who had first recognized Sullivan's talent, and Charlie Mitchell, the English heavyweight who had made Sullivan look bad during the worst of his drinking days. And guarding Kilrain's bottle, a key task, was none other than Bat Masterson, the old gunfighter from Dodge City.

Masterson, who was packing his iron that day, first became interested in boxing when he was Marshall Wyatt Earp's deputy. According to legend, it was Earp's custom to unstrap his gunbelt and whip wild cowboys with his fists while Masterson, armed, kept the cowboy's pards at bay. After the taming of Dodge, Masterson became a boxing promoter in Denver, and later came to New York to write sports.

But Mike, Charlie, and Bat couldn't do much for Jake Kilrain that morning (although Masterson tried, arguing with the referee to give Kilrain more time to recover between rounds). Muldoon had given the Strong Boy back his stamina, his powerful legs, his relentless attack, and his pride.

There was only one bad moment for Sullivan. In the forty-fourth round, he vomited the tea-and-whiskey he was drinking (smart-aleck reporters wrote that he vomited the tea and retained the whiskey) and seemed to lose energy. But he bounced back and continued to pound Kilrain's chest and face into a pulpy red mess. In fact, the heroism was Kilrain's—no one could understand what kept him going through seventy-five rounds in that 115 degree heat, absorbing awful punishment for more than two hours.

It was past high noon when Donovan threw in the sponge.

Sullivan would never be in such shape again, and the legal problems from that fight—he was actually arrested—drained much of the money he made from it. But he had hammered out his place in American history. The Strong Boy was Everyman's hero; he had flouted white Anglo-Saxon Protestant culture even as he picked its fruits. Yet he was also the Establishment's hero: he had gone straight, cleaned up his act, proven that anyone could get back up off the floor and be successful if he dared try hard enough.

Journalists gushed over him. Wrote Charles Dana of the *New York Sun*: "He has the strength of Samson and the fighting talent of Achilles. When he moves it is with a child's ease, and he hits with a giant's force.... If any one thinks that the physique of the human race is degenerating, let him consider the great John L."

Novelists used him as shorthand to promote their own agendas. In Abraham Cahan's 1895 *Yekl*, a Jewish immigrant in a sweatshop on New York's Lower East Side expresses his new American identity by telling fellow workers that when he was in Boston he "knew a feller" who was a friend of "John Shullivan's. He is a Christian, that feller is, and yet the two of us lived like brothers."

The message was that sport held possibilities for struggling immigrants, even if they weren't Irish. Few activities seemed so patently American. Where else were the values of competition and individual effort so transparently important—and rewarded? And even if you couldn't speak English or weren't a citizen, participation in sport, buying a ticket to a fight or a baseball game, rooting for one boxer over another, displaying your knowledge of the diamond, made you instantly American.

It also offered a splash of testosterone for the effete "brain-workers." E. L. Godkin, editor of the liberal, intellectual magazine *The Nation*, noted that John L. enjoyed the support of more than the "coarse and uneducated and vicious class ... Secret rills of sympathy" also "flow[ed] from higher sources." Some thirty years after the fight, Vachel Lindsay captured in verse what made the Boston Strong Boy America's idol of masculinity. Recalling his own childhood, when "Suffering boys were dressed like Fauntleroys" and "Louisa Alcott was my gentle guide," he wrote:

Then...
I heard a battle trumpet sound.
Nigh New Orleans
Upon an emerald plain
John L. Sullivan
The strong boy
Of Boston
Fought seventy-five rounds with Jake Kilrain....

So who could be surprised, a hundred years later, to see the current editor of *The Nation*, Victor Navasky, at a Mike Tyson championship fight at Atlantic City.

By the time Sullivan defended his title for the last time, in 1892, boxing was as respectable as it would ever get. The bout, against Gentleman Jim Corbett, was openly arranged by members of the elite Olympic Club of New Orleans. It was fought in an arena built especially for the fight rather than in a muddy meadow or on some floating barge. As one newspaper put it, "steady businessmen" and "society bloods... are eager and anxious to spend their wealth to see a glove contest."

Men of property in black tie mingled with the lower classes, even an occasional woman, in a crowd of 10,000 to see Corbett, a college-educated bank clerk who had never fought bare-knuckled, easily defeat the aging champion for a $50,000 prize. Fans gathered throughout the United States to hear the news coming over the telegraph wires. In New York, red and white beacons atop an office building, red for Sullivan, white for Corbett, signalled the result of each round.

Although he lost the fight, "the grandest slugger the world had ever seen" remained for many a promise that despite the close of the frontier, "overcivilization," and the immigrant "hordes," true Americans (the fact that Sullivan was born white in America eventually became more important than his Irish blood) would still rule the world.

American **men**, that is.

For women, it was still his-story, informed by the passion with which men rallied around the Great John L. and rushed to participate in sport. Men's growing passion for the physical was also fueled by mounting sexual fears. Writers of the time warned capitalists and white-collar workers left flabby and weak by desk jobs to steel themselves before they were overrun by women, by housewives raising effeminate "suffering boys," and by that small but vocal minority of the white middle class demanding the right to vote. Not to mention women moving out of the house and off the farm into professions formerly monopolized by men, especially in the clerical field. Living independently and eager to enjoy the new urban world, these women posed a threat to men with their very presence. And for those women with time and money, there were new opportunities to participate in sport.

Women were encouraged to see sport differently than men, as preparation for the private rooms of domesticity rather than the public sphere of business and politics. But some women viewed their participation as nothing short of revolutionary. Writing in *Munsey's Magazine* in 1901, Ann O'Hagan proclaimed that the "athletic girl" who played tennis, golfed, even rowed, at country clubs and colleges, challenged notions of the frail, weak female while promoting women's physical and mental health. And the great suffragette Elizabeth Cady Stanton declared that women were riding toward the vote on their bicycles.

Sullivan symbolically slammed the door on these female intrusions into a male world of power and dominance. Those who promoted sport as a male domain in which tough men were trained for real man's work concurrently denied women participation in any sports that would affect their "femininity." As the idol of American masculinity, Sullivan represented the extreme of what women were up against in their fight for full equality—in or out of the arena. The battle lines were drawn, to remain in place far into the twentieth century.

Sullivan never took a public stand on equality for women; he probably never even seriously considered it. On the subject of black equality, however, both by word and deed, he was outspoken. Despite public claims that he would meet any man alive if the price was right, he refused to fight black men. Such worthy challengers as George Godfrey, known as "Old Chocolate," and Peter Jackson, "The Black Prince," never got a chance. Even as Jim Crow laws and white racism dropped the lid on opportunities for African-Americans in and out of sport, there were occasional bouts between black and white boxers at the lower weight classes. In 1891, Jackson even fought Gentleman Jim Corbett to a sixty-one round, four-hour draw.

But not for the heavyweight championship of the world, the prize that personified the triumph of the fittest and the strongest. John L. was no scholar. He probably never discussed Charles Darwin or muscular Christianity. But he was a white American living at a time when most of his white countrymen believed that blacks were not their equal and did not deserve the opportunity to prove it. Sullivan declared he was willing to enter the ring with "all fighters—first come first served—who are white. I will not fight a negro. I never have and never shall."

When Jack Johnson became heavyweight champion in 1908, Sullivan—who had been traveling the country with Jake Kilrain reenacting their classic fight to standing-room-only crowds—became the front man for the syndicate that brought Jim Jeffries out of retirement as "The Great White Hope."

Despite his admitted "well-known antipathy toward the black race," Sullivan was at ringside in Reno, Nevada, on July 4, 1910, as a representative of *The New York Times*, when "Papa Jack" starred in the first major prizefight to be promoted as a race war.

CHAPTER TWO

JACK JOHNSON

A FEW HOURS BEFORE THE PRIZEFIGHT THAT WOULD CONFIRM HIS RETURN FROM exile, the once and future heavyweight champion Muhammad Ali sat in the darkened living room of a lakeside cottage outside Atlanta and watched Jack Johnson strut across a bedsheet tacked to a wall.

"This is my story," cried Ali, as the movie projector whirred and sixty-year-old documentary footage flickered on the sheet. "His fights are cancelled, too. Governors and Congress was involved. Threats against his life." He says to a reporter sitting nearby, "You notice Jack Johnson, Joe Louis, and me got the same kind of faces?"

Ali did not wait for an answer. He leaned forward as Johnson chased chickens to build up speed and stamina, challenged the top race car driver Barney Oldfield to a match, and went to jail on a trumped-up white-slavery charge.

"I was in jail for seven days for a traffic ticket," shouted Ali. He clapped his hands with delight as Johnson taunted an opponent in the ring. "What he say? I might say that tonight."

That night in Atlanta, October 26, 1970, there was little time for

talking as Ali quickly broke open Jerry Quarry's thin-skinned white face. The fight was stopped in the third round. George Plimpton, seated ring-side, recalls hearing Ali's trainer, Drew "Bundini" Brown, shout, "Jack Johnson's heah. Ghost in the house!"

By 1970, however, the ghost of Johnson had lost most of its power to scare white supremacists. The first black heavyweight champion was long dead, and his memory had been obscured by a hit play and movie, *The Great White Hope*, in which Johnson emerged as a flamboyant but basically decent man crushed by white oppression. Audiences in those sixties' days of racial rage and civil rights struggle found fiction more comforting than truth—Jack Johnson was a "bad nigger."

That highly-charged term means different things to different people. To white slave owners a "bad nigger" was like a "rogue bull" or a "rank horse," a piece of dysfunctional property. A "bad nigger" didn't do his job, talked back, was surly and uncontrollable. The slave master's biggest fear was that challenge to his authority would spread and the slaves would revolt. But to black slaves, as Al-Tony Gilmore has written, a "bad nigger" was a bold man who didn't react passively to the injustice of his condition. He was a fighter, a revolutionary.

The term "bad nigger" was a curse among whites and a compliment among blacks; even today the slang term "bad," meaning good or cool or admirable, comes from those days.

Johnson was also "uppity" and "smart." He was a dangerous character who wanted to live his life his own way at a time when Jim Crow laws were dismantling black progress. The color bar was firmly in place in American churches, schools, hotels, trains, and toilets. To create a rationale for discrimination, there were pseudoscientific studies claiming that blacks were mentally and physiologically inferior, that they were subhuman, savage, or childlike.

This propaganda campaign would be damaged if a black man beat a white man in the ring, especially since John L. Sullivan had done such a terrific job promoting himself and his championship as a symbol of virility and rough honor, as a protector of women and children. For all those young men who were leaving farms to come to the growing big cities of

America, Sullivan was the model of a poor boy who "made good" with his body—his only capital.

In 1875, three years before Johnson was born, a black jockey named Oliver Lewis won the first Kentucky Derby. Fourteen of the fifteen jockeys in the race were black. It was the continuation of plantation tradition; slaves raced their masters' mounts in betting races. In fact, many of the early "professional" athletes in America—jockeys, rowers, and boxers—were black slaves. Some even became the ultimate "free agents"—they won their freedom via athletic triumphs.

One black jockey, Isaac Murphy, won the Derby three times. The year of Murphy's first victory, 1884, Moses "Fleetwood" Walker became the first black man to play in baseball's major leagues. In 1899, a black cyclist, Marshall Taylor, won the professional world championship. He repeated in 1900.

But the black athlete's playing time in the nineteenth century arena was brief: Jim Crow laws were running him out of the ballpark. By 1894, blacks were forced out of major league baseball, not to return until Jackie Robinson broke in with the Brooklyn Dodgers in 1947. Black jockeys no longer rode mounts for white owners.

And by 1912, Johnson, the first black man to win the heavyweight boxing championship of the world, had been forced into international exile.

The North's victory in the Civil War brought with it real hope to many blacks. On their own, freed slaves found employment, built schools and churches, established mutual aid societies, and elected blacks to Congress. The thirteenth, fourteenth, and fifteenth amendments to the Constitution guaranteed freedom, citizenship, and, for black males at least, the right to vote. Government agencies like the Freedman's Bureau provided vocational training for former slaves while Radical Republican demands of "forty acres and a mule" for each newly freed slave, though unfulfilled, encouraged dreams of economic independence and full equality.

But the Republicans—the party of Abraham Lincoln, "the Great Emancipator"—sold them out with the agreement that became known as the Compromise of 1877, which withdrew federal enforcement of equal rights in exchange for the election of Republican Rutherford B. Hayes to the presidency. The pact, under the guise of states' rights, resulted in white terrorism—lynchings, beatings, rape, and race rioting.

It was a year after the Republicans' sellout, on March 31, 1878, that one of the twentieth century's least compromising black men, Arthur John "Jack" Johnson, was born into a world of restriction, discrimination, and humiliation. It scarred his roots and determined his future.

His parents, Henry and Tiny Johnson, did not suffer the sharecropper poverty of hundreds of thousands of Southern blacks after the Civil War. By the time Jack was born, Henry, a forty-year-old former Maryland slave, had worked his way to Galveston, the biggest city in Texas. As a school janitor he earned enough to own his own home and provide for his wife and five children, an impressive accomplishment but not uncommon to African-Americans given half a chance. Nevertheless, Galveston's black ghetto offered little promise of a brighter future. Like John L. Sullivan before him, Johnson wanted more than his father had, and like John L., he was born into a world with greater opportunities, however limited by racism and discrimination. Parents who knew nothing but slavery or the repression of their European existence were more willing than their children to passively accept the crumbs offered by their new freedom. But the new young citizens lusted after the full promise of American life and keenly felt its racial and class restrictions. The boldest met their frustrations head on; few were bolder than Jack Johnson.

Johnson was one of the first generation of free-born blacks. His mother remembered him as a sweet, sensitive boy who came home crying one day from school because he had been beaten up. She threatened a beating herself if he didn't go back and fight the bully. He did, of course, according to her story, and he won. Almost every champion's mother or father has told a similar story.

In his later years, Johnson turned out to be his own best mythologist. In his most vivid childhood memory, he claims to have traveled to New York, alone, at the age of twelve, to meet Steve Brodie, the man who claimed to have jumped off the Brooklyn Bridge. Although Brodie's boast was suspect, he became famous for it. Young Johnson traveled by rail and by boat, one time alone in a sailboat chased by "a monster shark twenty-three-feet long," according to his 1935 autobiography. He somehow made it to Manhattan, tracked down his hero, and hung out in the Bowery with Brodie before returning to Galveston, where he became famous as the boy who ran away to see the man who jumped off the bridge.

Most Johnson historians don't believe the story but find in it a clue to his character: he saw himself as a Horatio Alger hero with ambition, dash, vigor—all those prized American traits that bring fame and fortune by the final chapter. Like the young John L., young Jack had bought into the American dream; he believed Albert G. Spalding's promise that "Everything is possible to him who dares." Throughout his life, Johnson pushed the limits of American racism, seeking the pleasures he claimed as a human being, striving for goals his parents' generation believed to be out of reach.

Back in Galveston, Johnson, again like John L., drifted from one job to another—painter, bread baker, dockworker—finding little enjoyment and no future. And again like John L., he discovered that his natural gifts of strength and quickness could be the tools of a trade. But unlike Sullivan, who got to fight his opponents one at a time, Johnson had to begin with "battle royals."

It was brutal and humiliating. Young black men, as many as eight at a time, sometimes blindfolded or tied together, would brawl with no holds barred until only one remained on his feet. White men paid to watch, shouting racial epithets and throwing coins at the winner.

Johnson left no account of those early battles, but two black champions of the literary arena, the authors Richard Wright and Ralph Ellison, wrote about blacks fighting blacks for the pleasure of whites.

In the classic 1952 novel *Invisible Man*, Ellison's narrator, who has just graduated from high school, joins other young blacks to entertain the town's leading white males at a drunken party. Blindfolded, "everyone fought hysterically. It was complete anarchy. Everybody fought everybody else. No group fought together for long. Two, three, four, fought one, and then turned to fight each other, themselves attacked...."

I could no longer control my emotions. I had no dignity. I stumbled about like a baby or drunken man."

When it was over, the boys, sweaty and dirty, rushed to pick up their prizes; gold and silver coins scattered on a rug. But the rug was electrified. The audience found their painful contortions from the shocks hilarious.

"Then the men began to push us onto the rug.... We were all wet and slippery and hard to hold. Suddenly I saw one boy lifted into the air, glistening with sweat like a circus seal, and dropped, his wet back landing flush with the charged rug, heard him yell and saw him literally dance upon his back, his elbows beating a frenzied tattoo upon the floor.... When he finally rolled off, his face was gray and no one stopped him when he ran from the floor amid booming laughter."

In his 1937 autobiography, *Black Boy*, Wright and his friend Harrison, in Memphis, discuss an offer from white men to fight each other for five dollars. "To white men we're like dogs or cocks," says Wright. But Harrison wants money for a new suit.

"But those white men will be looking at us, laughing at us," Wright protests.

"What the hell," Harrison responds. "They look at you and laugh at you every day, nigger."

Eventually they decide to fight—but pull their punches. However, goaded on to "crush that nigger's nuts, nigger!" and to "hit that nigger," both forget their promise and start whaling away.

"The fight was on, was on against our will.... The shame and anger we felt for having allowed ourselves to be duped crept into our blows and our blood ran into our eyes, half blinding us. The hate we felt for the men whom we had tried to cheat went into the blows we threw at each other."

In the end, Wright wins but says, "I could not look at Harrison. I hated him and I hated myself...I felt that I had done something unclean, something for which I could never properly atone."

That theme of blacks fighting each other for money as whites enjoy the spectacle, the control, and sense of superiority, has been echoed throughout the history of boxing, particularly by black commentators.

It was made vivid in 1962, on the afternoon of the heavyweight championship fight between Sonny Liston and Floyd Patterson, two complex black men whose rivalry has often been unfairly reduced to a match between a "bad nigger" and an "Uncle Tom." Lipsyte tracked Malcolm X to a demonstration in Brooklyn and asked him what he thought of the fight.

"I'm pleased to see that the two best men in the sport are black," said Malcolm, then a leader of the Nation of Islam. "But they'll be exploited, of course, and the promoters will get all the bread. They let a Negro excel if it's going to make money for them."

By 1962, Malcolm X had already become a mentor to the very best man in the sport, then known as Cassius Clay, who within two years would be a force in boxing. The implications were not new, however; Jack Johnson would have understood everything that happened to Joe Louis or Muhammad Ali.

Like both of them, Johnson worked very hard to develop his boxing talent, and like both of them he rarely got credit for it. White commentators often refer to the "natural gifts" of black athletes, particularly fighters, as if they didn't have the mental ability to train and hone their craft or the emotional ability to be passionate about winning. It is a subtle way of labeling them "animals." Johnson became a great fighter by studying and by fighting, in and out of Galveston, up and down the West Coast, with occasional forays east to sharpen his skills working as a sparring partner for more experienced boxers. Against black and white opponents, both in legal exhibitions and, depending upon the city or state, illegal prize fights, Johnson won more than he lost. He also developed solid defensive skills, which are certainly part of a boxer's trade. Historian Randy Roberts suggests it was a good business practice; white fighters refused to fight blacks who carried the fight to them. It has been pointed out that defensive responses have traditionally been how African-American culture deals with whites, in the ring and out. Call it survival, call it finesse.

But everything else about Johnson was offensive, at least to most white men. Powerfully built, attractive to women, as bald as Michael Jordan,

"Papa Jack," as he liked to call himself, already exuded a confidence and enthusiasm that made good copy for fight promoters and boxing scribes—even as it increasingly troubled a white America intent on keeping blacks in their place.

Johnson flouted white expectations about how blacks should behave around whites. He relished public attention, dressed sharply, boxed in hot pink boxing tights that accentuated his manhood (he was known to stuff rags in his crotch to accentuate it further), flashed his gold teeth, affected a British accent, and carried on with white women in public, sometimes with more than one at a time.

None of this would have mattered, of course, if he hadn't been, like John L., a powerhouse puncher who could also absorb punishment. Johnson couldn't just be ignored or squashed. He was a gifted boxer who had worked hard at developing "combinations," an array of punches delivered in tactical sequence. By 1903 he was the premier black heavyweight boxer in the country.

He publically challenged Jim Jeffries, the world heavyweight champion, who replied, "When there are no white men left to fight, I will quit the business.... I am determined not to take a chance of losing the championship to a negro."

Even the white challengers refused to fight him, claiming to be unwilling to allow any opening that might lead to a fight for the crown jewel of masculine superiority.

And no major white sportswriters called them cowards. The same Charles A. Dana who had gushed so over the Great John L. wrote in the *New York Sun*: "We are in the midst of a growing menace. The black man is rapidly forging to the front rank in athletics, especially in fisticuffs. We are in the midst of a black rise against white supremacy."

Johnson released his rage during rare fights with second-rate white fighters who fought him because they needed the payday. He taunted them and waited until he felt he had punished them sufficiently before he knocked them out. Johnson was almost always in control of his fights, which were mostly against other blacks.

In 1905, Jim Jeffries retired undefeated, passing on his title to Marvin

Hart, who immediately lost it to a small, tough, scrappy but boring Canadian, Tommy Burns.

Johnson teamed up with a top white manager, Sam Fitzpatrick, and stalked Burns, who defended his title successfully over the next few years against nondescript opponents for small purses and little press attention. Burns was simply not box-office.

But Papa Jack was, slashing through the ranks of name fighters from the United States to Australia—from Robert Fitzsimmons to Bill Squires—until white sportswriters hungry for something fresh to write about, and boxing impresarios who didn't want boxing to wither, finally demanded a fight between the white champion and the black challenger.

The sportswriters, convinced of white superiority, expected Burns to win. And even if he lost, went the conventional wisdom, a "white hope" would quickly rise to thrash Johnson. Either way, the bout promised a fat payday for everyone.

On December 26, 1908, in Sydney, in front of moving picture cameras and a morning crowd of 40,000, Burns and Johnson squared off. Win, lose, or draw, Burns would receive $30,000, the incentive Fitzpatrick had dangled to nail the deal. It was cheap at the price.

From the first round when he knocked the champion down, to the fourteenth, when he finished him off with an uppercut, Johnson dominated the fight. Or as Jack London put it, "there was no fight. No Armenian massacre could compare with the hopeless slaughter that took place in the Sydney stadium today."

Johnson relished the slaughter, punishing Burns with his fists and his mouth. No history of sports trash talk would be complete without Jack Johnson.

"How does Burns want it?" he asked reporters before the fight. "Does he want it fast and willing? I'm his man in that case. Does he want it flat footed? Goodness, if he does, why I'm his man again."

In the ring, Johnson kept it up. "Poor little Tahmy," he taunted, "who told you you were a fighter?"

He even dragged in Burns's wife. "Poor little boy, Jewel won't know you when she gets you back from this fight."

After the fight, Johnson ridiculed his opponent, telling reporters how much he enjoyed taking revenge. And more openly than ever, he swaggered off with a white woman, this time one Hattie McClay, one of a series of white women he sometimes married, often beat, and always cheated on.

Some historians, such as Roberts, have suggested that Johnson's increasing defiance of established racial boundaries was part of a personal rebellion against a white world that constantly sought to keep him in check. "The more white society attempted to push Johnson back into the circumscribed borders of the black boxer's world," Roberts writes, "the more he balked at any restrictions."

Other historians see a fine line between acting out of a sense of rebellion and simply deciding to live your life as you see fit. Johnson responded to the American century's rhetoric, which encouraged ambitious men to make the most of their opportunities and enjoy as fully as possible all they had earned. He felt he had earned fast cars, loose women, high living, and the hot glare of public attention. Had Johnson been white, of course, he would eventually have been given that "boys will be boys" waiver that society handed John L. Sullivan, and later, Babe Ruth.

In a nation becoming increasingly comfortable with public spectacle and celebrity, what might have been acceptable, even laudatory, behavior for a white man—a measure of self-determination and success—became, instead, rebellion. The establishment had little patience with rebels, particularly black ones.

No less than Jack London, whose famous novel *The Call of the Wild* had been published seven years earlier, urged Jim Jeffries to come off his "alfalfa farm and remove that golden smile from Jack Johnson's face."

"Jeff, it's up to you," London implored in print. "The White Man must be rescued."

London's wild call for Jeffries as race redeemer reverberated from editorial page to pulpit, cynically peddled by promoter Tex Rickard, the self-styled "King of Ballyhoo." Just as Fox of *The Police Gazette* had whipped up class feelings about Irishmen for the Sullivan-Kilrain bout, so Rickard fed racial frenzy to hype the gate.

Rickard depicted Johnson as the "Negroes' Deliverer" and Jeffries as the "Hope of the White Race." Just to be certain that the reluctant white giant would take the bait, Rickard offered the fighters a $100,000 pot; seventy-five percent to the winner with additional money for both from the sale and rental of films of the fight.

Jeffries and Johnson agreed to terms in 1909, but the fight didn't take place until 1910. The three-hundred-pound ex-champion, who had been out of the ring for five years, needed time to get back into shape. Thus the nation had plenty of time to absorb the significance of the battle from popular songs, church sermons, editorial columns, and barbershop sportschat.

One song popular among whites, sung in a stereotypical Italian sing-song, offered advice to Jeffries with a racial subtext:

> Commence right away to get into condish,
> An' you punch-a da bag-a day and night,
> An'-a din pretty soon, when you meet-a da coon,
> You knock-a him clear-a out-a sight....
> Who give-a da Jack Jonce one-a little-a tap?
> Who make-a him take-a one big-a long nap?
> Who wipe-a da Africa off-a da map?
> It's da Jim a-da-Jeff.

Black response—at least published response—tended to be more dignified. The Reverend Reverdy Ransom's sermon, "The Negro and the Roped Arena," proclaimed a renaissance for African-Americans. It was reprinted in the *New York Age*, a widely read black newspaper, in December 1909.

"The darker races of mankind, and the black race in particular," maintained Ransom, "will keep the white race busy for the next few hundred years ... in defending the interests of white supremacy. The black singer is coming with his song, the poet with his dreams ... the scholar with his truth—in every domain of thought. The greatest marathon race of the ages is about to begin between the white race and the darker races of mankind. What Jack Johnson seeks to do to Jeffries in the roped arena will be more the ambition of Negroes in every domain of human endeavor."

This was gall to match Papa Jack's, predicting future struggles for racial power and place in arenas far more important than the ring! After all, Booker T. Washington, the prominent conservative black leader, urged his brethren to work for full equality in ways that did not challenge segregation or threaten white America.

And white America was easily threatened, as one gleans from this *New York Times* editorial two days before the fight: "If the black man wins, thousands of his ignorant brothers will interpret his victory as justifying claims to much more than mere physical equality with their white neighbors."

Reno, Nevada, was the place to be on July 4, 1910. The fight had been run out of California, and various legions of decency were calling for a ban against the sport, but every writer, fighter, politician, sportsman, thief, and high roller who could make it—an estimated 20,000—was there. Over 500 newspaper reporters pumped out more than 100,000 words a day, some of them under the byline John L. Sullivan, who was "covering" for the *Times*.

Writing for the *New York Herald*, this is Jack London: "This contest of men with padded gloves on their hands is a sport that belongs unequivocally to the English-speaking race, and that has taken centuries for the race to develop. It is no superficial thing, a fad for a moment or a generation. No genius or philosopher devised it and persuaded the race to adopt it as their racial sport of sports. It is as deep as our consciousness and it is woven into the fibres of our being."

As it turned out, Jeffries wasn't quite up to saving civilization that day, and Jack Johnson became the symbolic challenge to white supremacy and a beacon of black hope.

Defying convention, the men did not shake hands before the fight. Bare chested, wearing blue shorts with an American flag for a belt, Johnson took control from the outset.

Randy Roberts vividly recounts the fight. Papa Jack let Jeffries lead, then counter-punched with stinging lefts and rights. By the fourth round, as Johnson recalled, "I knew I was Jeff's master." And he let him know it. As he easily avoided the giant who charged at him with wild swings that rarely connected, Johnson taunted: "Don't rush, Jim, I can go on like this all afternoon."

Johnson kept the fight going for fifteen rounds, although many ringside observers agreed he could have ended it early. Even then, it was generally thought he did so because there would be a lucrative movie sale. Decades later, Ali would do that, too.

By the twelfth round, Jeffries was a bloody pulp—battered eyes and broken nose—with his blood covering both fighters. But he kept coming for three more bloody rounds. In the fifteenth round, as one round-by-round report had it: "He shambled after the elusive negro, sometimes crouching low...and sometimes standing erect. Stooping or erect, he was a mark for Johnson's accurately driven blows. Johnson simply waited for the big white man to come and chopped his face to pieces."

A flurry of punches to Jeffries's head put him on the canvas for the first time in his career. He struggled to his feet, and Johnson knocked him down again. The third time was the charm. When the count reached seven, one of Jeffries's corners rushed into the ring and the referee, Tex Rickard, ended "the fight of the century."

Writing for *Collier's* magazine, Arthur Ruhl described the "'hope of the white race,' with his crouch and his glare and all his hairy brown bulk hung over the ropes by his knees in a position quite primordial enough to satisfy even the red-blood novelists who have written so eloquently of late in the sporting pages of neolithic men and the jungle-born. And above him, with superb muscles of that terrifying left arm and shoulder taut and trembling to continue the battle if need be, stood the black man, Johnson...the undoubted champion."

Ruhl's descriptive prose—and his needling of London—reversed the accepted images of racial superiority so prevalent at the time. He went on: "The white race, whose supremacy this contest was going to establish, must, naturally, have been as dead as the Aztecs or the Incas."

More important than his sarcasm was his analysis. Most white writers and fans tried to convince themselves that Jeffries never had a chance, that he was a mere shell, that the fight proved nothing. Ruhl was one of the few white sportswriters to acknowledge Johnson's victory for what it was—the triumph of a tough, proud boxer "who stood on his own two feet and thought for himself, and fought and vanquished a brave opponent cleanly and like a brave man."

Ruhl was no less prophetic about the champion's future. "Mr. Jack Arthur Johnson … rode back to camp in his automobile," Ruhl reported, "with a harder road ahead of him than any he ever yet traveled—the gilded, beguiling pathway of him who is not climbing but has arrived."

The Great John L., his thoughts ghostwritten in the *Times*, found it "a poor fight … one-sided" in which Johnson "fought fairly." He went on to confide that because of that "well-known antipathy" he had not announced his prediction before the fight. He thought Johnson would win but didn't want to encourage the black man or discourage his friend, Jeffries. While Sullivan was clearly disappointed, he was not without the noblesse oblige of the old boy; not only did he offer Johnson pugilistic accolades, he wrote, "Since I know him better in the last few weeks, I am inclined to believe he hasn't many of the petty meanesses of human character."

Meanwhile, throughout an openly racist United States, Papa Jack's triumph gave his brothers and sisters a measure of revenge and a sense of empowerment even as they realistically assessed their situation.

Poet Lucille Watkins's "Jack Johnson," for instance, captured the fighter's symbolic importance as race savior.

> Jack Johnson, we have waited long for you
> To grow our prayers in this single blow
> Today we place upon your wreath the dew
> of tears—the wordless gratitude we owe
> We kiss the perspiration from your face
> And give—unbounded love in our embrace.

Rough-cut and pointed, another poem by an unknown writer, part of a rich oral folklore tradition passed down from generation to generation, clarifies both the meaning and the limits of Johnson's triumph.

Amaze an' Grace, how sweet it sounds,
Jack Johnson knocked Jim Jeffries down.
Jim Jeffries jumped up an' hit Jack on the chin.
An' then Jack knocked him down agin.

The Yankees hold the play,
The white man pulls the trigger;
But it makes no difference what the white man say,
The world champion's still a nigger.

Young black men took to the streets, boisterously proclaiming their victory and, in some instances, physically attacking whites. The response was predictably violent. Independence Day turned bloody, with injuries and deaths from race riots reported in every Southern state as well as in New York, Massachusetts, Ohio, Missouri, Oklahoma, and Colorado. Not surprisingly, as it had been since slavery, outnumbered and outgunned blacks suffered severely from a "lynching bee" in Wilmington, Delaware, to the murder of three blacks in Shreveport, Louisiana.

The white man also pointed "the trigger" at the champion himself. Determined to destroy him as a symbol of black pride and resistance, government officials embarked on a campaign to strip Johnson of his money and his title.

First, governors and mayors throughout the United States joined to prohibit showing of the Johnson-Jeffries fight film, ostensibly to quiet racial tensions. In reality, it deprived the fighters of ancillary income and helped keep blacks "in their place."

Some black journalists noted the hypocrisy of white colleagues who wrote editorials in favor of banning the fight film while their newspapers ran advertisements for Thomas Dixon's *Clansman*, a play based on his novel that violently proclaimed white supremacy and the Ku Klux Klan as society's salvation. (Six years later, President Woodrow Wilson enthusiastically screened D. W. Griffith's equally racist *The Birth of a Nation* at the White House with Dixon at his side.)

As would happen with Ali, there was no monolithic black opinion about Jack Johnson, at least not until it was clear that he was being set up for a fall. Some middle-class blacks criticized his wild ways and penchant for white women as inflaming prejudice and hurting the cause of black equality. The distinguished scholar and guiding light of black liberation, W. E. B. DuBois, was concerned lest Johnson's affairs with white women detract from building racial pride and self-esteem.

But most blacks were neither members of the middle class nor political leaders. They saw heroism in the new champion's confidence and swagger, in his exaggerated posture as his own man in a white world. They cheered the impotency of whites to control him or beat him. Here was the living embodiment of that folklore hero, the "bad nigger" who could "put it to the man."

Johnson moved to Chicago with his mother and presided over his Cafe de Champion, a large saloon and dance hall hung with paintings of himself, an immodest setting for an immodest man reminiscent of John L. Sullivan's own extravagant Boston saloon. Here was evidence that blacks, like the Irish, could make it in America.

While Johnson was never as political as Ali, he was not shy about declaring his rights as a free man. To an audience of prominent blacks in 1912 he spoke about his involvement with white women: "I want to say that I am not a slave and that I have the right to choose who my mate shall be without the dictate of any man." Then, with faint echoes of Shylock's claim to humanity, Papa Jack continued: "I have eyes and I have a heart, and when they fail to tell me who I shall have for mine, I want to be put away in a lunatic asylum."

Eventually the establishment did put him away, in prison, but it took some time. He was brought to trial in 1913, charged with various sexual violations of the Mann Act, better known as the White Slave Traffic Act, which allowed any man to be prosecuted for crossing state lines to have sex with a woman other than his wife. By all accounts, agents of the Bureau of Investigation—forerunner of the FBI—harassed and illegally detained one of their star witnesses, Belle Schreiber, a prostitute and Johnson girlfriend.

Even Judge Kenesaw Mountain Landis got into the act. The man best known for fining Standard Oil $29 million in 1907 and later becoming baseball's first commissioner in the aftermath of the 1919 Black Sox scandal, revoked Johnson's bail while lawyers on both sides prepared their cases.

Convicted unanimously by an all-white jury and sentenced to one year in prison and a one thousand dollar fine, Johnson fled the country. He said he escaped with the help of a black baseball team managed by Rube Foster, a founder of the Negro League. Changing clothes, jewelry, and places with a player who looked like him, Johnson took off for Canada with the team by train, his first stop on his way to Paris, France, and freedom. "The player resembling me, we believed, would be seized, permitting me to continue my trip," Johnson said.

Europe could not provide the stage that Johnson needed, however. Traveling with his wife, Lucille Cameron, he spent the next few years living on the margins, fighting exhibitions and performing in vaudeville shows. Finally, in 1915, he agreed to defend his title against a new white hope, Jess Willard, in Havana, Cuba.

Willard knocked Johnson out in the twenty-sixth round. It was part of a deal Johnson later said he made with the Bureau of Investigation for the right to go home.

More likely, the thirty-seven-year-old fighter, out of shape and out of practice, simply couldn't go the distance with a strong, well-conditioned, younger man. As it turned out, it wasn't until 1920 that Johnson returned to the United States. He spent one year at the federal penitentiary in Leavenworth, Kansas, where a friendly warden, a boxing fan, gave him "light time" and a chance to box exhibitions.

But Johnson's era as a public figure was over. White America didn't have to deal with him anymore, and black America had to wait for a champion who could represent them without seeming so threatening to whites.

The year Johnson got out of prison, 1921, the next black idol was only seven years old, a sweet Alabama sharecropper's boy named Joseph Louis Barrow, who said he got beat up by bullies until an older sister made him go fight back.

On June 10, 1946, on his way to watch Joe Louis defend his title, Johnson lost control of his speeding car and was killed.

Even in defeat and death, Johnson's legend endured. No evidence existed to corroborate his story that Rube Foster's team sneaked him into Canada or that he threw the Willard fight as part of a government deal. Those were Steve Brodie stories, exaggerations that made Papa Jack larger than life and enhanced his appeal. In his badness was hope.

Sixty years after Johnson whipped Jeffries, the folklorist William Wiggins was told a story by his father which he has retold in print.

"It was on a hot day in Georgia when Jack Johnson drove into town. He was really flying: Zooom! Behind his fine car was a cloud of red Georgia dust as far as the eye could see. The sheriff flagged him down and said, 'Where do you think you're going, boy, speeding like that? That'll cost you $50.' Jack Johnson never looked up; he just reached in his pocket and handed the sheriff a $100 bill and started to gun the motor: ruuummm, ruuummm. Just before Jack pulled off, the sheriff shouted, 'Don't you want your change?' And Jack replied, 'Keep it, 'cause I'm coming back the same way I'm going!' Zoooooooom."

While Johnson made a posthumous comeback in the sixties and seventies, thanks to Muhammad Ali, some of that zoom was muffled in Howard Sackler's *The Great White Hope*, starring James Earl Jones as a character based on Johnson. It opened on Broadway in 1969 to commercial and critical success, won a Pulitzer Prize, and later became a popular motion picture.

Levine, who saw the play in previews, had a particular interest; his aunt played the mother of Jack Johnson's first wife, Etta Duryea, who committed suicide soon after Johnson defeated Jeffries in 1910. Etta was abused and forsaken and she blew her brains out.

The mother's impassioned speech, offered center stage, attacked the champion for badly treating her daughter. It was cut before the show opened. Levine was disappointed that his aunt's big scene disappeared; in retrospect, he was not surprised and even more disappointed by the cosmeticizing of history.

Opening only a year after the assassination of Dr. Martin Luther King Jr., the play unequivocally chastised a white racist America for black oppression and offered its own call for black equality consistent with the civil rights movement sweeping the country. The play contained no room for a realistic appraisal of Jack Johnson.

Johnson was not simply a victim of racism. He lived large and he lived his way; he could be mean and cruel in and out of the ring. Historian Roberts writes: "He was not the ghost in the house, as the poetic Bundini told Ali. Where Ali was proudly black and political, Johnson's racial attitude was much more confused. His hatred of the white world was almost as deep as his longing to be part of it ... he refused the responsibility of leadership.... On only one point was Johnson consistent throughout his life: he accepted no limitations."

That, of course, may be his greatest legacy. The cultural critic, Nelson George, who is black, did not really know about Jack Johnson until Ali came around. And then he thought there might very well be a ghost in the house talking to disaffected black youth.

"Jack Johnson basically said f—— you to America in almost every way he could," said George. "The generation who've come up post-soul, post–Civil Rights, their vision is rebellion, not accommodation. Johnson's vision, not Joe Louis's.

"Jack Johnson took a risk when going out with a white woman was a dangerous political statement whether he saw it that way or not. He is a link from the past to Ali and even to Mike Tyson, whose mixed-up relationships are on a million rap records."

Johnson remains an invisible presence in a million soul and rap songs. "Strange Legacies," written in 1932 by a poet whose name has been lost, tells us why:

> One thing you left us Jack Johnson
> One thing before they got you.
> You used to stand there like a man.
> Taking punishment
> With a golden spacious grin;
> Confident.
> Inviting big Jim Jeffries who was boring in:
> "Heah ah is, big boy; yuh sees whah Ise at.
> Come on in..."
> Thanks, Jack, for that...

CHAPTER THREE

JIM THORPE

"DAD WAS RAISED AS A CHILD IN THE INDIAN WAY, AS THE CREATOR INTENDED IT to be," said Jim Thorpe's son Jack. "He and his father would go hunting at night and keep up with the dogs running along the river, barking and howling with them.

"I remember listening once to a tape of a radio interview and Vin Scully asked Dad, 'Of all the things you did in sport, what was most memorable?' and Dad starts to say, 'Well, I caught this fish that was ...' and you should hear Scully, 'No, no, no, no, I mean the Olympics, college football, major league baseball, pro football,' and Dad says, 'No, I caught this fish.'

"People didn't understand that Dad was an Indian, that sport was just competition, that's having fun, but when you are out there with the Creator and the things that are put here for you, the fishing and the hunting, you have a whole different perspective. You hook into a fish and you respect the battle it gave you, you say a little prayer, thank you, brother, that you would give your life to me so I may live."

The various legendary personae of Jim Thorpe—natural athlete,

innocent abroad, dumb jock, victim, hero—all take pieces of his "Indian-ness" for various traditional, progressive, radical, racist, and romantic agendas.

Yet the man himself—generous, warmhearted, rowdy, fun-loving, mean-streaked, stubborn, honest, direct—lived a far more rewarding and complex life than those who made him a symbol would concede. He was treated dishonorably by the amateur sports establishment, but no Indian in the early part of the century could take that personally; entire generations had been treated dishonorably, even murderously, by white men who cloaked simple greed in pseudo-religious ideology, whether they called it manifest destiny or the amateur ideal.

Native Americans believed then, and most still do, that Thorpe did nothing intentionally wrong that would justify his being stripped of his 1912 Olympic gold medals; in fact, there were dark plots swirling around him that would not begin to surface for decades.

Moreover, and perhaps most important to many Native Americans, Thorpe's life after the Olympics was not the sad slide into poverty and alcoholism that is often cited by historical apologists for the exploitation of celebrity (often minority) athletes. Thorpe went on to become pro football's first great star as well as a founder and front man for what has since become the National Football League.

Thorpe's name still resonates where it matters most.

"My grandfather gave a burst of life and spirit and energy to native people everywhere," says Dagmar Thorpe, the daughter of Grace Thorpe. "During his time, it was right after the Indian Wars, there was a lot of pain and suffering and loss among native peoples. My grandpa's ability to surpass all those things and use his gifts in a way in which he became recognized internationally has been an inspiration."

One key gift, insists son Jack, a former Sac and Fox chief, was his father's ability to imitate physical movement. Jim Thorpe threw the javelin and the hammer competitively after only a few hours of studying other athletes. As a hunter, he had been taught to mimic the movements of his prey; he was mimicking the movements of deer, wolves, and mountain cats as he darted and plunged through opposing football lines, said

Jack, as he reminisced about his father in 1994. Such oral legacies, passed down from uncles and old friends, give fresh dimension to the fossilized remains of old sportswriters' tales.

One afternoon in the fall of 1907, as one of the most enduring of those tales go, twenty-year-old Jim Thorpe barged onto the football field at the Carlisle Indian School in a borrowed uniform two sizes too large and asked to try out for the varsity. Everyone chuckled except Coach Pop Warner, who shouted, "Take that uniform off!" Jim was the star of the track team, and the coach didn't want him hurt.

"I want to play," Jim said. His mind was made up. Football was king at Carlisle as it was in most American schools by then, and Saturday's heroes got the cheers and the girls.

"If that's the way you want it," said Pop. He tossed Thorpe the first real leather football he'd ever held and pointed to the varsity players warming up on the field. "Give them some tackling practice."

Jim, of course, in true storybook fashion, slashed through the entire team, cutting and spinning, dodging, wriggling loose, then sprinting free. Warner was speechless when Thorpe trotted back to the sideline and grunted, "Nobody tackles Jim."

That was the tale that would appear, in lieu of real reporting, every time Thorpe led the Carlisle team to victory over the likes of Harvard or Penn or West Point. The idea of "the natural," a raw unstoppable power, played into America's self image, especially as personified by a tamed noble savage.

Thorpe was not America's only football hero of that era, nor even the most popular. Every region had its own shining Saturday son. And without the films and statistical analyses available today, who knows if he was even the best. But he was undoubtedly the best all-around athlete of his time—perhaps of any time—and the early twentieth century's handiest icon of American strength, stamina, and determination.

Half Irish, half Native American, modest and pleasant in public, Thorpe calmed the fears raised by Jack Johnson. Thorpe was a team player with old school ties, a copper-tinged white man who knew his place and respected the old white Anglo-Saxon Protestant values.

Most important, he played football, the game that was becoming a metaphor for the American century. Teddy Roosevelt—still celebrated for leading the Rough Riders during the Spanish–American War—lectured his countrymen that, "In life, as in a football game, the principle to follow is: Hit the line hard; don't foul and don't shirk, but hit the line hard!"

This was all part of his "doctrine of the strenuous life, the life of toil and effort, of labor and strife" as the only path to success. Roosevelt, who was president during most of Thorpe's time at Carlisle, insisted that sports—like football—were a good training ground for that life so long as everyone remembered that the games were not ends in themselves but instead important "preparation to do work that counts when the time arises."

By 1904, when Jim Thorpe arrived at Carlisle (Pennsylvania) Indian School, a rowdy game begun as an informal diversion for elite college boys was already a big money carnival promoted by robber barons, university presidents, sportswriters, socialites, and politicians. On Thanksgiving Day alone, more than 100,000 young men took to the field in 5,000 holiday matches played throughout the nation, involving colleges, high schools, and club teams. Sports was emerging as an important element of American culture.

As football's popularity spread, so did a national debate; some said it built character, others claimed it glamorized violence. Its language was militaristic: the quarterback was a "field general" and teams "crushed," "routed," and "demolished" their "foes." The debate continued. Was the game a preparation for war or a "moral equivalent"? Was football preparing youth for the new business world of factories and corporations or diverting them from real work? The debate still rages, of course, but nowadays it is drowned out by fight songs and "Bud Bowl" commercial simulations.

At Carlisle in the century's early years, however, football was primarily considered another way to "kill the Indian to save the man." As at all government schools, Indians were stripped of their clothes, their customs, their languages. Their long hair was shorn. Their games—snow snake, crooked path, fox and geese, long ball, lacrosse—were forbidden. Youngsters from different tribal cultures were thrown into the melting pot to be cooked "white." What seems a violation in these days of multiculturalism was considered in that era to be fuzzy-headed idealism. Clearly, America was not too far removed from its "the only good Indian is a dead Indian" days.

Carlisle's founder, Colonel Richard Henry Pratt, had impeccable Indian fighter-credentials which made it hard to call him soft on Indians. He had led the Tenth Cavalry, the so-called Buffalo Soldiers, African-American troopers commanded by white officers. As Pratt would explain to each new Carlisle class, his experiences with black soldiers and Indian scouts, as well as his conversations with captured Indian warriors, had convinced him that all people were created equal, and that Native Americans, because of their intelligence, character, and adaptability, could flourish in the white world if given the chance. Carlisle was that chance, said Pratt. In fact, it was their only hope of survival.

"I believe in immersing the Indians in our civilization," he had written, "and when we get them under, holding them there until they are thoroughly soaked. There is a great amount of sentiment among Indian teachers, but in the work of breaking up Indian customs there is no room for sentiment."

While Pratt's mission was specific, he was also part of a larger reform movement that used sports as a vehicle for assimilation and social control, particularly in cities struggling with waves of Irish and later Eastern European immigration. From the early social work movements, through so-called Organized Play, the growth of school, police, and parochial youth leagues, to the Midnight Basketball of the nineties, a ball has often been seen as the magic pill to make an outsider an American.

Like most settlement houses, YMCAs, and ghetto leagues, Carlisle was chronically under-financed by the government. Because too many politicians thought teaching "savages" a waste of time and taxes, Pratt hired a gruff young coach named Glenn "Pop" Warner to develop winning sports teams for cash and publicity. It was a pioneering concept that Knute Rockne would expand and refine a few years later at the University of Notre Dame, and it would eventually become institution-alized in American life.

Warner had been called "Pop" since his college days at Cornell University, where he played football for many years beyond his eligibil-ity. Warner was a prototype college coach: abusive, profane, protective, kindly, and absolutely relentless in his mission to make Carlisle a foot-ball powerhouse.

While his name lives on in contemporary football leagues for kids, Warner was certainly not the first, only, or even most important of the early coaches. As football became more popular, colleges recognized the game as a rallying point for alumni support and a revenue stream and thus removed it from student control. Paid coaches were hired to insure winning, or at least field competitive teams. Among the most notable were Amos Alonzo Stagg of Chicago, Fielding "Hurry Up" Yost of Michigan, and Walter Camp of Yale, who became the game's leading winner, promoter, and innovator. Camp led the drive to standardize rules and reduce brutality to a tolerable level of entertainment. Warner, who went on to coach at major colleges, was able to experiment in Carlisle's very special and sheltered environment.

The Indian Wars were still recent enough for games between Native Americans and whites to have a certain box-office appeal—perhaps not as powerful a lure as black versus white boxing matches, but certainly enough to draw press attention. Because Indians had been hyped by nineteenth-century newspaper reporters and cavalrymen as powerful and crafty foes, it was always big news when a white athlete beat an Indian. For example, in 1844 in Hoboken, New Jersey, 30,000 whites cheered the New York carpenter who beat John Steeprock, a Seneca, in a $1,000 long distance run. The sportswriter who covered the story declared the victory a triumph of white superiority.

Indian runners were actually the first American athletes; most nations had couriers in constant training, and the 1680 Pueblo upris-ing against the Spanish was successful because teams of runners de-livered messages coded into carved sticks and knotted strings. Tom

Longboat, an Onondaga (known as "The Bronze Mercury" when he won the 1907 Boston Marathon), and Louis Tewanima, a Hopi, ran in the 1908 Olympic Games. Ellison "Tarzan" Brown, a Narraganset, won the Boston Marathon in 1936 and the marathon for the U.S. in the 1936 Olympic Games in Berlin. In 1964 in Tokyo, Billy Mills, an Oglala Sioux, became the first American to win the 10,000-meter Olympic championship.

There were also such fine major league baseball players as Louis Sockalexis (the Cleveland Indians were nicknamed for him), Charles Bender, who was elected to the Hall of Fame, John Meyers, and Allie Reynolds—the "Big Chief" of New York Yankees fame.

But no one has ever come close, as athlete, celebrity, or American myth, to Thorpe. He was the grandson of an Irish-American from Connecticut, Hiram G. Thorpe, who turned up on the Sac and Fox Reservation in Kansas in 1842 looking for work and was hired to be the reservation blacksmith. White men were always given preference for jobs by the men who ran the reservations for the government, the so-called Indian agents. Thorpe married a native woman and had six children who were sent to free boarding schools.

Many Indian families tried to keep their children at home lest they lose their Indian roots, but Thorpe was less concerned with roots than with his kids making it in a white-controlled world.

When the U.S. government took back the Kansas reservation on which they had dumped the Sac and Fox, the Thorpes set out for Indian territory, in what is now Oklahoma. Thorpe's son Hiram P. grew up as raw and hard as the frontier, a top rider, hunter, and fighter, a trader who sold whiskey to other Indians, which was illegal. Hiram P. fathered at least nineteen children. His third wife, Charlotte Vieux, was also of "mixed blood," the large, strong daughter of a wealthy merchant of French descent and a Potawatomie woman. A devout Roman Catholic, she demanded that her children be baptized and attend Mass.

On May 22, 1887, she gave birth to twin boys. Moments after the elder of the two, James Francis, was born, Charlotte glanced out the window as the morning sun cut a trail of light toward the cabin door. The baby's Indian name became Wa-tho-huck, which has been translated as "Bright Path" and as "Light after Lightning," either one an optimistic name at a time when solving the "Indian problem" included a $500 reward in Arizona for each "buck Indian's scalp."

"This reward system," *The New York Times* explained to its readers, "while it may seem savage and brutal to the Northern and Eastern sentimentalist, is looked upon in this section as the only means possible of ridding Arizona of the murderous Apache....

"From time immemorial all border countries have offered rewards for bear and wolf scalps and other animals that destroyed the pioneer's stock or molested his family.... 'Extermination' is the battle cry now...."

Survival for Jim and his twin brother, Charlie, was based on having their feet in both worlds; they learned Indian ways from Hiram on the reservation and white ways at the Indian Agency boarding school. But after Charlie died during a pneumonia and smallpox epidemic in 1897, Jim, who never much liked school, ran home. Hiram is supposed to have said, "I'm going to send you so far you will never find your way home again."

Thorpe was twelve when he arrived at the Haskell Indian School outside Lawrence, Kansas, in 1899. Mornings he attended classes, afternoons he learned vocational skills such as baking, sewing, and electrical wiring. He continued to run away, getting as far as Texas, where he built fences and broke horses. Eventually disenchanted with the cowboy's low pay and hard life, he bought a team of horses as a gift to Hiram and returned home. He was welcomed, but his mother had died and Hiram's new white wife was busy with new children.

It was at this time that Thorpe discovered baseball—marathon games played on the prairies on Saturdays or before supper during the week. Thorpe was strong from his months on the range, and recruiters from semipro teams and colleges came to see him blast the ball over barn roofs, fire pinpoint throws to home plate from deep center, or pitch humming fastballs. Thorpe was only fifteen and raw, but he was smart and talented. He had a gift for games.

It is not clear whether it was Hiram's letter to Carlisle, the most prestigious Indian school in the country—"I want him to go make something of himself," Hiram wrote, "for he cannot do it here."—that touched Colonel Pratt, or the enthusiastic report of a recruiting scout, but Thorpe was admitted in early February 1904.

The rules were stricter at Carlisle than at Haskell, and the punishment for breaking them more severe. Students were kept occupied with classes and chores and rarely allowed to leave the campus except for "outings," periods of indentured servitude as maids, farmhands, or store clerks for white families with whom they lived. Ostensibly, the purpose was to acclimate the students to white ways, but it also generated money, good will, and political support for the Pennsylvania school. Academically, Carlisle was no more than a high school, although students were accepted all the way into their early twenties.

Life may have been easier at Carlisle for Thorpe than for many of the other youngsters; he was physically strong and tough-minded, he had survived on his own out in the world, and he was half-white—there was less Indian that had to be drummed out of him. And there was sports.

Pop Warner took care of his "athletic boys." They lived in a more comfortable dorm than other students, ate more and better food, and received spending money from the coach. There was a slush fund, just like at a real college. Downtown, at Mose Blumenthal's store, Jim could get a fancy suit on Warner's account and some extra cash from Blumenthal, who, like many merchants in town, was a team booster. The school's fame brought business to local stores, hotels, and restaurants. A varsity athlete never had to buy his own drink in Carlisle. Male or female students who were not athletes, however, would have to beg their local Indian agents to free up money in their own "allotment" accounts for new clothes or special books.

As Warner helped create the modern football factory, he was also shaping the game on the playing field. He came up with the "Indian Block," in which a player led with his hips and used his whole body to hit instead of just his shoulders, and he taught his passers to throw perfect spirals. From discarded wood and cloth he built the first blocking sleds. He invented the "hidden ball trick," during which a receiver would slip the ball into a pouch sewn into the back of a blocker's jersey. The blocker practically walked in for a touchdown while the other team searched frantically for the ball.

Thorpe was small for his age at 5-feet, 5-inches, 120 pounds, when he arrived at Carlisle not quite seventeen years old. He played intramural football that year, on the tailor shop team. His speed, however, made him a track and field star almost immediately.

By the time he turned twenty, in 1908, Jim's name dominated school cheers, press clippings, and football award lists. Many of the eleven games Carlisle won that season were decided at the last minute by his clutch kicking. In his first year of football, Thorpe was chosen a third-team All-American. He was a second-team All-American in basketball. That spring, he won nearly every track and field event he entered and in his first start for the Carlisle baseball team pitched a no-hitter. The record books have been less informative about his grades, class attendance, or homework assignments.

When the school year ended, Thorpe signed on as an infielder with Rocky Mount of the East Carolina League. Although playing for money violated college and amateur athletic rules, it was common practice and officials looked the other way. Many college athletes played under false names, including, the story goes, future resident Dwight D. Eisenhower, a West Point halfback who roamed minor-league outfields as "Wilson."

For reasons that have never been fully explained, Thorpe played under his own name. Did he think he'd never be caught? Was he too honest to lie? Or, most likely, did he think it didn't matter because he had decided not to return to Carlisle? His son Jack has an even more intriguing theory: his father's summer ball career was part of an "outing" assignment, with some of his pay kicking back to the school.

In any case, Thorpe's speed alone made him famous in semipro ball. One Fayetteville (North Carolina) shortstop remembered bending down to field a hard grounder only to see Thorpe already blazing past first base.

The league was a mixture of journeymen and college boys. Thorpe earned about twenty-five dollars a week, not luxurious but enough to live comfortably. Local kids often gathered outside the hotel of their favorite players and carried their gloves and bats to the park. Jim was a favorite, and he loved the friendly, small-town attention. After a while, he telegraphed Carlisle that he wouldn't be back. He asked his local Indian agent for some of the money in his account; it was grudgingly sent. When the baseball season ended, Thorpe went home to Oklahoma and found work as a hired hand. He was twenty-two years old.

The Carlisle football team struggled without him through the 1909 season. When Thorpe visited the school for Christmas, Warner begged him to stay for the track season, but Thorpe signed up for another season with Rocky Mount. Again, he returned to Oklahoma for the winter. This time, he began to miss the security and order of school; he was working and drinking too hard, living too aimlessly. And booming Oklahoma was becoming less hospitable to Indians. There were racial slurs and job discrimination. The latest craze, motion pictures, encouraged those attitudes; the "good" cowboys almost always whipped the drunken, foolish, rapacious redskins. Protests by Native American groups were ignored.

One assumes all this helped persuade Thorpe to return to a place where Indians were treated as human beings, (even as they were being de-Indianized), a place where he was a hero, even in the downtown stores. Academic officials weren't sure if he was "worthy" of an education; Thorpe's dropping out had disappointed them. And he was, after all, twenty-four years old now.

But Coach Warner was thrilled at the chance for another powerhouse football team, and maybe even a trip to the Stockholm Olympics that summer with Thorpe and Louis Tewanima. Warner convinced the administration that Carlisle could not afford to refuse Thorpe. After all, hadn't he always been "worthy" enough to sell tickets?

An innovator in sports public relations, Warner had his staff hype the 1911 team into a national powerhouse and dub Thorpe "greatest all-around athlete in the world." The label stuck before it proved true.

In football, he was a wonder. Jim's most feared tactic during those games was a punt kicked so high that he could race downfield before the ball landed, in plenty of time for a bonecrushing tackle or even a recovery and touchdown. After one of the mighty Thorpe exhibitions that fans came to expect every time he played, the *Pittsburgh Dispatch* printed this poem:

This person was a host in himself.
Tall and sinewy, as quick as a flash
And as powerful as a turbine engine,
He appeared to be
Impervious to injury.

Not quite. Out of action for two weeks with an ankle sprain, Thorpe returned unhealed but ready to beat mighty Harvard University. The media buildup was intense, and nearly 30,000 people attended the game in Cambridge, although arrogant Harvard coach Percy Haughton was so convinced that Carlisle was no match for his team that he didn't deign to attend. He ordered his assistant to play only the second stringers. By the time the varsity rode in to save the day, the massacre was over. Nobody tackled Thorpe. When his ankle finally gave out and he hobbled off the field, a stadium filled with Harvard fans let out a wild cheer. Later, the Harvard coach was quoted as saying, "I realized that he was the theoretical superplayer in flesh and blood."

Thorpe was a bona-fide superstar. The next morning's newspapers hailed him as a legend in the making. And somewhere in the white American psyche, thinks Onondaga Chief Oren Lyons, an American Studies professor at Buffalo University, a button was pushed; Jim Thorpe would have to be brought down.

"He showed up the white world," says Chief Lyons, a former all-American lacrosse player at Syracuse University and an international spokesman for the Iroquois Confederacy. "They were trying to prove we were savages, how else could they justify stealing our land and killing us? But here was Jim Thorpe and this raggedy group of savages from Carlisle, who just recently got shoes, and they're whipping West Point and Harvard. The white world took it as an insult. They had respect for us in a way, but they had to beat us down."

On July 14, 1912, Thorpe took his first ocean voyage, a trip on the *USS Finland* bound for the Stockholm Olympics. Under Warner's supervision, Thorpe and Tewanima worked out on deck with their one hundred fifty American Olympic teammates. They spent hours every day on the cork track that circled the jumping mats and swimming pool. Thorpe's teammates said that no one trained harder. Yet there were newspaper stories that Thorpe, the natural man, snoozed in a hammock for most of the trip.

The Stockholm Olympics were the fifth "modern" Games, and the first that Americans took seriously. Women competed for the first time in 1912. From Baron de Coubertin's first modern Games in 1896 through 1908, rich young men from club teams comprised the core of the U.S. squad. But by 1912, Americans saw the Olympics as another venue in which to flex their muscles to the world. Competition for spots on the team became fiercer and more organized.

One regional track and field champion who made the squad was Avery Brundage, a sturdy engineer from Detroit. He was a few months younger than Thorpe, and a rival. He expected to do well, maybe even beat the Indian in the pentathlon and decathlon, the most demanding tests of the all-around athlete.

Brundage saw himself as something of a Horatio Alger character, a plucky lad who would overcome his impoverished upbringing by working hard and making good connections. An Olympic medal would be a major step up commercially—the publicity would help him get better jobs—and spiritually—de Coubertin's "Olympism" had become a religion for Brundage.

Eventually, Brundage would become a construction and real estate millionaire in Chicago and the most powerful figure in amateur sports. He was de Coubertin's apostle, and he guided the Olympic movement through hot war, cold war, protests, drugs, and commercialism with a heavy and sometimes hypocritical hand. His credo—during the so-called 1936 Nazi Olympics in Berlin and after the murder of Israeli athletes at the 1972 Munich Olympics—that the Games must go on at all costs, has been judged with increasing harshness. His refusal through the years to return Thorpe's medals may have come from his obsession with keeping amateur sports "pure" of "tainted" professionalism, and it may have come from his personal shame at finishing far behind the Indian in 1912.

Warner had entered Thorpe in the pentathlon, which in those days consisted of the running broad jump, the javelin and discuss throws, the 200-meter dash, the 1500-meter race, and the decathlon—the pentathlon plus the 100-meter dash, the high jump, the 110-meter hurdles, the shot put, and the 400-meter run. Thorpe won gold medals in both events and set a decathlon record that lasted for sixteen years.

Along with his gold medals, Thorpe received a valuable bronze bust of the King of Sweden and a jewel-encrusted silver chalice in the shape of a Viking ship from the Czar of Russia, as well as overwhelming worldwide attention. It was the first Olympics covered en masse by the press. Thorpe became the first global sports star, predecessor to Pelé, Muhammad Ali, and Michael Jordan. And like them, his image was accessible to interpretation.

When King Gustav, placing a laurel wreath on Thorpe's head and a gold medal around his neck, said, "Sir, you are the greatest athlete in the world," Thorpe replied, "Thanks, King."

To the press, it was an amusing example of the barely-civilized native with amazing natural abilities meeting his master, the tolerant, sophisticated royal. That was the prism through which most people viewed Thorpe.

To his granddaughter Dagmar, however, it was another example of the Native American's harmony with all beings; he was "very simple and a direct and a truthful man."

After exhibitions in Europe, the U.S. team returned to a tickertape parade in New York City. Thorpe rode in his own car and waved to millions of cheering fans. There was a letter from the White House (no phone calls to the locker room just yet), offers from pro football and baseball teams, and vaudeville impresarios. Thorpe returned to Carlisle, perhaps out of loyalty to Warner, perhaps because he figured that after another great football year he would be worth even more.

And Thorpe had that great year indeed, capped by the famous game against West Point, publicized as a classic match of Indian speed and savvy versus Army size and power. Nineteen-hundred-twelve was still early enough in the century to appreciate that metaphor: a troop of future Army officers, the sons of Custer, seeking revenge against a new generation of warriors out to prove they deserved better than confinement on a reservation. Of course, a clearer lens would have two sides of jocks getting free educations at taxpayers' expense and playing their hearts out for pride and glory.

Thorpe orchestrated touchdowns for his teammates and scored one himself on a brilliant run, only to have it nullified by on an offside penalty. Two cadets tried to take Jim out with a high-low tackle, but he pulled up in time to let them collide and knock each other into a daze. They staggered out of the game. One of them was "Ike" Eisenhower, future president.

It was a tough victory, and after several lackluster games on the road, Warner let the team recuperate and train in Worcester, Massachusetts. Roy Johnson, a young editor for the local *Telegram*, came by to watch and was chatting on the sidelines with Charley Clancy, a baseball manager, when Thorpe jogged by. Clancy pointed excitedly, "Hey, I know that guy!"

A few years back, Clancy explained, he had managed against Thorpe's Rocky Mount team in the East Carolina League. Johnson tasted a career scoop. The greatest amateur athlete in the world was really a pro!

This, of course, is the accepted version, which seems plausible enough. Jack Thorpe thinks that Brundage dug up information from Rocky Mount and fed it to contacts in the press and the Amateur Athletic Union, which controlled sports at that time. In any case, Johnson was the man on the spot, and years later his son talked about the young editor's dilemma. Johnson didn't want to hurt Thorpe. He believed the amateur rules were hypocritical; they favored rich athletes who didn't need to make a living. As did many people, he felt the rules were unfairly strict. Johnson sat on his big story.

On Thanksgiving day, Thorpe ended his college football career with three touchdowns and two field goals in a swirling blizzard, beating

Brown University, 32-0. "The greatest football player, ever," said the referee. Thorpe was selected first-team All-American for the second year in a row.

Jim returned to Oklahoma for the holidays and then to Carlisle, where he gave inspirational speeches to the students in a pleasant, straightforward style and won a school dance contest. It was noted that he brought the first prize, a chocolate cake, back to the dorm. Thorpe was always generous with his possessions and his money.

Johnson broke his story in January, and the Amateur Athletic Union (AAU) called a hearing. Clancy, the baseball manager, denied talking to Johnson. Warner said he never knew his athletes played summer ball. Later, when players from the Carolinas confirmed the truth, Thorpe was left to twist in the wind alone.

Warner wrote a letter and persuaded Thorpe to copy it over in his own hand. Warner then read it as Thorpe's own words at the AAU hearing:

"I hope I will be partly excused by the fact that I was simply an Indian schoolboy and I did not know all about such things. In fact I did not know I was doing wrong because I was doing what I knew several other college men had done.... I have always liked sport and only played or ran races for the fun of things and never to earn money."

As an admission of guilt, the letter got everyone off the hook except Thorpe. The Olympic Committee, Carlisle, and Warner were officially cleared of charges that they had known Thorpe played pro ball and yet had still allowed him to compete as an amateur. The bust of King Gustav and the Russian Czar's chalice were returned to the Olympic Committee, never to reappear, and the gold medals, which Thorpe had given to Warner for safekeeping, were awarded to the second place finishers. The name James Thorpe was stricken from Olympic record books. The AAU, however, halted its investigation before other American athletes could be charged with professionalism and disqualified; it was better to scapegoat one Indian schoolboy than risk wiping out future Olympic teams.

To the sporting press and most Americans, Thorpe's was a sad but unsurprising story; straight from the woods, Indians were dumb, naive hedonists who needed protection. A logical extension of that included the government "protecting" them out of their land, mineral rights, and money. They'd just drink it up anyway, was the conventional wisdom.

To Native Americans this was just another broken treaty; no matter how white their ways or how many touchdowns they scored, they would never be treated fairly. After Thorpe had bested the whites at every game they taught him, he was being punished for being too good.

Thorpe's story has had particular resonance for Chief Lyons, who met him as a reservation youngster when Thorpe toured upstate New York with an Indian pro wrestler he managed, Sonny War Cloud. Thorpe would stop at Onondaga to visit with old Carlisle teammates, including Lyons's uncle Ike. As a lacrosse player, Lyons found in the history of his own sport a parallel to Thorpe's biography.

In 1880, after more than a century of teaching Europeans how to play "Bump Hips," the Iroquois national lacrosse team was charged with taking money in violation of amateur rules, even though they only used the money to travel to international tournaments in Europe. It was just a white scheme to push them out of the way because they were winning too much, maintained the Indians. The Iroquois were banned from international play for more than a hundred years, until a fierce campaign led by Lyons resulted in reinstatement in 1984. Indian men and women from all over America celebrated by joining the Jim Thorpe Longest Run, from Onondaga near Syracuse, New York, to the Los Angeles Olympics. By that time, another fierce campaign led by Thorpe's children had resulted in the reinstatement of his name on the Olympic winners' list and duplicate medals for the family.

Both campaigns have tended to be covered by the mainstream media in modern times as sentimental crusades "to clear the name" or to bring closure to a painful chapter, rather than as a window into ongoing patterns of systemic corruption. Rules defining "amateurism" were used in Jim Thorpe's time as they are still used today—to control sports. The enforcement of the rules by various Olympic organizations and the National Collegiate Athletic Association (NCAA) has always seemed arbitrary. The outspoken and the outrageous, those "bad apples" who might bring too much attention to what many feel is a totally spoiled barrel, are punished, as are the vulnerable, those without strong connections to politicians or the media.

It wasn't too long after Warner got Carlisle off the hook during the Jim Thorpe scandal that the school was closed for a range of financial irregularities. By then Colonel Pratt was long gone, and Jim was playing major league baseball for the New York Giants. Warner had tried to make up for letting Thorpe take the rap by helping him negotiate a $6,000 salary plus a $5,000 signing bonus, an enormous amount in those days for an untested rookie. Thorpe was twenty-six. He married a classmate and moved to Manhattan.

Baseball in 1913 was still the pre–Babe Ruth "inside" game of hit-and-run, squeeze bunts, and managers who prided themselves on using players as chess pieces. Cocky John McGraw, the Giants' manager, was a strict disciplinarian and his traditional, textbook approach to baseball clashed with Thorpe's free-wheeling style. McGraw seemed jealous of Thorpe's fame. He mocked his unpolished skills and made no effort to utilize his enormous natural gifts or willingness and ability to learn quickly and work hard.

Their relationship deteriorated after Jim missed a steal signal and McGraw called him a "dumb Indian." Thorpe chased McGraw around the field until teammates restrained him. McGraw insulted Thorpe publicly, suggesting he was not smart enough for the complexities of the game, and that he "couldn't hit the curveball," even then an old baseball putdown. He accused Jim of drinking too much and risking injury to other players by challenging them to wrestling matches. Actually, it was usually Thorpe's teammates that challenged him, eager to boast of pinning the world's greatest athlete.

It was football, which he played and coached into his forties, where Thorpe got his athletic kicks. During baseball's off-season, he would volunteer as an assistant to Warner at Carlisle and later at the University of Pittsburgh. And when the American Professional Football Association, forerunner to the National Football League, was created,

Jim became player-coach-owner of the Canton (Ohio) Bulldogs. In 1920, he was elected president of the Association. Pro football at that time was a raucous game played by former All-Americans of varying ages. Jack Thorpe remembers stories told by his uncles about his father at Canton. "Dad would come up to the bench and say, 'Watch number 34, boy, this guy's sure been playing some dirty ball. Watch the next play.' Invariably they'd take the guy off the field on a stretcher. The one thing that upset Dad was if you played dirty sport. He would sure find a way to get even."

Thorpe never lost his kicking leg, and even when running and tackling he could still dominate most players in their prime. Ernie Nevers, a football star in his own right, was tackled by a thirty-nine-year-old Thorpe and said he had never been hit so hard in his life. Thorpe's love for the game increased as he packed the Bulldogs with old Carlisle teammates. The postgame parties were often wilder than the games themselves.

Newspaper stories about Thorpe in later life portrayed him as a pathetic, broken spirit, as "Poor Jim," especially when he turned up tapped out or drunk or bar-brawling. In 1932, when he supposedly couldn't afford a ticket to the Los Angeles Olympics, vice-president Charles Curtis, himself part Native American, invited him to sit in his box. They may have watched a lacrosse exhibition starring a young Iroquois who would be spotted by a Hollywood talent scout. Renamed Jay Silverheels, he played the Lone Ranger's sidekick, Tonto.

That was the same Olympic Games competed in by Babe Didrikson, perhaps the greatest all-around woman athlete in American history. In 1950, the *Associated Press* named her Female Athlete of the Half-Century and Thorpe the Male Athlete. He finished far ahead of runnerup Babe Ruth.

On March 28, 1953, in the Lomita, California, trailer in which he lived with his third wife, Patricia Askew, Thorpe died of a heart attack. He was not quite sixty-six years old. It was also the year that Ike Eisenhower, the West Point cadet who knocked himself out trying to tackle Thorpe on the gridiron, took office as the thirty-fourth president of the United States.

Jack Thorpe takes issue with the perception that his father died a penniless alcoholic. "That's as far from the truth as there is. I think my stepmother was trying to play on the sympathy of the public. He owned a couple of bars in Lomita and San Pedro. He was the sports director for the beach cities in the Los Angeles area. I guess people find it easy to believe the stereotype, the bloodthirsty, drunken savage."

The year Thorpe died, *Jim Thorpe—All-American*, starring Burt Lancaster, was a box-office hit. Thorpe had sold the film rights to his life story for $1,500 and didn't share in the profits. While the film captured Thorpe's joyous athleticism, it portrayed him as a magnificent animal who needed to be ridden—by white men.

"Jim Thorpe was beaten, but he was never tamed," said Chief Lyons. "He was too strong an individual for that. He suffered, but he survived. And that is the story of our people."

Jim Thorpe was not only a Native-American icon; as an All-American hero he embodied "hope" for the bustling, powerful, confident American century.

PART II

THE GOLDEN AGE

CHAPTER FOUR

KNUTE

ROCKNE

KNUTE ROCKNE OF NOTRE DAME WAS FORTY-THREE YEARS OLD WHEN HE PASSED into legend on March 31, 1931. His plane crashed in a Kansas cornfield on its way to Hollywood. The football coach was reportedly set to sign a deal for an astounding $50,000 to play a football coach in a movie musical.

Cynics might claim that tells you all you really need to know about American college football then and now—"One of the last great strongholds of genuine old-fashioned American hypocrisy," according to Paul Gallico. But the cynics kept their mouths shut. The *United Press* actually reported that "the first flash from Emporia that Rockne was dead shocked the entire world."

"And who was he?" intoned the Reverend Charles L. O'Donnell, Notre Dame's president, in the funeral oration. "Ask the president of the United States, who dispatched a personal message of tribute. Ask the King of Norway, who sends a special delegation.... Ask the thousands of newspapermen, whose labor of love in his memory has stirred a reading public of 125,000,000 Americans; ask the men and women from

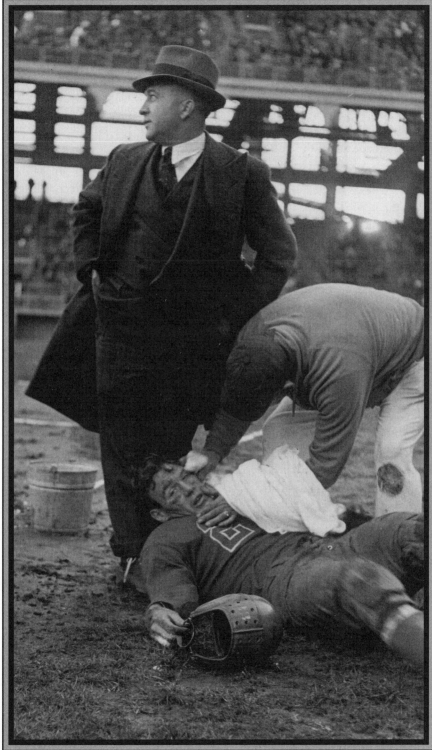

every walk of life; ask the children, the boys of America, ask any and all of these ... whose death has struck the nation with dismay and has everywhere bowed heads with grief.

"What was the secret of his irresistible appeal to all sorts and conditions of men? Who shall pluck out the heart of his mystery and lay bare the inner source of the power he had?"

On a superficial level, Rockne had the power to win football games and, better yet, sell thousands of tickets to see them. On a deeper level, Rockne, like Sullivan, Johnson, and Thorpe, offered connections to that tradition of individualism and masculinity that so many felt was threatened in a modern, fast-changing world.

But the "heart of his mystery" may have been his control over other men. Unlike those individual athletes, Rockne could not be ultimately dismissed as a performing animal of the arena, a civilized son of slaves or immigrants, a sanitized savage. Rockne was hailed as one of the true elite—a manager of men who could mold individuals into a team, into a whole greater than the sum of its parts. Throughout American history, that has been the role of the tribal headman and the war chief, the ship's captain and the wagonmaster. By the twentieth century, the platoon leader and the factory foreman had become the main managers of men. The football coach did battle without killing, hard work with a romanticized joy.

In the ten years between the exuberant optimism of 1919—when the boys came home from World War I, that war to end all wars—and the dark pessimism of 1929 when the stock market crashed, the football coach assumed mythic proportions; leader, father-figure, boss, teacher, puppet-master, psychologist. And when hard times hit, he became also a symbol of survival, hanging tough, getting on. It was with no trace of irony that the historian John A. Krout wrote in 1929, "During depressions, with thousands out of work, sports help refocus our attention on the Great American values and ideals, and also help us remember that life does not begin and end with the dollar."

No wonder, then, that it was the Depression that shaped Rockne's most famous coaching descendants—Bear Bryant of Alabama, Woody Hayes of Ohio State, Eddie Robinson of Grambling, and Bud Wilkinson of Oklahoma, all of them regional folk heroes who will be remembered long after the governors of their states are forgotten.

Knute Rockne was not the first celebrated college football coach— Pop Warner, Amos Alonzo Stagg, Percy Haughton, and Walter Camp, among others, preceded him—but he has become the model for all who follow. His funeral services were broadcast nationally by CBS Radio. *The New York Times* proclaimed that "his death produced a sensation in this country which reveals college football as a national institution."

A Youngstown, Ohio, newspaper remembered Rockne for his ability to "fire the manhood of others" and went on to say, "We all have latent powers that need to be stirred and awakened; Rockne did this, not merely for the men of Notre Dame...but for all the healthy young men of the country."

To a nation reeling from unemployment and bank closings, frightened of economic collapse, the Rev. O'Donnell's eulogy made Rockne a saint of altruism: "In an age that has stamped itself as the era of the 'go-getter'—a horrible word for what is all too often a ruthless thing—he was a 'go-giver,' a not much better word, but it means a divine thing."

Actually, Rockne *was* more of a "go-getter" than a "go-giver," a hard-driving charmer intent on winning on and off the field, by any means necessary. His legend, crafted by himself, sportswriters, and by Notre Dame, has obscured his enormous gifts of leadership, public relations savvy, and athletic innovation, as well as his complicity in the corruption of higher education. It requires no great stretch of the imagination to find Rockne's influence in the creation of models of masculinity and femininity that have limited and repressed the lives of millions of American men and women.

College football has made liars and cheats out of thousands of recruiters, boosters, coaches, and faculty members. It has made thousands of athletes both victims and crooks. It is a world of entertainment that defines itself as a crucible of manhood, a school of positive values and hard knocks. Many of the college football stories we read today about unnecessary roughness, untreated injuries, exploitation, no-show jobs, payoffs, substance abuse, and gang rapes could have been written at any time throughout the century. As could the testimonials of successful men, presidents of major corporations as well as presidents of the United States, that the lessons of football—teamwork, hard work, taking and giving orders, playing through pain and focusing on a goal— were the most important of their lives.

The pigskin propaganda that football pays its own way and even supports other university activities is almost always a lie. Few football programs are self-supporting, much less budgetary contributors to the library or women's sports; many large universities have mortgaged their souls for a stadium that can never sell enough tickets to break even.

Rockne didn't create the system although he certainly manipulated it. And while Notre Dame has profited from this abundant "fakelore" as much or more than most colleges, it has also compiled a far better record than most for the graduation and fair treatment of its athletes.

While Rockne and Notre Dame seemed happy to cooperate in gilding the Golden Dome, they certainly could not have done the job without the sports press.

The so-called Golden Age of Sport may really have been the gold-plated age of sportswriting. The great troubadours of the arena— Grantland Rice, Ring Lardner, Damon Runyon, Paul Gallico—wandered from ballpark to racetrack to ringside strumming their typewriters as if they were lyres. They lived well, made a lot of money even during the Depression, and became household names often bigger than the ball players they "Godded up," in the words of later critics.

Historians of sportswriting divided the Golden Agers into the "Gee Whiz!" and the "Aw, nuts!" schools, depending on whether they were "boosters" or "rippers." But even at their most sarcastic they rarely knocked the burgeoning sports industry's belief system, almost religious in its passions, that playing and watching competitive sports were healthful activities and a positive force on the national psyche. Children would learn courage and self-control, old folks would find nostalgic bliss, and families—whole towns and cities!—would communicate. The melting pot might be a myth, but once at the ballpark we would all come together.

The Black Sox scandal of 1919 was portrayed as an aberration, and the occasional bad apple (like the "Georgia Peach," Ty Cobb) was excused as an intense competitor. Sportswriters became the "homers" of a just-add-hot-prose-and-serve American mythology, making up for our lack of Greek, Roman, Indian, or Chinese gods and goddesses. Nowhere were they more successful than in college football where young Thors and Hermeses strove and sacrificed for their temples of learning.

College football is "even dirtier than prize fighting, because it insists, every so often, in proclaiming and harping upon its virtues, which prize-fighting does not" wrote Gallico in his 1938 book, *Farewell to Sport.*

After a celebrated sportswriting career, Gallico was off to Europe and an even more distinguished career as a fiction writer. Yet he never named names. That wouldn't happen until the sixties. Gallico was vicious but vague; the coach, he wrote, "owes the school nothing but the services for which he is paid, and has no loyalties except to himself."

Sportswriters in the Golden Age were insiders who knew where the bodies were buried as well as where they were playing. But the best of them either wrote general cynicism, like Gallico, or sentimental hokum like Grantland Rice, the first nationally important American sports-writer. Here are a few lines from old Granny's famous poem, "Alumnus Football," in which the "wise old coach, Experience," gives this advice:

> Keep coming back, and though the world may romp upon your spine,
> Let every game's end find you still upon the battling line;
> For when the One Great Scorer comes to mark against your name,
> He writes—not that you won or lost—but how you played the Game.

Rice and Rockne were co-conspirators in turning a prairie parochial school into a national powerhouse. The most famous paragraph in sportswriting history is the lead of Rice's story after the Fighting Irish beat Army, 13-7. It appeared on the front page of the *New York Herald Tribune* on October 19, 1924.

"Outlined against a blue-gray October sky, the Four Horsemen rode again. In dramatic lore they are known as Famine, Pestilence, Destruction, and Death. These are only aliases. Their real names are

Stuhldreher, Miller, Crowley, and Layden. They formed the crest of the South Bend cyclone before which another fighting Army football team was swept over the precipice at the Polo Grounds yesterday afternoon as 55,000 spectators peered down on the bewildering panorama spread on the green plain below."

The inspiration for that lead is a story unto itself. In Jerome Holtzman's collection of the oral histories of Golden Age sportswriters, *No Cheering in the Press Box*, the retired sports editor of the *Chicago Tribune*, George Strickler, recalled his undergraduate days at Notre Dame as Rockne's public relations man.

At halftime of that famous game, young Strickler mentioned to Rice that the Notre Dame backfield was "just like the Four Horsemen." Several nights earlier Strickler had seen Rudolph Valentino's first big hit, *The Four Horsemen of the Apocalypse.*

Rice had a different recollection. In his memoir, *The Tumult and the Shouting*, he wrote that in the 1923 game, during which he had roamed the sidelines, the four backs had swept off the field on an end run and leaped over him. "It's worse than a cavalry charge," he told a colleague. "They're like a wild horse stampede." A year later, he refined the line.

Either way, the lead was a press agent's dream. When Strickler got back to South Bend, Indiana, he hired four horses and a photographer and posed the Apocalyptics in the saddle. The photo galloped around the country. It helped make Stuhldreher, Miller, Crowley, and Layden immortal, and it made Strickler $10,000 richer.

Was Rockne's hand in all that? It's hard to believe it wasn't. As Rice tells it, four years after the Horsemen rode, on a night before the 1928 Army–Notre Dame game in New York, Rockne came up to Rice's Fifth Avenue apartment. They drank and stared at the fire, and Rockne told Rice about George Gipp, the brilliant young athlete who died of pneumonia after the 1920 season. It was the role Ronald Reagan played in the 1940 film *Knute Rockne, All-American.*

A talented, all-around player discovered by Rockne while still an assistant coach, Gipp led the Fighting Irish to brilliant victories, none more impressive than a 1920 triumph over a mighty Army team in which the halfback rushed for 150 yards, passed for 123, and racked up another 207 yards returning punts and kickoffs.

As Rockne told Rice, on his deathbed Gipp whispered to his coach: "Someday, Rock, sometime—when the going isn't so easy, when the odds are against us—ask a Notre Dame team to win a game for me, for the Gipper. I don't know where I'll be then, Rock. But I'll know about it and I'll be happy."

Eight years later, Rockne stared into Rice's fireplace and said, "Grant, I've never asked the boys to pull one out for Gipp. Tomorrow I might have to."

Tomorrow, of course, Rockne pulled the Gipper out of his halftime hat and the Irish beat the Cadets. Rice wrote the next day that Notre Dame "knew they were playing with a twelfth man, George Gipp" who "must have been very happy."

Gipp had come to Notre Dame as a twenty-two-year-old freshman, far more interested in football, pool, and poker (not necessarily in that order) than in pursuing a degree. Gipp regularly cut classes, lived off-campus, and spent much of his time hustling in local billiards parlors. But he was, according to the *Chicago Tribune*'s Arch Ward, "a rangy athlete, 175 pounds ... adept at faking plays. After taking the ball from center, he would grip it in his right hand, simulating throws until the defense started to run back to cover receivers. As soon as he would see an opening, he would tuck the ball under his arm and skirt end or drive off tackle. In the huddle he improvised plays which sometimes caused the great heart of his coach to skip a beat. But they usually clicked for long gains."

On March 8, 1920, three months after being named captain of the football team, Gipp was expelled for cutting too many classes. As legend has it, he claimed he had been too sick to attend class and asked Rockne to arrange an oral examination to prove that he was on top of his studies. Rockne and the university complied, and George passed with flying colors. Alas, the story is as false as Rockne's claim that he never knew his star player was a gambler until after his death. While Gipp hustled pool and considered offers from other colleges, local South Bend boosters—

no doubt with Rockne's support—petitioned university officials to have George readmitted. The Gipper was back in plenty of time to lead the lads to another unbeaten season.

The presence of what were then called "tramp athletes" like George Gipp was the cause of controversy at Notre Dame even in those days. University officials publicly questioned the conflict between the school's image as a football factory and its vision of becoming a nationally-recognized academic institution. In 1929, for example, Rev. O'Donnell deplored "the excessive and almost exclusive eminence of Notre Dame as a place where a football team is turned out."

It has been a valid complaint ever since. Fast-forwarding a half-century, Notre Dame's most famous president, the Reverend Theodore Hesburgh, often refused to discuss the football team with reporters because he was so uncomfortable with that image, even at a time when Notre Dame had moved far beyond it.

In the mid-eighties, almost all male undergraduates interviewed said they first heard about the school while following college football with their dads. Once there, they were swept up in a religious spirit that seemed as much Saturday afternoon as Sunday morning. Michael Oriard, an English professor who played NFL and Canadian football, was one of those recruited as a child by radio and TV broadcasts of Notre Dame games. In his football memoir, *The End of Autumn*, Oriard recalls "sacred objects on the Notre Dame campus ... transformed into secular shrines to the football team." One was a statue of Moses with forefinger raised. He was said to be calling Notre Dame No. 1. The huge stone mosaic of Christ on the library wall, arms upraised, was known as "Touchdown Jesus." Rockne was still recruiting.

In the twenties, Rockne was seen as a lightning rod for positive publicity, revenue, and the support of a vast network of "subway alumni," particularly those in New York and Chicago who attended the school vicariously. The muscular image of Fighting Irish (the hefty percentage of Italians and Poles, not to mention Protestants like the Gipper, never seemed to mind publicly) football was critical in a time of generalized anti-Catholic prejudice and specific Ku Klux Klan activity. The key to the future was this charismatic, demanding, charming, shrewd convert from Lutheranism.

Unlike those poor, marginalized boot-strappers, Sullivan, Johnson, and Thorpe, Rockne was a product of the middle class. He was born in Norway and brought to America in 1893, at age five, a few months after his father, a talented artisan, exhibited his prize-winning two-wheeled carriages at the Chicago World's Fair. Taken by his newfound American possibilities, Lars Rockne sent for the rest of the family.

For the only boy in the family, middle class life meant school, music lessons, and sport—baseball, football, and especially track and field, in which he excelled. Slight in appearance, only 5-feet, 3-inches and 110 pounds as a high school freshman, Rockne sprinted and pole-vaulted. Caught training for a track meet instead of attending classes in his senior year, he was asked to transfer to another school as punishment. He refused and quit without a diploma, eventually going to work for the U.S. Postal Service.

In 1910, with money saved on the job and a body fit from running and vaulting for local track clubs, Rockne passed admission exams and entered Notre Dame, like the Gipper a twenty-two-year-old freshman. He, too, spent the rest of his life there.

A gifted student, he did well in the classroom, dressed in drag for varsity shows, played the flute in the orchestra, set school records in track and field, and edited the yearbook. Football was small-time when he arrived, but as a speedy end he caught quarterback Gus Dorais's innovative forward passes to help post a 24-1-3 record during his three varsity years, including an upset victory over Army.

Rockne stayed on after graduation, first as track coach and assistant football coach. In 1918, he became head football coach and athletic director. Over the next thirteen years, his teams won 105, lost 12, and tied one, including five undefeated seasons and a 1925 Rose Bowl victory over Stanford University. His winning percentage of .881 is still a major college coaching record, and he set it with big, flashy, crowd-pleasing plays like long forward passes. As he helped transform Notre Dame into a national university, Rockne built a lucrative business career as entrepreneur, camp owner, corporate spokesman, inspirational speaker, and author. He was the model of the modern big-time coach. Others may have made more money, but few have done as much for a school.

In 1918, Notre Dame played its home games at Cartier Field (seating capacity 2,500). Competing against the likes of Case Tech, the Great Lakes Naval Station, and Purdue University, the football team ran up expenses of $17,000. Its net profit to the college was $234.

Twelve years later, the school opened Notre Dame Stadium, seating capacity 58,000. Playing a coast-to-coast schedule against the nation's best teams, the Irish capped the last of Rockne's five undefeated seasons with a 27-0 shutout of the University of Southern California before almost 90,000 people in the Los Angeles Coliseum. Rockne's juggernaut generated income close to $900,000 and a profit in excess of a half-million dollars for the season.

But even Rockne, with what one of his biographers called "a mind that touched genius, a blowtorch spirit, physical courage, infectious humor, rare charm," could not have won the games and sold the tickets alone. He needed the horses. Murray Sperber's *Shake Down the Thunder: The Creation of Notre Dame Football* provides chapter and verse, even an occasional song, to document the ways Rockne successfully competed for the nation's high school stars. This sexist, racist ditty was sung to the coach in 1923 at a reception for Cleveland's Notre Dame Alumni Club:

> The Notre Dame Alumni
> To keep the their team alive
> Are enrolling all the first-born
> As soon as they arrive;
> At each birth they wire Rockne
> And he tries to put them right
> I'm not interested in girl babies,
> And be sure the boys are white.

Working with a growing body of alumni, Rockne scoured the nation for talent, guaranteeing blue-chip prospects that boosters would pay for their tuition, room, and board. Once they were on campus, the coach found jobs for his most deserving players in violation of formal school policy. Rockne put the Four Horsemen in charge of selling home football game programs and soliciting advertisements for them, jobs worth $1,500 for each man, which was not bad for part-time work in 1924.

Rockne could have paid them out of his own deep pockets. When college football burst into the popular consciousness in that post-war consumer era, Rockne became America's consumer coach, too. In the dawning of the age of the automobile, who but Rockne could be sales promotion manager for Studebaker Motors; there were plans to bring out a car called The Rockne. As electric power helped create America's new leisure, there was Rockne hawking Wilson Sporting Goods. In 1929 alone, Americans spent more than $1.7 million on golf equipment and $3.4 million on tennis gear, at the same time making celebrities of those sports' best athletes. With money left over from buying such labor-saving devices as washing machines, Americans used their newly created free time to watch the new professional hockey and football leagues.

While baseball and college football were the main beneficiaries of the Golden Age, an entrepreneur like Rockne left no sport unturned. He was a celebrity tour guide to the Olympic Games. His inspirational speeches were worth $2,000 apiece. His off-season football camps at Notre Dame brought him $15,000 a summer, more than his annual coaching salary. He endorsed shaving cream ("It's the right play at the right moment— that's why I use Barbasol") and his byline appeared atop a nationally syndicated, ghost-written column peddled by Christy Walsh, who was also Babe Ruth's agent. One can only imagine how he might have operated in our time of competing athletic shoe companies. Sometimes Rockne had to miss games to meet business commitments, but his assistants kept the horsemen riding and Notre Dame kept winning and selling tickets.

While not cited specifically as the villain, Rockne was certainly on the minds of Carnegie Commission members when they issued their famous denunciation of intercollegiate sport, particularly football, in 1929. The report documented such abuses as illegal subsidies for players, grade tampering, the exploitation of athletes, and the violation of admissions requirements. It accused colleges of financial greed and a desire to win at all costs that were destroying the very purpose of higher education.

Henry S. Prichett, the head of the Carnegie Foundation, stated bluntly that "the question is not so much whether athletics in their present forms should be fostered by the university, but how fully can a university that fosters professional athletics discharge its primary function." He called for faculty and university presidents to restore meaning and purpose to higher education by reforming college football and curbing its excesses.

Rockne, who countered every challenge to his power at Notre Dame by threatening to leave, met the reformers head on. He declared it unfair to discriminate against "the brawny boy because he is not good in math" and added: "Four years of football are calculated to breed in the average man more of the ingredients of success in life than almost any academic course he takes."

Rockne was particularly adept at perpetuating that twentieth-century jock-frontier theory of sports as a preserve of American manhood. He urged Jazz Age college boys to spend less time socializing, dancing, and debating and to instead play football, to "get out where the going is rough." He told readers of *Collier's* magazine in 1930 that the world needed "rugged men, not flabby ones."

Rockne regaled after-dinner audiences with a comic vision of an unmanned future in which "gaily-clad" Northwestern players in "purple-mauvette tunics...the hosiery specially designed with beige tasseled garters by Patou, perfume by Houbigant," prepared to receive the ball from Notre Dame's eleven, themselves resplendent in "green shirt waists." In a game where plays ended when one was "tagged by a deft tap on the shoulder" and referees "dressed in regulation costume of plus fours and crepe de Chine blouse" kept order, both teams sipped tea at halftime as they contemplated how to break a scoreless tie.

On the very last play of this future contest, a Northwestern back, one Bickerdash, would break into a "rhythmical gavotte" on line to the Notre Dame goal. Thankfully for the Irish, however, one of their players stopped him in his tracks by shouting, "I say, Bickerdash, old thing, there's a terrible run in your stocking."

"Imagine the intense embarrassment and mortification of poor old Bickerdash," Rockne would tell an audience roaring with laughter. "What could he do to hide his discomfiture but drop the ball and sneak away to the clubhouse. So the game was saved."

Sometimes Rockne would just sock it to them. "Football isn't commercialized enough," he liked to say, "because there are only about twenty-five out of a thousand colleges making any real money out of it."

Notre Dame, of course, is still one of the twenty-five (if such a figure is accurate). Its Dome was gilded further in the 1990s by another fiery little coach, Lou Holtz, who threatened to leave for greener pastures even more frequently than did the Rock. In 1992, Notre Dame sold its games to NBC television for $35 million over five years.

The impact of television on college football and, more recently, basketball, only complicates an old problem. Aware of the high financial stakes and the opportunity for national attention, alumni—and coaches who, at big-time powers typically earn more than university presidents, let alone professors—urge their young charges to cut corners to stay eligible and build bodies to risk them. As one investigation of the state of big-time college athletics concluded in 1980, "From the moment the student-athlete sets foot on campus, the name of the game is 'majoring in eligibility.'"

Reported almost daily now are accounts of the illegal recruitment of athletes, transcript tampering, bogus courses, and the use of drugs for performance enhancement and recreation. The death of Len Bias in 1986 brought national attention to these concerns. Bias, an All-American basketball player from the University of Maryland, died from a cocaine overdose soon after having been picked No. 1 by the NBA's most storied franchise, the Boston Celtics. An investigation of the school's basketball program following Bias's death revealed that he had either failed or withdrawn from five classes that spring and that the grade point average for the entire basketball team was barely above a D.

The National Collegiate Athletic Association (NCAA), ostensibly created to self-police college sport, spends most of its time making mul-timillion dollar deals with television networks and dividing the spoils among select member schools. Most NCAA penalties seem to affect less select schools, or hapless youngsters caught violating rules that few bother to (or, indeed, can effectively) follow.

African-Americans, in particular, have been held hostage to a system that exploits their athletic talents while denying them a real chance at an education. Prior to World War II, American blacks participated primarily in intercollegiate sport on a segregated basis. Over the last half-century, however, thanks in part to television, blacks have come to dominate the so-called "revenue sports." Consider the appearance of black-dominated teams in the 1980s at Deep South institutions such as the University of Alabama; twenty years earlier, force was often used to keep African-Americans from their classrooms.

But black athletes, enticed with scholarships to play football and basketball as a prelude to the starry life of a pro, are usually sold a false bill of goods. Many find themselves unprepared for the rigors of college or encouraged to take meaningless courses in order to stay eligible. They graduate at far lower rates than comparable groups of white athletes and in the end are confronted with the sad fact—by one estimate, odds of over 20,000-to-1 for any college athlete dreaming of a career as a professional football or basketball player—of how illusory sport is as a lifeline to a better life.

Although the life of a megabuck professional athlete is even more of a fantasy for women, in the interests of equal opportunity and the chance to strut their stuff on national television in their own Final Four, women's basketball players have recently been caught up by the ratings chase, too.

Periodic attempts to clean up college sport have been either purposely weak or subverted by the media's refusal to follow up charges and findings. The reason? Because sports became too important a moneymaker for newspapers, magazines, publishing houses, and now television. That first twentieth-century fox, Richard Kyle Fox of the *Police Gazette*, found a formula in John L. Sullivan's time, and soon

Grantland Rice appeared to open the throttle on the gravy train. His syndicated *New York Herald Tribune* columns appeared in more than eighty newspapers with a combined circulation of ten million. That was a lot of readers for the time; more importantly, as dean the of sportswriters, Rice set the tone for everyone else's coverage. Ultimately, he even had his own newsreel show.

Rice was an intelligent, educated writer, a former minor league baseball player, and a golf enthusiast all his life. He also personified the so-called "Gee Whiz" sportswriter—described by his most recent biographer, Charles Fountain, as the "optimist, anticipating heroics and triumph...both heartbroken and exhilarated in defeat."

Using the language and allusions of Greek mythology and Shakespearean drama, Rice and his colleagues embellished their descriptions of events with extravagant hyperbole that extended the entertainment even as it dehumanized the athlete and obscured the reality of corruption. A case could be made that their coverage of college sports was corrupt itself; certainly Rockne's relentless courting of Rice, the free tickets for family and friends, the special access and private interviews, made sure that nothing damaging would ever appear in the columns of a sportswriter who set the standards for the trade.

Not that Rice was out to dig dirt; he had come to polish the SportsWorld silver and his published opinions were conventional for the time. Jack Johnson, he wrote, was "a bad actor socially" who "was a poor representative of his race." Jim Thorpe, who was "pilloried by ... shabby treatment," should have been "utilized by the Department of the Interior where he could have helped his own people." Rockne was "a man of great force, deep charm ... the greatest personal salesman I've known."

While Rockne's eulogist was a clergyman, Rice's was America's most important advertising executive, Bruce Barton, the founder of the giant agency BBDO (Batten, Barton, Durstine & Osborn), the man who sold Jesus to American Christians as a fun-loving guy who was God's best salesman. It seemed fitting.

At Rice's funeral in 1954, Barton described the sportswriter as "the evangelist of fun, the bringer of good news about games ... forever seeking out young men of athletic talent, lending them a hand and building them up, and sharing them with the rest of us as our heroes."

Had Rockne lived longer and perhaps broadened his stage, even to politics, Rice would have brought us more good news about him; to a nation conditioned to accept the values of sport, the *Father Knows Best* appeal of a gruff but lovable coach could sell anything from football tickets to cars to international adventures. Not that Rice lacked for copy. Of all the heroes the evangelist of fun shared with us, none profited so handsomely from his buildup than the most compelling athletes of the first half of the twentieth century, the two Babes.

CHAPTER FIVE

BABE RUTH

"I HAD A ROTTEN START," SAID BABE RUTH, "AND IT TOOK ME A LONG TIME TO get my bearings."

That may have been about as introspective as George Herman Ruth Jr. ever got. Not that it was necessary; daydreaming about Babe Ruth, talking about Babe Ruth, and writing about Babe Ruth has absorbed a lot of other people's time. This spindle-legged, pot-bellied, throw-away man-child not only became the Sultan of Swat for baseball fans, he appealed also to everyday Americans caught in changing times. Here was a man who not only embraced the greedy new consumerism of the twenties but also evoked nostalgic longings for a less complicated society where traditional values ruled.

And incredibly, he did all this while becoming the prototype jock, the loud, vulgar, rambunctious, cocky male athlete whose excesses, irresponsibility, total self-absorption, and commercial greed were all excused as necessary parts of the winning whole.

Of course, how else could he play ball with such supreme confidence if he wasn't larger than life?

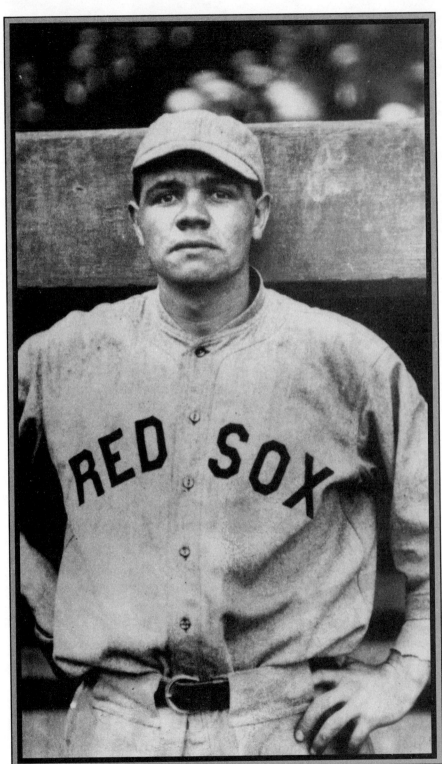

Especially if, like the Babe, there wasn't a mean bone in his body. He was, said a Yankee teammate, "the kind of bad boy it's easy to forgive."

And the Babe *was* a bad boy. He ate too much, he drank too much, he stayed up too late, he used foul language, and he screwed himself silly. But almost all of the damage he did was to himself. Ruth's tragic flaw was hedonism, if his farting, slobbering, messy lusts deserve such a fancy name, and if indeed it was truly a flaw, much less tragic.

People found it lovable, especially since he was the best baseball player in the world and made more money than almost anyone drawing a paycheck. And his comments about it could stand up today.

"It isn't right," he said in 1922 when criticized for his $52,000 salary, "to call me or any ball player an ingrate because we ask for more money. Sure I want more, all I'm entitled to. The time of a ball player is short. He must get his money in a few years or lose out. Listen, a man who works for another man is not going to be paid any more than he's worth. You can bet on that. A man ought to get all he can earn. A man who knows he's making money for other people ought to get some of the profit he brings in. Don't make any difference if its baseball or a bank or a vaudeville show. It's business, I tell you. There ain't no sentiment to it. Forget that stuff."

That was about as serious as Ruth got. On a blistering day in Chicago, he shook President Calvin Coolidge's hand and said, "Hot as hell, ain't it, Pres?" Shades of Jim Thorpe's "Thanks, King." At an elegant dinner he passed on the asparagus salad, saying "It makes my urine smell." Ruth was capable, in the same day, of visiting sick kids in the hospital, which he did often, and standing on a table at a team party and bellowing, "Any girl who doesn't want to fuck can leave now."

It was somehow excusable. Not only was Ruth generous, jolly, and good-natured, but his early life had been grimly Dickensian. Raised in an orphanage because his parents didn't want him, it wasn't until he was a celebrity and applied for a passport that he found out his date of birth.

Babe was born in Baltimore on February 6, 1895, in a third-floor shotgun flat over his parents' saloon, a rough waterfront dive for dockworkers and whores. "I hardly knew my parents," said Ruth. Of German descent, they were a tired, angry, beaten couple who occasionally took out their frustrations on their young son with hand and belt. Kate Ruth gave birth to seven children, only two of whom lived to adulthood. Neither she nor Big George had much time for "Little George," who grew up wild on the streets. He stole, skipped school, chewed tobacco, drank whiskey, "hated the coppers," and threw apples and eggs at truck drivers.

"I honestly don't remember being aware of the difference between right and wrong," he told his official biographer in a book he dictated while dying in 1948. "I was a bum when I was a kid."

When Little George was eight-and-a-half years old, Big George and Kate committed Ruth to the Catholic St. Mary's Industrial School for Boys as an "incorrigible." He spent most of the next ten years inside a complex of stone buildings surrounded by high walls on the outskirts of the city.

St. Mary's was run by the Xavierian Brothers as a reform school, orphanage, and shelter for eight hundred boys between the ages of five and twenty-one. It was described as a "moral hospital which treats poor maimed souls and deeply wounded spiritual natures." The school relied on regimentation and discipline as medicine, keeping its poor maimed souls busy from 6 A.M. to 8 P.M. with chapel, chores, basic schooling, and vocational training in a variety of trades from shirtmaking to plumbing. There was, of course, in the spirit of channeling energy and civilizing savages, a lot of sports, particularly intramural baseball.

St. Mary's regimen was not unlike Carlisle Indian School. Like Jim Thorpe, Little George majored in tailoring (years later when a Yankee superstar, he would turn his own shirt collars), and he found his own Pop Warner in Brother Matthias, the 6-foot, 5-inch, 250-pound disciplinarian who apparently loved the urchin.

Brother Matthias taught him baseball. He would spend hours hitting fungoes to Little George in the concrete outfield and coaching him on which base to throw to in a given situation. It is often overlooked that the homerun king was probably the most complete player of all time—

not only was he a superb major league pitcher but his fielding and base-running were far above average, too. In twenty years in the big leagues, teammates have said, Ruth rarely made a tactical mistake and never threw to the wrong base.

Although there is no evidence that Brother Matthias read such reformers as Jane Addams of Chicago's Hull House or was aware of the Playground Association of America and the Public Schools Athletic League (whose motto was "Duty, Thoroughness, Patriotism, Honor, and Obedience"), many physical educators, psychologists, and social workers of the day believed that children's play recapitulated stages in the evolutionary process of the human race. In YMCAs, YMHAs, and settlement houses concerned with teaching Jewish and Italian immigrant children American ways, baseball was key. As one settlement house worker put it: "We consider baseball one of the best means of teaching our boys American ideas and ideals."

Baseball was Little George's salvation at St. Mary's. He was a gawky, unattractive boy when he arrived, tagged by his schoolmates with the nickname "Niggerlips" or "Nig" for short. (Years later, his popularity with Negro Leaguers was based not only on his willingness to barnstorm with them but the rumor that he had African-American ancestors.)

Little George barely learned to read and write at St. Mary's, but in a baseball-mad school in a baseball-mad city, he simply played his way to acceptance, and then fame, first as a catcher and then as a pitcher. And always as a hitter. In his last year there, Ruth did not lose a single game and hit at least one home run in every game he played. He also filled in for local semipro and amateur teams

By the time he was nineteen, no one dared call Ruth Niggerlips to his face. He was 6-feet, 2-inches tall, 180 pounds of rippling muscle, much of it in his shoulders and chest. His overpowering left-handed pitching rivaled his thunderous slugging. Jack Dunn signed him to a contract with the Baltimore Orioles—once a premier major league team of the 1890s, then in the minor International League—for one hundred dollars a month. Dunn took custody of Little George and brought him down to spring training in Fayetteville, North Carolina, where he doted so on the boy that Oriole players began calling him Dunnie's Baby, and eventually, just Babe. The "new" nickname stuck.

In Ruth's fifth day as a professional, March 7, 1914, in his first game and second at bat, he hit a home run that local fans claimed was sixty feet farther than Jim Thorpe had hit when he played at Fayetteville. The next day Ruth's name appeared in headlines in the Baltimore newspapers. The city didn't have too long to enjoy him; before the season was over, desperate for cash to save his franchise, Dunn sold his baby to the Boston Red Sox.

We sometimes forget how good he was as a pitcher. In his first four full seasons with the Red Sox, Ruth became the left-handed ace of a fine staff, winning 77 and losing 38, compiling an average ERA of 2.10. The Red Sox won the World Series three of those four years. Although not yet known as a hitter, the young Ruth batted .321 in 1915 and hit four home runs, one-third of the team's total. In the war-shortened 1918 season, Ruth filled in for players who had gone off to the army and tied for the home run title with 11.

Babe's outsized personality—open, egotistical, generous, selfish—also emerged early. His eating habits were gross even by ball players' standards; all those years shoveling down reform-school food before bigger boys grabbed it had left him with enormous appetites and little taste. Other players lost their own appetites watching him gorge and belch and fart. Boston's professorial right fielder, Harry Hooper, saw Ruth inhale six ham-and-cheese sandwiches and six sodas as a late-night snack and cautioned him to "take it easy." Ruth was bewildered. "About what?"

He approached sex with the same gusto, snacking outside an early marriage; at twenty, right before the opening of the 1915 season, he married seventeen-year-old Helen Woodford, a hotel coffee-shop waitress and the first woman he dated as a big leaguer. By all accounts, she was a "nice" girl.

The marriage didn't have a chance. Both Catholics, they eventually separated but never divorced. After Helen's death in 1929, Ruth married his longtime mistress, a sophisticated, widowed model and actress named Claire Hodgson, who managed to control some measure of

Ruth's physical and fiscal excesses and winked at the rest.

Generations later, Jim Bouton, the author of *Ball Four* and a former twenty-game winner for the Yankees, recalled the stories of Jimmy Reese, one of his old coaches, who had once roomed with Ruth. True or not, this is as good as any example of Babelore.

"Jimmy's job," said Bouton, "depended on getting him to the park on time. One time, the Babe had locked Jimmy out of their hotel room while he was in there with some women. It was Babe's custom to have sex, smoke a cigar, and when he was finished he was ready to go to bat again. Jimmy was out of his mind, it was less than an hour to game time, and finally he broke into the room, and the Babe said, 'What took you so long, kid?' He was exhausted and there were six cigar butts in the ashtray."

But it was the Babe's hunger for attention that put off teammates at first. Ball players hate a "hot dog" until he has proven himself a winner. Here was this big, loud, city boy who swaggered into clubhouses as if he owned them and never bothered to learn the names of his teammates—even the older ones. There was locker-room justice, however: Ruth's straw boater was once filled with horse manure and unknowingly he clapped it on his head. There was a brawl, of course, and then Ruth began wearing soft cloth caps, which became a twenties' fashion statement.

Once Ruth showed he could put money in his teammates' pockets, they applauded him and became his mythologists and apologists. Waite Hoyt, a Yankee pitcher and eventual broadcaster, may have had the bottom line on his old teammate. "Wives of ball players," he said, "when they teach their children their prayers, should instruct them to say, 'God bless Mommy, God bless Daddy, God bless Babe Ruth.' Babe has upped daddy's paycheck by fifteen to forty percent."

Ruth's excesses thus became heroic, his crude ways proof he was a "natural man." Said his teammate "Jumping Joe" Dugan: "Babe Ruth wasn't born. The sonuvabitch fell from a tree."

For the scribes of the Golden Age, the sonuvabitch fell from heaven, a gift from the Prose God. Then, as now, the relationship between sportswriter and athlete was an edgy one, made even more complicated in those days by train travel. Baseball was the premier sport, and the first-rank columnists like Grantland Rice, Ring Lardner, and Paul Gallico often traveled with the teams on those long rides in close quarters. A great athlete who was also great copy, who could be depended on for daily stories, made for happy trips and easier lives. Ruth was open, funny, and rarely seemed to complain about stories, if indeed he read them. In return, sportswriters never wrote about his relentless debauchery. Besides losing access to the story, it might mean losing your job; it was not what fans wanted to read about, and editors knew it. Write about whether or not he actually "called" that homerun in Chicago, about his salary squabbles with management, his occasional battles with umpires and Judge Landis. Let your imagination soar as far as one of his homers.

Gallico wrote: "There has always been a magic about that gross, ugly, coarse, gargantuan figure of a man and everything he did.... He was kneaded, rough-thumbed out of earth, a golem, a figurine that might have been made by a savage."

Or a scribe. Rice, whose happiest moments, he said, were hunting, fishing, golfing, drinking, and swapping stories with Ruth, liked to recall a network radio broadcast in which Ruth was supposed to refer to Wellington's famous line about the Battle of Waterloo being won on the playing fields of Eton. What Ruth actually said, according to Rice, was this: "As Duke Ellington once said, the Battle of Waterloo was won on the playing fields of Elkton."

Afterward, Rice asked how he'd managed to bobble that one.

"About that Wellington guy I wouldn't know," he said. "Ellington, yes. As for that Eton business—well, I married my first wife in Elkton, and I always hated the goddamn place. It musta stuck."

The wonderful copy and wondrous batting statistics made money for players, owners, sportswriters, and the products he endorsed, as well as for him. Ruth stormed into the national consciousness just when baseball and the nation needed a happy hero. But defining what happened next has never been easy.

"I saw it all happen, from beginning to end," said the thoughtful outfielder Hooper. "But sometimes I still can't believe what I saw: this nineteen-year-old kid, crude, poorly educated, only lightly brushed by the social veneer we call civilization, gradually transformed into the idol of American youth and the symbol of baseball the world over—a man loved by more people and with an intensity of feeling that perhaps has never been equaled before or since. I saw a man transformed into something pretty close to a god."

The game and the society surrounding it were being transformed at the same time, which helped. Ruth's major league career began in the so-called "dead ball" era, when the home run was not only a rarity but somewhat déclassé, considered a crude gesture without the finesse of true craft (as once was the slam dunk and the long touchdown pass). Pre-Ruthian baseball was a game of skillful, spit-balling, nine-inning pitchers and such cunning managers as John McGraw and Connie Mack who called every pitch. The scientific "inside" game was low-scoring and relied on strategy, speed, base stealing, the sacrifice bunt, and the hit-and-run.

The quintessential inside player was Ty Cobb, the Detroit Tigers' hard-pitted "Georgia Peach," who won the American League batting title twelve times (his twenty-four-year average was .367, the all-time record) and led the league in stolen bases six times (in 1915 he stole ninety-five, a record which stood for sixty-five years). He even won the home run title one year; in 1909 he hit nine.

Ten years later, the Babe hit twenty-nine, and it was a brand-new ballgame. No wonder that Cobb, jealous psychopath that he was, sneered that Ruth had been able to perfect his home run swing because, as a pitcher, he could experiment at bat without the pressure a real hitter would have had—who cared if he struck out those early years? In 1920, in his first year as a New York Yankee and as a non-pitching regular, Ruth slammed a then-record fifty-four homers and saved the sport, or at least obscured its problems.

Baseball was never the agrarian dream land of its Golden Age "fakelorists," and trouble had been brewing for years. Between 1913 and 1915, the upstart Federal League challenged the monopolistic control the American and National Leagues had established over professional baseball through their so-called National Agreement and the reserve rule, a long-standing, unwritten rule that bound a player to the club that owned him. Federal League clubs offered higher salaries and contracts without a reserve clause. Eighteen players jumped to the new circuit as did a number of former major leaguers, although he game's stars stayed put, waiting to see how the competition would shake out.

Eventually, the established leagues won out by raising the salaries of players who threatened to jump and by buying out the owners of struggling Federal League franchises.

The Federal League battle was just one of many challenges to the major leagues' monopoly. Ball players, perennially upset with the reserve rule, with salary ceilings, with manipulations by management to keep them in their place, rose up from time to time with leagues of their own, labor actions, and the threat of fixing games for gamblers. There were always rumors of "dumping;" in fact, it is claimed still that Ty Cobb and Tris Speaker retired before their time rather than face an investigation into allegations they bet on games in which they played.

In 1919, members of the Chicago White Sox conspired to lose the World Series. Because they were favored to win by 5-1 odds, a fortune could be made betting against them. Chick Gandil, the tough White Sox first baseman, apparently conceived the idea and convinced seven of his teammates, including the illiterate star outfielder, "Shoeless Joe" Jackson, to participate. Gandil had been feeding inside information to gamblers for years. Charles A. Comiskey, the tight-fisted owner of the White Sox, unwilling to pay decent salaries to his players, no doubt helped provoke the eight into corruption. So, too, did one of America's most prominent gangsters, New York's Arnold Rothstein. This labyrinth tale of intrigue, deception, and double-crossing involving ball players and gamblers has been well told by Donald Gropman in his book *Say It Ain't So, Joe!* and (with a somewhat different judgment on Joe) by Eliot Asinof in his classic *Eight Men Out*. The fix was successful. The Series was thrown, and the powerful Chicago team was beaten in eight games by the Cincinnati Red Stockings.

Even during the Series, some sportswriters wondered out loud if the fix wasn't in, and some even hinted it in print. But it wasn't until a year later, as part of a Chicago grand jury investigation into a gambling incident involving the Chicago Cubs and Philadelphia Phillies, that the story broke.

On September 28, 1920, Joe Jackson and Eddie Cicotte confessed what Comiskey and other baseball men had suspected all along. All eight players and a clutch of gamblers were indicted for their alleged crimes, but by the time the case came to trial in 1921 the grand jury confessions of Cicotte, Jackson, and Claude Williams had mysteriously disappeared. On August 2, 1921, all the ball players and gamblers were acquitted.

Rothstein, who was never directly linked to any of the White Sox players and never indicted, denied accusations that he paid $10,000 to have the confessions stolen. The "Black Sox" scandal remained front page news for more than a year, damaging the game's standing and its business potential. Baseball's owners moved quickly to cosmeticize the game, hiring Judge Kenesaw Mountain Landis as baseball's first commissioner. This was the same Landis who had denied Jack Johnson bail and who, in 1915, had helped craft the agreement that ended the Federal League. In this matter, Landis promptly declared his own "law." The day after their acquittal, Judge Landis banned the eight White Sox players from baseball for life. With less fanfare, other players on other teams disappeared as well.

The commissioner's decision set the tone not only for baseball governance to this day but indeed for the future development of the sport as a business enterprise run by capitalists determined to regulate competition, maximize profits, stabilize their markets, and control their labor force.

Baseball was helped immeasurably by a Supreme Court decision in July 1922 involving an antitrust suit brought by the Baltimore Federals against the major leagues. The majority decision, written by Justice Oliver Wendell Holmes Jr. determined that although organized baseball was a business, it wasn't what typically passed for trade or commerce and therefore was exempt from antitrust prosecution. Typical of the close cooperation between big business and government that marked the twenties, this particular decision gave baseball executives free rein to govern themselves. Despite such challenges to their control as free agency in the 1970s, the owners' iron grip lasted until the summer of 1994, when the players struck and the owners closed down the season.

Ironically, that was the season when half-a-dozen spiritual sons of the Babe, including Frank Thomas, Ken Griffey Jr., Barry Bonds, and Matt Williams, were swinging free and reviving interest in the game with the home run. People were talking about Ruth again.

In the 1920s, Babe the Big Swinger was more important than Judge Holmes or Judge Landis, at least in the short term, in refurbishing baseball's popularity. The big guy with the big stick, the voracious young powerhouse, became a reflection of his country's image of itself.

In his biography of the Babe, Robert W. Creamer quotes him on hitting: "I swing as hard as I can, and I try to swing right through the ball.... I swing big, with everything I've got. I hit big or I miss big. I like to live as big as I can."

That might just as well have been a metaphor for the Roaring Twenties. Bursting with the power of natural resources, throbbing factories, and a large and growing labor pool, America could afford to swing from the heels, miss ... and swing again. Maybe it didn't have the finesse of the Europeans (the equivalent of "inside" baseball), but it did possess the circuit-clout that changed the game. You didn't have to dither and dance diplomatically for years when you could step up in the bottom of the ninth, come from behind, and win it all.

America was moving away from its rural mindset and a belief in Victorian morality and the Protestant work ethic toward a new mentality that encouraged immediate gratification from the abundant material riches of a modern industrial world.

Babe Ruth might have patterned his swing after Shoeless Joe's, but it somehow seemed fitting to leave that hick behind, a victim of history. Jackson might well have been a scapegoat, as Gropman maintains, or indeed a conspirator, as Asinof theorizes, but it was most comforting to think of him as the country boy caught in changing times who couldn't even come up with an answer to that apocryphal kid's "Say it ain't so, Joe!"

Babe would have known what to say, booming, "How are ya, keed," as he moved on toward a plate of franks and a glass of bicarb, then on to a roadhouse party, two dames in the backseat. He'd be wearing a camelhair coat and a silk shirt. After all, he was no hick. He was cool.

Ruth was completely in tune with the new attitudes toward leisure and consumption fostered by the new urban markets for consumer goods, aided and abetted by a communications revolution heralded by the radio, and a new, aggressive advertising industry that persuaded—no, demanded—that Americans live big with their new free time and disposable income.

Americans were urged to have fun, take a break, see a movie, buy something at a department store, ride the loop-de-loop at an amusement park like New York's Coney Island, take a spin in a shiny new Ford. Buy, spend, acquire, dispose. And if you were really rich, buy yourself a ball player, a really hot commodity.

Right after his twenty-nine-homer season for the Red Sox in 1919, the year of the fix, Ruth was sold to the Yankees for $125,000, by far the most ever paid for a player. The Red Sox's owner, Harry Frazee, wanted to invest his money in Broadway musicals.

During the 1920 season, while news of the fix was leaking out, Ruth delivered on the investment. He hit fifty-four homers. Before midseason, one baseball writer declared that "Babe Ruth is a bigger show this year than baseball itself.... The infant heads a procession whenever he walks abroad. They bring their babies to the park and point him out. And that hand that shook the hand of Babe Ruth is looked upon with quite as much awe as the hand that shook the hand of John L. Sullivan used to be."

Ruth continued his prodigious hitting the following year, belting a record 59 home runs. Everyone who could was swinging for the seats now, using lighter, whippier bats. In 1917, the total number of home runs hit in the majors was 338. By 1924, the total was 1,167, a substantial percentage by the Babe and his Yankee teammates, known collectively as "Murderer's Row."

Led by the Bambino (as Ruth's many Italian fans called him; some headline writers just called him "Bam"), the Yankees were baseball's dominant team in the 1920s, winning six pennants and three World Series. After 1922, the team played its home games in Yankee Stadium, the biggest and best ballpark in the majors with a seating capacity of 62,000. With his wonderful sense of drama, Ruth hit a homer on opening day.

The 1923 World Series, the first to be played "in the house that Ruth built" was the ultimate triumph of baseball's new muscular era. The New York Giants manager, John McGraw, predicted an easy victory for his scientific team over the power-hitting Yankees, the third in a row. But Ruth hit three home runs and batted .368, and the Yankees won in six games.

The *New York Tribune*'s Heywood Broun mocked the Giants' skipper in Homeric cadences that marked the game for the next decade.

"Ere the sun had set on McGraw's rash and impetuous words," Broun intoned, "the Babe had flashed across the sky fiery portents which should have been sufficient to strike terror into the hearts of all infidels. The Ruth is mighty and shall prevail."

Prevail he did. By the time he retired from the game, the Babe had set 56 major league records including most home runs in a season (60), in a career (714), most seasons with 40 home runs or more (11), most walks in a single season (170 in 1923), most strikeouts in a career (1330), highest career slugging average (.690), and most runs batted in (2,211).

And everybody heard about them. By 1927, the year Babe hit sixty home runs, even an American of modest means living in a medium-sized city could marvel at the first talking picture, *The Jazz Singer*, starring Al Jolson (though Jewish, he was also a St. Mary's alum), tune in to the World Series, follow Charles Lindbergh's historic solo flight across the Atlantic, or join the estimated fifty million who heard Graham McNamee broadcast Jack Dempsey's unsuccessful attempt to regain his heavyweight crown from Gene Tunney at Chicago's Soldier Field—a fight that attracted 104,000 paying customers, including Jack Johnson and Charlie Chaplin.

This combination of radio, the movies, newsreels, the booming advertising industry, and fiercely competitive sportswriters who took great liberties with their subjects to sell papers, created the perfect climate for a former sportswriter, Christy Walsh, to become the model for the modern sports agent. He turned his biggest client, Ruth, into a one-man conglomerate, SportsWorld's first great commodity.

Ruth was not the *only* sports celebrity in this Golden Age of sports celebrity, merely the biggest and brightest star in a galaxy that included golf's Bobby Jones, football's Red Grange, boxing's Dempsey, and tennis's "Big Bill" Tilden. Even a woman or two occasionally twinkled in that company, usually to be mocked as what Gallico called "a muscle moll."

As baseball's biggest draw, Ruth led annual national barnstorming tours featuring, for a time, the "Bustin' Babes" and Lou Gehrig's "Larrupin' Lous." The Babe even starred in *The Babe Comes Home*, a low-budget feature film made in 1927. Ghostwritten sports columns and children's books, appearances on the vaudeville circuit and on the radio, and endorsements of everything from cigarettes to automobiles generated close to $2 million over the course of his career.

Ruth also cashed in at the ballpark, far surpassing what other ball players earned. In 1927, he received $70,000. The next highest-paid player on what many experts consider to be the greatest team of all time was Herb Pennock, who received $17,500. Over his career, Ruth's salary rose from $20,000 in 1920 to its peak of $80,000 in 1930 and 1931. His income from baseball alone was more than a million dollars. Remembering that he played through the 1929 stock market crash and the early years of the Great Depression, the mind boggles at how much his worth would be valued in today's dollars.

When asked if he found it unusual to be making more money than the President of the United States at a time of national economic collapse, Ruth's supposedly retorted, "Why not? I had a better year than he did." (1930.)

In a society fascinated with things that could be measured and counted, Ruth's records on and off the field received constant attention. Though juicy anecdotes contain much of the fascination, his story also touches on a major conflict of his time. In a modern, industrialized society characterized increasingly by complexity and bureaucracy, where individualism itself seemed a threat to order and performance, Ruth's rise from rags to riches reminded people of a mythological tradition that guaranteed fame and fortune to anyone—regardless of background—who was willing to work hard to get it.

Although rarely a keen observer of his times, Ruth tended to explain his success in just such terms. It is unlikely he actually wrote the following in his autobiography, but the sentiments are probably his:

> Too many youngsters today believe that the age of opportunity has passed. They think it ended about the time people stopped reading Horatio Alger. There are more opportunities today than when I was a boy. And all these opportunities are open to every type of American. The greatest thing about this country is the wonderful fact that it doesn't matter which side of the tracks you were born on, or whether you're homeless or homely or friendless. The chance is still there I know.

Not surprisingly, in an atmosphere where many intellectuals still lamented the close of the frontier and its potential consequences for America's future, Ruth, like Charles Lindbergh, or even Al Capone, was often pictured as a throwback to a less complicated, primitive time where the exceptional individual mattered. One baseball writer, for example, described Ruth as a "superman" who "throws science itself to the winds and hews out a rough path for himself by the sheer weight of his unequalled talents" much in the way that commentators referred to Lindbergh as another Davy Crockett or Daniel Boone.

Ironically, of course, neither Ruth nor Lindbergh, as John William Ward reminds us, could have achieved such acclaim outside of the new modern world in which they lived. Where would Lucky Lindy, the "Lone Eagle," have been without his plane, "The Spirit of St Louis," invented, built, and serviced by others? Even "Scarface" Al Capone needed technology—the apparatus to brew illegal alcohol, the trucks to transport it, the tommyguns to protect it.

And for all the talent and personality that earned him the sobriquet "our national exaggeration," even Ruth would not have been so universally heard and seen without the advent of new communications technology.

Not all Americans living in the 1920s participated in, nor welcomed, this new culture of abundance. Farmers in the Midwest or South found much of this urban, technological reality both out of reach and repugnant to their rural, Protestant upbringing. They must have been appalled by Jazz Age flappers, and while they drank their own illegal "white lightning," the gangster-controlled speakeasies of the cities seemed like another stop in Sodom.

Italian and Jewish immigrants living in crowded city slums may well have dreamed of partaking of the fruits of the Promised Land but, for the most part, remained preoccupied with practical matters of survival. And blacks, whether on the farm or in the city, experienced systematic and harsh discrimination that denied them any hope of full participation in white American society.

Nevertheless, all could find in Ruth some piece of their American Dream. Hank Greenberg, the great Detroit Tigers slugger who grew up in the Bronx and was later known as the "Jewish Babe Ruth," recalled that Ruth was every boy's hero in his neighborhood. Once Ruth arrived in New York, the Yankees became the city's most popular team, easily surpassing both the Brooklyn Dodgers and the New York Giants at the gate.

Crafty John McGraw began a search for good Jewish baseball players, hoping to attract immigrant New York Jews and their children living in Manhattan and the Bronx to the Polo Grounds. At the end of the 1923 season, Giants' scouts turned up Mose Solomon, a hard-hitting minor league outfielder who had hit forty-two home runs that season. The New York press immediately dubbed him "the Rabbi of Swat." The nickname stuck, but Mose didn't.

Next came Andy Cohen, a solid-hitting second baseman who joined the club for a trial at the end of the 1926 season and became the Giants' regular second baseman in 1928. On opening day, before 30,000 fans, Andy led the Giants to a 5-2 victory, scoring twice and knocking in two runs.

The crowd's reaction was overwhelming; thousands of Jewish fans rushed onto the field and lifted him to their shoulders. They carried him around the Polo Grounds as they would a Jewish bridegroom. He had to be rescued by his teammates.

"Cohen at the Bat," an anonymous parody of "Casey at the Bat," captures the excitement of a day inadvertently made possible by Babe Ruth.

> The outlook wasn't cheerful for the Giants yesterday
> They were trailing by a run with but four innings left to play...
> It was make or break for Andy, while the fans cried 'Oy, Oy, Oy,'
> And it wasn't any soft spot for a little Jewish boy.
> And now the pitcher has the ball and now he lets it go.
> And now the air is shattered by the force of Casey's blow.
> Well nothing like that happened, but what do you suppose?
> Why little Andy Cohen socked the ball upon the nose.
> Then from the stands and bleachers the fans in triumph roared.
> And Andy raced to second and the other runner scored.
> Soon they took him home in triumph amidst the blare of auto honks.
> There may be no joy in Mudville, but there's plenty in the Bronx.

The Giants did so well at the gate that Harry M. Stevens, the famed concessionaire, instructed his Polo Grounds vendors that they were "no longer selling ice cream cones, but ice cream Cohens." However much they may have been exploited by the Giants' management, Jewish audiences took advantage of Cohen's presence, feting him with special "days" and demanding his appearance at their synagogues and organizations, seizing the moment to identify themselves with a young Jewish man making good in a very visible American way, thus proving that a person didn't have to give up ethnic identity to be a successful American.

Cohen stayed with the Giants just for two seasons. Long after a successful career as minor league player and manager, he fondly recalled his brief moment as an ethnic hero. Although he did not enjoy the anti-Semitic remarks of ball players, newspaper cartoons that highlighted his "hook" nose, or writers that described his "black beady eyes" and "thick eyebrows," Cohen relished his position as a role model for young Jewish boys and memories of loyal but ignorant Jewish fans who asked to sit right behind second base at the Polo Grounds so they could be close to him.

Thank the Babe for this, but don't be sure he knew much about it. Italian fans were thrilled that second-baseman Tony Lazzeri was playing with the Bambino, but it's likely Ruth didn't know his name either. As is typical of many sports heroes of any era, Ruth seems to have cruised through in the bubble of his own celebrity. During his twenty-year major league career, America fought a world war; banned liquor, only to repeal its prohibition; allowed women to vote; and entered the New Deal with President Franklin D. Roosevelt.

But the Babe's opinions went unrecorded. The Panama Canal was opened and the first telephone call was made without him. He does not seem to have been involved in the fierce debates on birth control and evolution, or to have read the important new books by Hemingway, Dreiser, Fitzgerald, Sandburg, or Sherwood Anderson. In a time of the new Red Menace (Communists instead of Native Americans), of unions and strikes and brawls and bombs, Ruth was totally self-absorbed in baseball and his daily pursuits.

As one dimensional as he was, Ruth was still unable to fulfill his dream of managing the New York Yankees. Was it because, as Yankee owner Jacob Ruppert supposedly said, "Manage the Yankees? You can't even manage yourself!" or were the owners glad to unload such an expensive and difficult employee and send a message to anyone else who didn't know his place?

Ruth was still The Babe, of course, but during the Great Depression a hero of consumption and abundance made little sense. Had he helped lead the country into disaster, urging people to buy and enjoy too many goods for which, ultimately, they didn't have the money? Once his bat was silent, he became less compelling; like so many athletes past their prime, he was a faint embarrassment. Ruth had outlived his time—but his time would return again in legend. During World War II, it was reported every so often, attacking Japanese would scream, "To hell with Babe Ruth."

For awhile, the modest, hardworking, clean living, penurious momma's boy, Lou Gehrig, the Yankee cleanup hitter, was baseball's beau ideal. After the Iron Horse died of amyotrophic lateral sclerosis, or what is still commonly known as "Lou Gehrig's disease," Hollywood set to film his life story. Gehrig, as played by the handsome Gary Cooper, was "The Pride of the Yankees." Ruth played himself and was the most natural actor in the film.

The Babe's autobiographical movie, which came out while he was dying of cancer, had been hurriedly produced to cash in on the publicity value of his death. It was the ultimate commodification of an idol, but certainly in keeping with Ruth's outsized life. Unfortunately, Ruth was played by the comical and supremely ordinary looking William Bendix, "a terrible shame," as Creamer wrote: "Lots of men look like William Bendix, but nobody else ever looked like Babe Ruth. Or behaved like him. Or did all the things he did in his repressed, explosive, truncated life."

The Babe, himself, staggered into the premiere but had to leave early. Those who knew him were shocked, unable to reconcile this gaunt, cancer ravaged fifty-three-year-old with the bursting boy who had made the country smile. Perhaps sport's most comparable contemporary idol, Muhammad Ali, today evokes something of the same shock and sadness; people who remember Ali's handsome, magical youth bite their lips upon glimpsing this shuffling, frozen-faced man.

The death of an idol is a release, a chance to turn back all the clocks. The outpouring of emotion at Ruth's funeral was real. He lay in state in Yankee Stadium, and more than 75,000 passed his coffin. The Yankee equipment manager, Pete Sheehy, cried as he mopped the stone floor. He remembered that the Babe had taken up a collection for the clubhouse staff back in the days before they were cut into World Series shares. Old-timers remembered how the big kid at St. Mary's would use the money he earned in the tailor shop to buy candy for smaller kids, especially the orphans.

Yankee teammates talked about Ruth's pretty swing and all the girls. In the exchange that has become something of a final eulogy, "Jumping Joe" Dugan, sweating in the August heat at the Requiem Mass at New York's St. Patrick's Cathedral, turned to Waite Hoyt and said, "Christ, I'd give a hundred bucks for a cold beer."

Hoyt replied, "So would the Babe."

Once he could no longer embarrass, no longer tarnish the legend or contradict the mythmakers, the Babe was cast in bronze, an American demigod. His two greatest records, 60 homers in a single season and 714 in a career, were considered unbreakable until, of course, some modern hero came like a pinstriped King Arthur to draw the sword Excalibur from the stone. For a while it was thought that Mickey Mantle would be the new Babe.

Ruth's records were eventually broken by two splendid ball players, fine young men, decent, hardworking, discreet, and totally without the charisma that sells cereal. Roger Maris, who hit 61 home runs in 1961, was never forgiven for that "sacrilege." The Commissioner of Baseball at the time, Ford Frick, a former sportswriter who had been one of Ruth's ghostwriters, briefly affixed an invisible asterisk to Maris's record; Ruth had hit 60 homers in a 154-game season, Maris 61 in a 162-game season. No one mentioned all the night games and airplane rides Maris had to endure.

"You know, 1961 was an easy season. It was fun. It was exciting. How could it not be?" Maris said in 1984, a year before he died. "But what happened afterward, well, it still bitters me up to talk about it."

The asterisk didn't stick, but the scarlet letter for Unworthy did. Fans booed Maris, and he never got the kudos he deserved. Even old ball players grumbled. Jimmy Dykes said, "Maris is a fine ball player, but I can't imagine him driving down Broadway in a low-slung convertible, wearing a coonskin coat."

It was even tougher on Henry Aaron, who hit his 715th homer in 1974 as an Atlanta Brave. "Hammerin' Hank" got hundreds of death threats that began, "Dear Nigger," and twenty years later he is still struggling to understand the lesson of his life; Aaron had been inspired by one great idol, Jackie Robinson, to surpass another idol—yet somehow the promise of sport, of the level playing field, had not been fully kept.

But Maris and Aaron at least were male. For that other Babe, and a female Babe at that, Babe Didrikson, life was far more complicated. Ruth could be a shameless hedonist, covered—and routinely covered up for—by a male press. He has spawned generations of baby Babe cockjocks. In 1991, when Magic Johnson announced that he had been infected with the virus that causes AIDS after having sex with more than 2,000 women, he was treated by the media as a victim and a tragic hero.

Martina Navratilova, the Babe Didrikson of her time, was one of the few critical voices. "If it had happened to a heterosexual woman who had been with 100 or 200 men, they would have called her a whore and a slut," she said. "It's a very big-time double standard."

Babe Didrikson had to lead a secret life. She lowered her official age and obscured her sexual preferences, although the word "tomboy" was often invoked with a wink. While balls were thrust into little boys' hands so they would grow up to be like Babe Ruth, balls were snatched from little girls' hands, parents warning, "Do you want to grow up to be like Babe Didrikson?"

BABE DIDRIKSON

AT THE AGE OF TWENTY-FOUR, ALREADY A FORMER ALL-AMERICAN BASKETBALL player, Olympic gold-medalist, and vaudeville star, Babe Didrikson won the first championship golf tournament she ever entered. It was a typical triumph for the greatest all-around female athlete of the American century.

Typical, too, were the snide remarks about class and sex that became par for her course.

The favorite to win that 1935 tournament, Peggy Chandler, was so miffed when Didrikson showed up she sniped aloud that the Texas Women's Amateur Golf Championship didn't need "any truck driver's daughters."

And after Babe used her own driver, as well as her putter and sand wedge, to beat Chandler in the final round, it was that Golden Age sportswriter, Paul Gallico, who wondered in print if "it was Mrs. Chandler's neat and feminine clothing that made Didrikson mad. The Texas Babe seems to be working out a lifelong vendetta on sissy girls."

Gallico and Grantland Rice would never have covered that tournament in Houston, yet another exclusive affair for rich white women, if the

Babe had not decided to add golf to her personal dominion over every sport she ever played. To a reporter who once asked if there was anything she didn't play, she snapped, "Yeah, dolls."

Babe Didrikson became something of a pet to the scribes of the Golden Age; even more important than her wondrous athletic gifts were her accessibility and her willingness to say anything that could be quoted. Who else would say after a bad round of golf, "I couldn't hit an elephant's ass with a bull fiddle today."

Rice wrote poems about her and rhapsodized thus: "the most flawless section of muscle harmony, of complete mental and physical coordination the world of sport has ever known."

Gallico had a different angle in his report on that 1935 golf tournament: "I wrote a few years ago, that when the Babe learned a little more golf and grooved her swing, steadied herself and learned how to approach a putt, she would raise hell with the average competing ladies by her wholly masculine aggressiveness and pugnacity."

Gallico wrote off her phenomenal athletic success—"simply because she would not or could not compete with women at their own best game—man-snatching. It was an escape, a compensation. She would beat them at everything else they tried to do."

Some of this was the routine sexism of the time and some of it was personal. Rice had an impish streak and once matched Didrikson in a foot race against Gallico, a former college athlete. Didrikson ran him into the ground. Gallico was shamed. How could a real man be beaten by a woman? Unless, of course, she wasn't a real woman. From then on, Gallico rarely wrote about her without a reference to her Adam's apple or the down on her upper lip. Even his highest praise was qualified: "The best all-around performer the country has ever known was a hard-bitten, hawk-nosed, thin-mouthed little hoyden from Texas."

Hoyden, huckster, pioneer, and product, Didrikson not only started the women's professional golf tour but had as much impact on her sport's playing style as did Babe Ruth in baseball or Martina Navratilova in tennis. And like her spiritual daughter, Billie Jean King, she was as much defined by class as by gender.

Mildred Ella Didrikson was born June 26, 1911, in the oil boom city of Beaumont, Texas, the sixth of seven children of Ole and Hannah Didriksen, Norwegian immigrants like Knute Rockne's parents. Two of those facts were fudged in her own 1955 autobiography; she claims to have been born in 1914 and doesn't explain that she anglicized her name. Like most idols, Didrikson invented herself as she went along.

Her interest in sports was encouraged by her father, like Rockne's dad a highly-skilled carpenter, who built his children a backyard gym. Mildred, called "Baby" until the seventh child arrived, quickly developed a reputation as the local "tomboy"—a short, wiry girl who was chosen in neighborhood games over boys twice her size. The neighborhood was tough and poor; sports meant status and was a safety valve, a testing ground—and for some a ticket out.

Early in her teens, she got the nickname "Babe" because she was hitting the ball farther than any of the boys she played against. During the 1932 Olympics she explained that she wasn't nervous because, "All I'm doing is running against girls." Her advice to young female athletes was to "get toughened up playing boys' games."

Tough, strong, hardworking, and fiercely competitive, Babe dominated every team the Miss Royal Purples of Beaumont High School fielded. An English teacher in those years, Ruth Scurlock, later said: "Babe's excellence at sports made her unacceptable to other girls. And these frothy girls, in her eyes, were simply not useful. Babe was bucking society even then."

A sniggery poem called "The Baseball Girl," written in 1905 by Grantland Rice, captures the prevailing male attitude toward athletic women, double entendres and all:

The type of girl which keeps each head cavorting in a whirl,
Is the nectarine of nature which we dub "The Baseball Girl."
She's got "proper curves," you know, well rounded out and neat,
She has the "speed"-nor do we refer to her feet.
She always "makes a hit" to boot, and, what is very nice,
She's ready at the proper time to "make a sacrifice."

Babe was no nectarine; she was a tough nut. As an all-city and all-state forward, she led her high school basketball team to an undefeated season and the 1930 state championship game in Houston during her junior year. In the stands that night was Colonel Melvin Jackson McCombs, coach and promoter of the women's athletic teams of the Employers Casualty Insurance Company of Dallas.

By the 1920s, men's and women's industrial league sport had become important for public relations, especially in the Midwest and South. McCombs offered Didrikson $75 a month as a stenographer/basketball player, good pay in that first year of the Great Depression. According to one of her biographies, *Whatta-Gal!*, by William Oscar Johnson and Nancy Williamson, Didrikson seemed less excited by the offer than by leaning out of her hotel window after the game and keeping score of how many people below she could hit on the head with her spit.

Didrikson talked her parents into letting her quit high school in February of her junior year to go to Dallas; as much as they wanted her to graduate, they needed the money. She sent $45 a month home, she has said, and her first purchase from the money she saved was a radio for her mother. Didrikson subsequently became known all her life for being cheap, for trying to get things free or at discount, and for sending presents to her family.

Within a month she was averaging an amazing 42 points a game for the Golden Cyclones in the national Amateur Athletic Union championships. They lost the title game by one point, but Didrikson was ecstatic. She wrote to Ruth's husband, Tiny Scurlock, sports editor of the *Beaumont Journal*, that "everybody is talking about yours truly."

Her boastfulness and her constant hunger for attention quickly alienated her teammates, but she was deluged with offers from other companies. Didrikson stayed in Dallas, leading the basketball squad to the championship in 1931 while taking up track and field. In that year's national AAU meet, she led her team to second place by scoring 15 of its 19 points. The following year she won the team championship all by herself, competing in eight events, winning six gold medals, and setting world records in the javelin, the 80-meter hurdles, the high jump, and the baseball throw. She also won a berth on the Olympic team.

Babe loved the limelight even as it complicated her relationship with teammates who resented her crude, obnoxious, boastful, blunt, flamboyant, and immodest style. She would stride into locker rooms all her life, braying, "The Babe's here, who's going to come in second?" Didrikson was in-your-face before it was cool. Some of it was clearly superficial sports psyching. In golf, she could throw an opponent off her short game with a casual, "You always hold your putter like that?"

And some of it was deeper.

In the beginning, she seemed proud of her lack of socially-accepted feminine graces and her preference for sweatshirts, close-cropped hair, and an unadorned face. Was she showing her disdain for the "frothy girls," or defensively masking her feelings of inferiority? Clearly, Didrikson was too different, even for other competitive, conditioned women, who themselves were an American anomaly.

The dedicated female athlete in the first half of the twentieth century was a kind of political statement-in-motion. The mainstream style was playing at sports. The pretty Peggy Chandler who Babe beat in 1935 was fond of saying, "I've missed a few putts but never a party." Didrikson hated to lose at anything; if she was being beaten at gin rummy she would throw the cards out the window.

Meanwhile, most Americans saw competitive sport as a masculine arena, and most women were ambivalent about why and how they should participate. They knew they were supposed to be helpmates for men. Women sweating and competing was unacceptable to many, and to some it was a sign of imminent social collapse. The debate over female athleticism was a major and visible part of the larger struggle for full equality.

One important line of thought had been laid out in 1848, when America's first organized political feminists, led by Elizabeth Cady Stanton, met at Seneca Falls, New York, and demanded the right to vote, declaring that women were entitled to the same rights and opportunities guaranteed to men by the *Declaration of Independence* and *Constitution*.

In 1920, the nineteenth amendment to the *Constitution* finally gave women the vote, but only after a campaign engineered by women suffragists that denied the feminist position staked out by their sisters seventy-two years earlier. Reflecting their own beliefs and the realities of American politics, they asked for the vote not on the basis of their equality with men but by arguing that women were different; that somehow their frailness, morality, and sentimentality would help civilize the rough male beast of American politics.

Thus it was easy, in 1923, for congressmen to vote against the Equal Rights Amendment by claiming, as one did, "There are differences in physical structure and biological function. Indeed there is more difference between male and female than between a horse chestnut and a chestnut horse."

Women's increased involvement in sport assumed a variety of forms. Between 1870 and 1920, the number of women going to college increased from 11,000 to 283,000, precipitating the rise of physical education programs, run by women, that offered a full range of activities for female students including calisthenics, swimming, fencing, tennis, track and field, rowing, and even basketball.

"Temples of feminine sport and gymnastics" such as the Ladies Berkeley Club of New York and the bicycling craze of the 1890s, catered to the health demands of white, urban middle-class women who took to their gyms and their two-wheelers in a desire for exercise and fresh air. But a lid hovered over competitive sport; the Vassar College baseball team was disbanded after a girl fell and injured her leg. Critics of women's sports argued that God or "natural selection" had made men and women suited to perform different worldly functions. Luther Gulick, a prominent physical educator who founded the Public Schools Athletic League and was a stalwart proponent of the cult of masculinity, invoked the Stone Age and Charles Darwin. It was natural for men to love sport, Gulick argued, for ever since prehistoric times, a "man's ability as a hunter and fighter depended very largely upon his ability to run, to throw, to strike." Women, on the other hand, who "always cared for the home" and were destined to do so in the future, never had any need for these athletic skills.

In an editorial titled "College Sport and Motherhood," *The New York Times* opined: "Every girl, it seems, has a large store of vital and nervous energy upon which to draw in the great crisis of motherhood. If the foolish virgin uses up this deposit in daily expenditures on the hockey field or tennis court, then she is left bankrupt in her great crisis and her children have to pay the bill."

There were brave female physical educators who counterpunched, arguing that by learning about teamwork, aggressiveness, competition, and winning—habits and attitudes traditionally considered for "men only"—women might break down restrictive gender barriers and prepare themselves to participate fully in American life.

But the moderates were more vocal and numerous. Appalled by such promoters as Didrikson's Colonel McCombs—who dressed his girls in yellow satin shorts and publicized them as alluring "beauty queens of sport"—and by the destructive notion fed by the Gallicos that female athletes had to be "muscle molls," those female college physical educators whose careers depended upon the growth of women's athletics offered their own perspective: A woman should play sport to bring blood to her uterus so that she could make better babies and better prepare herself for her life's work—having children and taking care of the home.

Rules were put into place curbing the rough play, competitiveness, and win-at-all-costs-tactics that marked men's games. One of the clearest examples of this was the creation of six-woman basketball, a slower, less aggressive version of the game that Dr. James Naismith's wife helped develop. It was not a full-court game; women stayed in prescribed zones. Nevertheless, most famously in Iowa, it became an important social and athletic tradition. Farm women took their daughters out to the barn in winter and showed them how to shoot and pass. Iowa girls' basketball often outdrew boys' high school games. (Six-woman basketball was a victim of equal rights by the 1980s. Once there were college athletic scholarships for women, even the traditional high school teams switched to the five-player, full-court game.)

The taming of the strong, independent woman of the twenties was a hot issue in this time of dramatic social change. Women were flooding colleges and the workplace, and they were voting. The athlete, a highly visible symbol of the new woman, became icon and target.

Didrikson was not the first American woman to crash the arena. Annie Oakley, the sharpshooter, and Helen Wills Moody, the tennis champion known as "Little Miss Poker Face" for her cold precision, were major celebrities, as was the aviator Amelia Earhart, the Olympic swimmer Eleanor Holm, and Eleanora Sears, equestrian, golfer, squash and tennis player. In 1926, Getrude Ederle became the first woman to swim the English Channel. She also became the fastest person, beating the previous record by almost two hours.

But no woman made a bigger splash than Babe Didrikson. The 1932 Olympic Games in Los Angeles were her personal debutante ball. Her country wit and lack of social graces were celebrated in that year of the Depression as proof that she was real, and the Hollywood crowd appreciated her larger-than-life ways. Clark Gable, Bob Hope, and Bing Crosby all became pals. Rice and Gallico became her Boswells and took her golfing. She met her namesake, Babe Ruth, who, according to Didrikson, gave her the best advice she ever got: "I wish someone had told me this when I was your age. I know you're making money. Put some of it away. Get yourself an annuity."

Everyone loved the idea of a sassy nineteen-year-old immigrant's daughter who could "whup" the arrogant ladies of sport. Of course, she was lying about her age; she was twenty-one. But she knew a "teenager" would get cut more slack and receive more ink.

Didrikson had an impact on many young athletes as well. Betty Hicks was eleven years old when she sat in the Los Angeles Coliseum and saw "the geometric, bosomless, narrow-thin Texas kid with the hacked-off hair, skimming the low hurdles to an 80-meter world record. I had dreamed adolescent dreams of being a star athlete; now I knew what a woman athlete had to be." Hicks would become a golf champion herself, a rival and critic of the Babe, but on that day the Texas kid showed her the future.

Actually, not everyone was inspired or charmed. Didrikson's teammates on the women's track and field squad resented her cockiness and publicity. She could also be a nuisance, loud when people wanted to sleep, a towel snapper, a pillow puller. Although they publicly cheered her victories in the 80-meter hurdles and the javelin throw, they privately cheered when she was denied a third gold medal in the high jump after officials ruled her head-first western roll style illegal. The winner that day, Jean Shiley, recalled forty years later that "the other girls on the team were delighted like children at Christmas because I had beaten the Babe."

Didrikson was even more of a problem for those female physical educators who had worked so hard to maintain noncompetitive "play-day" sport for college women well past World War II. To them, Babe represented the competitive "she-man" manipulated and exploited by promoters.

Ironically, while Didrikson clearly flouted the ideals of women who saw sport in moderation as preparation for motherhood, she never did become the feared lascivious sexpot. In fact, those who promoted women athletes as "beauty queens" had their own problems with Didrikson's disdain for makeup, stockings, dresses, and the opposite sex. A 1933 *Redbook* article on her Olympic triumphs, pointedly titled "How Can a Woman Do It?" noted that Didrikson liked men to play around with but not to "make love" to, and that she showed greater affection for her girlfriends than for any man.

The Babe never quite fit anyone's easy definition—she was neither a beauty queen nor an unnatural aberration, and she never became a mother—which may have been why she was able to be, uniquely, just the Babe. Women who saw her naked in the locker room testified that she was obviously a woman. It was her naked drive for money and fame that so concerned the boys that they needed to question her sexuality. This was printed in a Dallas newspaper after the Olympics: "Perhaps she supplies the proof that the comparatively recent turn of women to strenuous field sports is developing a new super-physique in womanhood, an unexpected outcome of suffragism which goes in for sports as well as politics and threatens the old male supremacy even in the mere routine of making a living."

She returned from the Olympics to a tumultuous parade through Dallas. The police band played "Hail to the Chief." A local dignitary called her "the Jim Thorpe of modern women athletes." (A portent of that 1950 *Associated Press* award when they were named female and male athletes of the half-century.) She waved, cracked jokes and talked Colonel McCombs into upping her pay to $300 a month so she wouldn't jump to another company. Then she settled down to make a buck.

In a somewhat murky chapter of her life, the AAU, those guardians of athletic purity who had found Jim Thorpe guilty of professionalism, began an investigation after Babe was seen driving a shiny red Dodge coupe. The AAU didn't think she could afford it on her Employers Casualty salary. There was no shortage of jealous people to turn her in. Didrikson claimed she was paying off the car on time. Then her name and photograph appeared in a Dodge ad. Didrikson claimed that the Chrysler Company had used her off-handed enthusiasm for her new car without permission and the company backed her up.

Eventually, the AAU declared her an innocent exploited by the new hidden persuaders of advertising, but Didrikson realized that there was little money and no control in being an amateur. She turned pro. Her options were limited, but she merrily took them to gender-bending extremes. She became the leading lounge act in sports.

After working the 1933 Detroit Auto Show as a come-on at the Dodge booth, Didrikson followed the greasepaint trail blazed by the Great John L., Papa Jack, and the boy Babe. She hit the boards, receiving top billing on the RKO vaudeville circuit in a show featuring one Fifi D'Orsay and Bob Murphy and his Collegians. Babe said she earned $2,500 a week (this was 1933!) for an act that basically consisted of eighteen minutes of banter and song that flirted with the ambiguity of her sexual identity.

While one George Libbey played the piano and sang on stage, Babe would sashay down the aisle "wearing a cute panama hat...a green swagger coat and high-heeled spectators," and join him for a parody of "I'm Fit as a Fiddle and Ready for Love," singing the key line, "I'm fit as a fiddle and ready to go." Then Babe would trade her high heels for track shoes, peel off her coat to reveal red-white-and-blue satin shorts and jacket, and proceed to work out—hurdling, hitting golf balls, running on a treadmill—before closing the act with a harmonica solo. Naturally, she was a terrific harmonica player.

After Broadway there was Babe Didrikson's All-Americans, a barnstorming coed basketball team. She pulled down $1,000 a month. Come summer she was back on the road with the old major league pitching ace Grover Cleveland Alexander, each making $1,500 a month as stars of the House of David, a baseball team of whiskered gents from a midwest religious cult.

"I didn't even travel with the team," Didrikson recalled. "I was an extra attraction to help them draw big crowds.... I had my own car, and I had a schedule, and I'd get to whatever ball park they were playing at in time for the game. I'd pitch the first inning, then I'd take off and not see them again until the next town."

While Didrikson earned more than $40,000 between 1932 and 1935, Johnson and Williamson point out in *Whatta-Gal!* that she did nothing to advance the cause of women's sports, becoming instead "a symbol of the negative effects competitive sport could have on women." Female physical education instructors certainly portrayed her that way, but it is clear also that women who loved sports felt empowered by her talent and grit. And her size. For all the Amazonian prose about her, Didrikson stood about 5-feet, 6-inches and weighed, at most, 140 pounds.

Her message outlived her. Mariah Burton Nelson, pro basketball player, coach, and author, who was born the year that Babe died (1956), vividly remembers reading Didrikson's answer to reporters who asked her how she was able to hit the ball so far.

"She said, 'I just loosen my girdle and let it fly.' I loved that," said Nelson. "We don't technically wear girdles anymore, but we do remain constrained by many ideas of femininity, traditional standards of beauty. I like to tell college students, don't hold back, go after what you want. Achieve anything you can. Let's loosen our girdles and let her fly."

That image of freedom and possibility may have been Didrikson's single greatest legacy. But no woman with less determination, with less of that "mean streak" so prized in male athletes, could have dared to crack the cultivated, upper class world of women's golf.

"Animosity," wrote golfing rival Hicks in a 1975 *womenSports* article, "was the primary fuel for Babe's competitive fire."

That she channeled her "animosity" into golf, a precise game of killer control surrounded by polite society, may be a clue to Didrikson's psychic needs. The Hall of Fame pro golfer, Betsy Rawls, a Phi Betta Kappa from the University of Texas, has offered this analysis: "I think the potential to make money attracted her to golf and the potential to become more of a celebrity, to be a real star. Also, I think she picked golf because it was such a genteel sport.

"It was probably the most respectable sport for women there was in this country. Golfers were a very refined group. Being in that group gave Babe instant respectability in her eyes."

In late 1934, when Didrikson got serious about golf, she was already a name on those "Where are they now?" lists—a has-been. She had lost her luster, her earning power was slipping, and sportswriters no longer gathered for quotes. Her own description of her golfing apprenticeship is standard fakelore; we are led to believe she rarely played until the day she "whupped" Peggy Chandler. Actually, Babe began hitting golf balls in high school, and her sister Lillie remembers visiting her in Dallas when Babe was eighteen and begging her to leave the driving range because it was dark and blood was seeping through the tape on her hands.

During the 1932 Olympics, Rice took her golfing and was impressed with her "lashing style" and her "forearms of steel." Using a baseball grip, Didrikson consistently drove the ball 250 yards, unusual for a woman in those days. Over the next few years, she took many lessons, spent hours at driving ranges and practiced putting obsessively. She was still raw as a golfer and as a personality when she arrived at the Texas Women's Amateur Golf Championship in the spring of 1935. It is not clear whether the women who withdrew from the pre-tournament driving contest were frightened off by her power game or offended by her mouth.

Women golfers were country club ladies back then. Babe was known to shout after a bad shot, "Man! All that work and the baby's dead." Other golfers shuddered, the gallery howled, and Didrikson—beaming—swaggered on. Women's golf was mostly match play in those days, and in head-to-head competition the intimidating psych-out artist has an enormous advantage. A genteel game would fall apart against a hearty "Step back, kid, and watch this!"

Didrikson's come-from-behind victory over Chandler, a doyenne of Houston society married to a West Pointer, was later fictionalized in Gallico's "The Lady and the Tiger," and accorded class and cultural significance. Certainly, Houston's posh River Oaks Country Club had never before seen the likes of Didrikson's cheering, hooting gallery.

Nor did River Oaks want to see it again. Two days later, the United States Golf Association announced an investigation into her amateur standing, and several weeks later, citing the old AAU charges, barred her from further competition "in the best interests" of golf. Didrikson quickly signed a promotional contract with a sporting goods firm and went off on a $150 per day exhibition tour with golfing great Gene Sarazen, who remembers that they did very well, if not always for the best of reasons: "People wanted to come out and see this freak from Texas who could play golf, tennis, and beat everyone swimming up and down the pool."

Sarazen gave her golf tips. R. L. and Bertha Bowen, a wealthy Texas couple who befriended her, offered tips on etiquette and clothes. The rougher edges were being sanded down. According to Hicks, while Didrikson remained "back-alley tough and barroom crude" she did "develop the sensitivity to acquire certain layers of the veneer of femininity. She painted her fingernails, curled her hair, put on high heels and wore lace-trimmed dresses."

So veneered, in fact, that she was swept off her feet in 1938 by George Zaharias, the "Crying Greek from Cripple Creek," a 250-pound professional wrestler and promoter. Leo "The Lip" Durocher, then the Brooklyn Dodgers' volatile shortstop, and later best known for saying "Nice guys finish last," was the best man at their wedding.

With Zaharias supporting her, Babe was able to regain her amateur status by giving up professional sports for three years. Early in 1943, smoother, better-dressed, now married to a man who exuded hearty heterosexuality, she began a furious charge down the fairway that confirmed her as the most popular woman golfer in the world, and—eventually—helped to establish women's golf as a viable professional sport.

For the next four years, Didrikson dominated the women's amateur game and spooked the men's. In 1945, after she was voted the outstanding woman athlete of the year by the *Associated Press*, she said she might play in the all-male U.S. Open. The newsies bolted the press conference to phone their papers. The next day, the USGA held a special meeting to specifically bar women from the event and change the official name of the tournament to the U.S. Men's Open. Didrikson later told friends she had no intention of playing against men, she just thought it would make a good story.

Just spell my name right, she would cackle, and after she added on Zaharias she would sometimes pronounce it "Za-hairy-ass" to get a laugh.

Anything for a laugh, a raised eyebrow, for attention. People came out to see her at first, not women's golf. They enjoyed themselves, but they seemed to need to convince themselves they were seeing a new, improved, feminized model.

In 1938, *Life* magazine reported that "the world's most amazing athlete has learned to wear nylons and cook for her huge husband." The story noted that the happy newlyweds slept in a specially-made eight-foot square bed, and that this "lonely girl" whose "lips were too thin and her Adam's apple too big...who hated girls and only lived to beat them," was now a wonderful housewife who liked to wear makeup and dress up in silk and nylon.

By 1947, the *Saturday Evening Post* could reveal that Babe had finally taken off "her mask" of masculinity to reveal the true woman that was always there.

"Babe is no longer button-breasted," the *Post* observed. "The bust measurement of this ex-Texas girl," once described as "born halfway between masculine flats and angles and the rubbery curves of femininity ... is now a Valkyrian forty inches," a full inch and a half larger than "Hollywood's leading sweater-filler," Jane Russell.

Now, "perfume, lipstick and fingernail polish lie on her dressing table. Style and class hang in her closets.... Such frills and fripperies are a far cry from the cotton union suits she once wore and the makeup she defiantly didn't wear."

Babe wasn't the only object of wartime America's confusion and ambivalence over gender and sexuality. Between 1940 and 1945, as American women marched into factories to help build the arsenal of democracy, their numbers in the work force increased from twenty to thirty-five percent. "Rosie the Riveter" became an idol of the assembly line. Yet when working women requested federal and state child-care assistance, they met strong resistance—a reminder that even if they did a "man's job" they were still expected to fulfill their responsibilities as mother and housekeeper.

Perhaps because their work was so essential to the Allies' cause, these women in men's clothing frightened men. Would they become defeminized by the experience, would they be reluctant to return full time to their special and proper roles as mother and homemaker when the war ended, would they be out of men's control?

In 1943, Philip K. Wrigley, chewing-gum magnate and owner of baseball's Chicago Cubs, launched the All-American Girls Softball League to help fill his Wrigley Field as major league baseball players went off to war and attendance dwindled. Two years later, the game became baseball, in part to distinguish it from the softball played by thousands of working-class women throughout the country. AAGBL contracts stipulated that players attend charm school, "learn how to take a third strike like a lady," and wear makeup and short skirts. On the road they were accompanied by chaperones.

As Susan Cahn points out in *Coming On Strong*, Wrigley cashed in on the tension between sport and femininity by selling the league "as a dramatic spectacle of gender contrasts, presenting women's baseball as a unique combination of feminine beauty and masculine athletic skill."

Or as the league handbook put it in a section called "Femininity with

Skill," it was "more dramatic to see a feminine-type girl throw, run, and bat than to see a man or boy or masculine-type girl do the same things. The more feminine the appearance of the performer, the more dramatic the performance."

Like Didrikson, the women who played professional women's baseball put up with, and often even encouraged, the gender hype and hypocrisy. They earned good money and enjoyed the camaraderie and teamwork usually reserved for men. In its best years, the league fielded teams in ten midwestern cities and played before as many as one million people.

By 1954, the "league of their own" was over; post-war America needed its factory and baseball jobs for its returning veterans. A conformist, cold war era demanded that women return to the kitchen.

By that time, however, Didrikson had the Ladies Professional Golf Association up and running. It was backed by the Wilson Sporting Goods Company and by Fred Carr, former director of the men's pro tour. There were fine young golfers like Louise Suggs and Patty Berg. An expanding suburban leisure class who played the game wanted to watch it, too.

Though prize money was negligible at first, Didrikson, through endorsements and appearances, made more than $100,000 a year when total yearly purses were around $25,000. Didrikson was aware of the disparity, but was concerned mainly with getting hers. As she once told Hicks, "Ah can remember them hamburger days in Beaumont. Ah want nothing but filets now." There were resentments, of course, but the bottom line was simple—no Babe, no LPGA. Happily, there was a trickle down effect: By the mid-1950s, prize money was around a quarter of a million dollars.

But the Babe got hers first. Peggy Kirk Bell, LPGA charter member and now a well-known teacher to the pros, remembers Didrikson in New York passing a jewelry store, looking in the window and saying, "They're making a woman's Rolex. I got to have one of those."

As Bell tells it: "So she goes into the telephone booth and finds out where Rolex is and gets in a taxi and goes up to the office and says, 'I'd like to see the president, you just tell him Babe Zaharias is out here,' and in about two shakes the president was out shaking her hand, 'Hey, Babe,' and she says, 'I got to have one of those Rolexes,' and he said, 'Fine, we'll meet tomorrow at Toots Shor's. We'll have a little press conference, and I'll present you with a Rolex. And then we'll go out and play some golf.'"

As would happen, George Zaharias and friends of hers ended up with watches, too. And when several dress companies began sponsoring the women's tour, Didrikson got her cash but saw to it that other golfers got free clothes.

Betty Hicks, a runner-up to Didrikson in several major tournaments, seems to have been her harshest public critic among women golfers. She has admitted to feeling "puny and brittle" beside Didrikson's "rampant brutishness," and she tends to dismiss some of the modern feminist praise. Men did not feel threatened by her, maintained Hicks, because "men could convince themselves that she was not quite all woman."

Didrikson's message was consistently mixed. She was "masculine-type" crude. Yet she wore backless high heels and plumed hats. Even as her marriage to Zaharias deteriorated ("When I married him he looked like a Greek God," she repeated with an increasing edge over the years, "now he looks like a god-damned Greek"), she did not flaunt her live-in friend, the golfer Betty Dodd. It was never clear whether they were lovers as well as intimate friends although there was intense speculation. Some straight women who were beaten by Didrikson and some men who were threatened by her power game and aggressive ways insisted she was a lesbian, as have some lesbians who want to claim this foremother of American sport as one of their own.

It may be enough just to label her "Babe," a woman athlete who was a unique force. American sports did not see another one until Billie Jean King came along in the 1960s.

Babe Didrikson Zaharias died on September 27, 1956, at the age of forty-five. The last round of her life was so quintessentially Babe-like that it cemented her legend as a courageous scrapper. She came back from cancer operations and a colostomy to win five tournaments, including the U.S. Women's Open. The *Associated Press* voted her Woman Athlete of the Year for an unprecedented sixth time. Along the way, in a time when the word cancer was barely whispered, she publicized her illness, appeared at fund-raisers, and encouraged other cancer patients. She approached her cancer as if it were a sand trap or a water hazard to be conquered, but this time she didn't know the course—she had never been told that her disease was terminal. Critics say her unwarranted optimism let down other cancer patients. Boosters say she helped eradicate the false shame of the disease and saved lives.

Didrikson is controversial still. Some say she set back the progress of women's sports with her gender-bending antics and some claim she jump-started it. In any event, she can't be judged by a modern feminist perspective. Or by suffragist standards.

When Billie Jean King played Bobby Riggs in 1973, it was a conscious political act that recognized SportsWorld as a stage from which to challenge male power and exclusivity. Babe played the clown through the Depression, World War II, and then the conformist fifties, when survival came before equality. But she helped make Billie Jean possible.

And in her own way she lived the athletic declaration of independence voiced a few years after her death by another braggart who delivered, Muhammad Ali: "I don't have to be what you want me to be, I'm free to be who I want."

The LPGA runs a fine and profitable tour these days, and its teaching division has done far more to reach out to poor and minority youngsters than has the men's game or most other sports. Women are proud to play a power game, thanks to Didrikson. Day care is a fixture on the tour, as is a counselor known as "the image lady" who advises individual golfers on clothes, makeup, and etiquette. Mixed messages play through.

Babe was an unabashed jock before it was fashionable for women to loosen their girdles and let it fly. She lived for the applause and for the game. After her death, George Zaharias recalled: "She told me when things were tough, 'George, I hate to die.' I said, 'why'—she said, 'I'm just learning to play golf.'"

PART III

CREDITS TO THE RACE

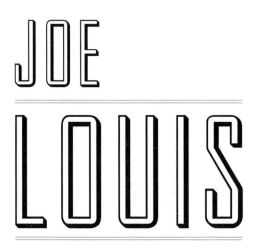

JOE LOUIS COULD HIT. HIS HANDS WERE FAST, WHICH MEANT HE COULD THROW a furious combination, and his punches were short, which meant he didn't need much space to throw them. Crowding him wouldn't work, nor would dancing away, because he was a stalker. "You can run but you can't hide," was his warning.

If Louis had not been such a smart boxer, such a dream-street slugger, he could never have been such a shining symbol in such a dark time. As in the core of every idol's appeal, Louis possessed a startling talent and a ferocious will to prevail, to win. His jab could rattle your brain and set you up for either his right cross or his left hook, both knockout blows. Sparring partners felt sore for days. After James J. Braddock lost his title to Louis, he said, "When you're hit by Louis it's like a light bulb breaking in your face."

The light-bulb image is especially apt because Louis was an idol spanning both grinding Depression and terrifying war. He would eventually become a hero to all Americans, "a credit to his race, the human race," to quote sportswriter Jimmy Cannon, which seems patronizing now but

was powerfully progressive when he wrote it. But before Louis was a national hero, he was an important and rare symbol of hope for African-Americans.

In her autobiography, *I Know Why the Caged Bird Sings*, Maya Angelou recalls a childhood night with friends and family in a tiny store in Arkansas as the radio broadcast a Louis knockout. "Champion of the world. A Black boy. Some Black mother's son. He was the strongest man in the world. People drank Coca-Cola like ambrosia and ate candy bars like Christmas.

"Those who lived too far had made arrangements to stay in town. It wouldn't do for a Black man and his family to be caught on a lonely country road on a night when Joe Louis had proved that we were the strongest people in the world."

John Thompson, the Georgetown University basketball coach, lived with his parents in the basement of the house his mother cleaned for a white family. The Thompsons were invited upstairs to hear the fight.

"When Joe knocked the fighter out, however, the people jumped up and turned the radio off," recalled Thompson. "So my mother and father quickly said good night and went downstairs. The minute they got downstairs they yelled like hell in celebration of the win."

In his autobiography, Malcolm X wrote of his youth, "Every Negro boy old enough to walk wanted to be the Brown Bomber."

Louis was the most important black sports hero whom blacks and whites could cheer together. World War II's unifying threat of an outside enemy made that possible as did Louis's willingness to conceal his private life. He allowed himself to be merchandised as the anti-Jack, the non-threatening black superman.

Louis was probably as hedonistic as Jack Johnson or Babe Ruth, and he apparently had an abusive side like John L. Sullivan. He probably slept with more famous white women than Johnson ever met. But very little of that information leaked out during his time; he was protected by his managers and by sportswriters. Submerging his personality may have been emotionally costly, however. Louis descended into madness and addiction in middle age. But people who knew him in his prime still catch their breath trying to describe his beautiful, deadly grace as he sprang across the ring, his fists a brutal blur.

He was born Joseph Louis Barrow on May 13, 1914, in a forsaken pocket of America—a sharecropper's shack in the red clay Buckalew Mountains of Alabama, near the town of Cussetta. He was the seventh of eight children of Munroe and Lillie Barrow. From a distance, it is easy to say that Louis spent the first twelve years of his life surrounded by the oppressive rural poverty of most American blacks. They could not vote, go to the same schools as whites, or, for most, find more than menial work. The threat of beatings, humiliations, and lynchings hung in the soft southern air.

But for Joe Barrow, doted on by older sisters, it was a sweet time of ponds to swim in and thick elms to scurry up. The game of his childhood was "skin the tree," a tag game played among the tangled branches. Even then he was bigger, stronger, more graceful than the others. And he would remember that there was always plenty of food—ham and corn and baked chicken legs and cakes that would never last long enough to grow stale.

Beyond the Buckalew Mountains the world was turning upside down. Years of turmoil in Europe and Asia had brought twenty million new-comers to America, and their muscle and energy helped industrialize the northern cities. Kick-started by World War I, America's economy boomed. Between 1910 and 1930, more than two million African-Americans headed north for urban factory jobs.

Crossing the Mason-Dixon line was not quite fording the River Jordan. For African-Americans, there was more economic discrimina-tion, social segregation, and racial violence than milk and honey either in the so-called Progressive era or in the abundance of the 1920s. But cities such as New York, Chicago, Pittsburgh, and Detroit provided opportunities for community, education, and even political participation that far exceeded anything they had left behind. In particular, New York City's Harlem was a savory black stew of art, music, and intellectual ferment, bubbling with aspirations and demands.

When Joe was but two years old, Munroe Barrow, who bore the last name of the white slaveholder who had owned his parents, was committed to a state hospital for "the Colored Insane." Soon after, Lillie Barrow moved in with Pat Brooks, a widower with five children of his own. The blended families chopped cotton on rented land until 1926, when they joined the great black migration north. The Barrow-Brooks bunch settled in Detroit where Pat and his older sons got jobs at the Ford plant.

Joe was a big, shy, stuttering teenager who quickly fell behind in school. Lillie Barrow was not without hopes and dreams for him. She enrolled him in after-school violin lessons. Joe was no gangster. He hauled coal, delivered ice, and fought on the street only when he had to. One day, urged by an older boy he admired, an amateur boxer, he used his music money to rent a locker at a local gym. Everyone could see the basics were there—speed, strength, and the willingness to hit and be hit.

Like the world champions Benny Leonard (Leiner), Barney Ross (Rosofsky), and hundreds of other ghetto boys who changed their names so their mothers wouldn't know they were boxing, Joe dropped Barrow and became Louis. He was soon sorry; he was so good right away that the merchandise checks he won as prizes piled groceries on the table. The family was delighted. In 1933, fighting as an amateur light-heavyweight, Louis won fifty bouts, forty-three by knockout, and the world began to open up for him—Chicago, Boston, Golden Gloves matches that took him all the way to a fight for the National Amateur championship. He lost that bout, one of only four defeats all year, but "I saw things I wanted that I had never really known about," Louis later recalled. "I met important people and I wanted to be important, too."

The most important was John Roxborough, an African-American who operated in Detroit real estate and "the numbers," the illegal lotteries that dominated the dream-life and finances of poor neighborhoods. Well-dressed and smooth, Roxborough proposed himself as Louis's manager. He offered him a fifty-fifty split of purses once Louis turned professional and agreed to pay all expenses out of his half. It was a fair deal. He began teaching Louis how to dress, how to act among strangers, how to hold his knife and fork. He was clearly grooming him for the big time. Roxborough was also what was then known as a "race man," a proud pillar of racial pride and consciousness. Much later, he would tell the story of a call from a New York promoter who said, "I can help your boy."

"We can use help," Roxborough reported as his reply. "We think Joe is ready for big things."

"Well, you understand he's a nigger and can't win every time he goes into the ring."

"So am I," said Roxborough, hanging up.

Apocryphal as the story may be, it helps explain Roxborough's attraction to Louis not only as cash cow (he could have made quicker dough dealing with the white mob) but as a racial hero. And as a black man, Roxborough understood the youngster in ways that would never become apparent to the predominately white press and boxing establishment: Joe Louis, for all his fury in the ring, was an internal person, shy and careful among whites and strangers, stoic and laconic in that American frontier way so prized in movie heroes.

By June 1934, Joe was at Trafton's Gym in Chicago, where Julian Black, Roxborough's friend and partner, introduced him to Jack Blackburn, a black trainer who had fought a hundred times as a lightweight, sparred with Jack Johnson, and done prison time for murder. Blackburn was dubious. He preferred to train white boys. They had a future. The meeting between the shy twenty-year-old and the tough, middle-aged, alcoholic trainer is supposed to have gone something like this.

"You know, boy," rasped Blackburn, his shaven head gleaming under a naked bulb, "the heavyweight division for a negro ain't likely. But if you really ain't gonna be another Jack Johnson, you got some hope. You got to listen to everything I say. Jump when I say jump, sleep when I say sleep. Other than that, you're wasting my time."

"I promise," said Joe.

Blackburn nodded. "Okay, Chappie."

"Okay, Chappie," Joe echoed.

Blackburn grinned. "Chappie" became their nickname for each other in that complex relationship between trainer and fighter that may be the closest in all of sport. The blackness of Louis's management, the fierceness with which the three men protected him from white hoodlums and black hustlers, and their faith in his future were all critical shaping factors. They were not only able to see beyond the shadow of Jack Johnson but helped Louis create a persona that allayed white fears. By the time of Muhammad Ali, it was deemed hip for militants to call Louis an "Uncle Tom" for what seemed like his passive social role. That was unfair, self-serving, and ignorant; Louis did the best he could to stand up with finesse. Blackburn's advice was earthy and to the point. Don't look like those "little black toy dolls ... with thick red lips," he told Joe.

"I got the message," Louis recalled. "Don't look like a fool nigger doll. Look like a black man with dignity."

Blackburn drilled into Louis that as a black fighter the odds would be against him every time he fought a white man. "It's mighty hard for a colored boy to win decisions," said Blackburn. "You gotta knock 'em out and keep knocking 'em out to get anywheres. Let your right fist be the referee. Don't ever forget that. Let that right fist there be your referee!"

It seemed fitting then that Louis fought his first professional bout on July 4, 1934, twenty-four years to the Independence Day that Jack Johnson beat Jim Jeffries. And he followed Blackburn's advice. White Jack Kracken went down within two minutes of the first round. A week later, Willie Davis fell in three. That first year, fighting primarily in the Midwest, Louis won all twenty-six of his bouts, twenty-two by knockout. Each outing earned him a little more money, as much as $6,000 for one fight, a heady payday for a twenty-year-old black man in the depths of the Great Depression.

But there was a lid that needed to be lifted, and Louis couldn't do it with fists alone. The path to the title went through New York, then the capital of American boxing. Madison Square Garden was the most famous boxing arena in the world. But there was no way a black boxer, managed and trained by black men, would get the opportunities he needed. Even for Joe Louis, clearly the best fighter of his time—some say, any time—it would take the twists of both world and boxing politics, and the juxtapositions of such characters as William Randolph Hearst, Mike Jacobs, Benito Mussolini, and Adolph Hitler to make Louis an idol of the arena.

Three weeks before Louis's professional debut, Max Baer had defeated Primo Carnera to become heavyweight champion of the world. Roxborough was convinced that Louis could beat either of them if only he could get the chance.

It was during Baer's one-year reign that Roxborough met Mike Jacobs, who claimed to have the key to that chance. Jacobs said he could book Louis to a succession of important bouts that would give him national exposure and force the Garden to set him up with a title fight. But he wanted a percentage of Louis's purses and his future. Roxborough signed it over. If Jacobs came through, it would be cheap at the price.

Jacobs was also an outsider, the son of East European immigrants, born and raised in the crowded Jewish ghetto of New York's Lower East Side. He had learned the fight promotion racket from Tex Rickard, the preeminent sports impresario of the Golden Age who ran Madison Square Garden. When Rickard died in 1929, Jacobs expected to take over the Garden. When he was shut out, Jacobs organized the rival Twentieth Century Sporting Club and began to compete with the Garden. But to achieve his own dream of gaining control of boxing, he needed a superstar fighter, a heavyweight champion who could hold the title for years.

Ultimately, he did become boxing's dominant figure because of Louis. Over twenty years, Jacobs staged 61 championship fights and 320 boxing cards at the Garden alone. The sidewalk outside his offices on New York's West Forty-eighth Street was called Jacobs Beach because it was always crowded with boxers, trainers, and managers often sitting on beach chairs, waiting for an audience with "Uncle Mike."

Jacobs's dominance of boxing began with a plan using Joe Louis. In the early 1930s, the Hearst Milk Fund took a cut from fight proceeds at the Garden to feed hungry children. The Garden monopoly arrogantly reduced the amount of money that could be donated to the Fund, which was the favorite charity of newspaper publishing magnate William Randolph Hearst. The powerful publisher, whom some have credited with helping to start the Spanish-American War to sell papers, became enraged. Jacobs let it be known that the Milk Fund would get more money than ever before if he were running boxing.

Suddenly, Hearst sportswriters, including Damon Runyon, began writing stories about fighters Jacobs controlled, especially this new sensation, Joe Louis.

Jacobs realized that Louis's talent as a boxer would not be enough. As had Roxborough, he insisted that Louis comport himself in a manner inoffensive to white Americans. He made sure newspapers published copies of the Roxborough commandments:

Never be photographed with a white woman.
Never gloat over a fallen (read white) opponent.
Never go into a night club alone.
Live and fight clean.
Keep a "dead pan."

To further Louis's public image as a serious, polite, and well-intentioned black man who just happened to be a boxer, a tutor was hired to polish his English. Delighted by all the money, new clothes, and his growing status as a celebrity, Louis gladly went along for the ride, even as he "discreetly" enjoyed the company of both black and white women, as he did throughout his career.

Later, he would choose from a flock of admirers that included Lena Horne, Sonja Henie, and Lana Turner. Publicly, it was another story. As his ghostwriter declared for him in *Joe Louis' Own Story*, a pamphlet about his life, "I can't throw my race down by abusing my position as a heavyweight challenger. It is my duty to win the championship and prove to the world that, black or white, a man can become the best fighter and still be a gentleman."

And that was pretty much the official line on Louis, "as different a character from Jack Johnson" wrote one New York sportswriter "as Lou Gehrig is from Al Capone.... He is a God-fearing, Bible-reading, clean-living young man to be admired, regardless of creed, race, or color."

He was also the Brown Bomber, the Sepia Slugger, the Dark Destroyer, the Shufflin' Shadow, and the Tan Tornado. Few white sportswriters could give Louis much credit for dedication or hard work. The dean of that brotherhood, Grantland Rice, called Joe a "bushmaster" with "the speed of the jungle, the instinctive speed of the wild." He also wrote that "the great Negro boxer is rarely a matter of manufacture, like many white boxers. He is born that way."

But as they said in those days, a knock is just a plug that came in the back door, and Mike Jacobs was happy with any plug as he cranked up his pugilistic public relations machine. Sportswriters might, as did Paul Gallico, misread the stuttering Louis's shyness as surly coldness and concoct a "mean man, a truly savage" animus for him, but as long as they were writing about his fighter, even as "a magnificent animal," Jacobs was happy. It would sell tickets because it fit into his own promotion of Louis as Democracy's fighter against Fascism and Communism.

Jacobs's first match for Louis, against former champion Carnera at Yankee Stadium on June 25, 1935, fitted neatly into his ideological hype. Carnera was an Italian national and, at 6-feet, 5-inches and 260 pounds, the largest man ever to hold the heavyweight crown. He had won the title from Jack Sharkey in 1933 and lost it a year later to Maxie Baer, who wore a Star of David on his trunks to attract Jewish fight fans. He was supposedly part Jewish. The only reason he won, wrote one sportswriter, was "because he was in there with a bigger bum."

But in the time of Benito Mussolini's invasion of Ethiopia, when newspapers carried stories of brave, black Ethiopian warriors facing Italian tanks with their spears, Jacobs could not have found a better opponent for his "meal ticket." Mussolini's huge "emissary" became a metaphor for fascist aggression against a small, African nation and, more subtly, against American democracy. America's Brown Bomber would stop the tanks—even if Ethiopia's emperor, Haile Selassie, could not. At least that's how many sportswriters, especially those in Jacobs's pocket, "steamed up" the fight.

Joe trained hard for his big chance, insulated from most of the political subtexts although at least one visitor to his camp, a black professor, seriously suggested that Louis pull his punches lest he enrage Mussolini and cause more Ethiopian deaths.

Louis was apolitical, but as the world intruded he began to catch on. It was while training for Carnera, he noted later in his autobiography, that "a lot of black people would come to me and want to kiss me, pump my hand. I thought they were congratulating me for my fighting skills. Now they started saying things like, 'Joe, you're our savior,' and 'Show them whites!' and sometimes they'd just shout, 'Brown Bomber, Brown Bomber!'"

On another day, while training for Carnera, a photographer asked Louis to pose with a slice of watermelon. He kept refusing and the photographer kept insisting. Exasperated, the photographer asked why. "I don't like watermelon," Joe lied. He refused, according to Harry Markson, then a sportswriter covering the camp, because he "instinctively knew this was a racist kind of a thing."

When black reporters were refused the same ringside working-press seats as white reporters, Louis became actively involved. The official explanation was that those seats were reserved for daily newspapers—almost all the black newspapers were weeklies; Louis lent his support to a protest and some ringside seats were found for black reporters.

What they saw was even more satisfying close up. The fight was Joe's from the first punch. It took him a while to get used to Carnera's size and his awkward style, but the giant was powerless to stop the Brown Bomber from slipping in his long punches and working himself inside. He battered Carnera with short, chopping body punches. Carnera was hurt and flustered.

In the sixth round, Louis put Carnera down three times with hard crosses. The third time, Carnera, dazed, his mouth pooled in blood, could not get up.

The *New York Sun*, the same paper that forty years earlier had warned of the humiliation of having a black champion, wrote in 1935 that Louis had "the skill, strength and courage of which champions are made." But the editorial went on to state that the "American Negro is a natural athlete. The generations of toil in the cotton fields have not obliterated the strength and grace of the African native."

Two months later, Louis went after the lesser "bum." Baer was a better boxer than Carnera, but he lasted two fewer rounds. Louis said later it was the peak of his power, that he never felt so sharp or so strong. When he knocked Baer out in the fourth round, it was his second victory over a former heavyweight champion.

Richard Wright's depiction of black Chicago's response to that victory is among the best in capturing its meaning for black Americans as well as the frenzy and joy of the moment: "Two hours after the fight the area between South Parkway and Prairie Avenue on Forty-seventh Street was jammed with no less than twenty-five thousand Negroes, joy-mad and moving to they didn't know where. Clasping hands, they formed long writhing snake-lines and wove in and out of traffic. They seeped out of doorways, oozed from alleys, trickled out of tenements and flowed down the street; a fluid mass of joy."

Wright, already acclaimed for *Black Boy*, and an avowed Communist, put his own interpretation on the celebration: "Something had happened, all right.... Something had popped loose all right. And it had come from deep down.... Four centuries of oppression, of frustrated hopes, of black bitterness, felt even in the bones of the bewildered young, were rising to the surface.... From the symbol of Joe's strength they took strength, and in that moment all fear, all obstacles were wiped out, drowned."

Mike Jacobs was also thrilled with the Baer victory although his analysis was more commercial; it was proof of Louis's potential of becoming boxing's top attraction. The next major step up would be over Max Schmeling, a third former champion and an even bigger political symbol than Carnera. The fight was originally set for June 18, 1936. It would be delayed one night by rain.

A genial, not particularly political man married to a German movie star, Schmeling had emerged as champion from a pool of heavyweight contenders for Gene Tunney's vacated throne by beating Jack Sharkey in

1930 on a foul. He lost the title to Sharkey two years later in a rematch that most experts thought he had won. By 1936 he was thirty years old and desperate to get back on top. He was also the most legitimate contender for James J. Braddock's title. A victory over the German boxer would make Louis the most legitimate contender as well as provide a striking opportunity to make him acceptable to white America as the champion of democracy against Nazi Germany. (Beating Schmeling in a fight where nationalism and political ideology were more important than race would guarantee Louis a championship fight.)

That's how Mike Jacobs had figured it. As it turned out, he had his work cut out for him. Jewish organizations already engaged in promoting an American boycott of the 1936 Olympic Games, scheduled that summer for Berlin, demanded that Jacobs cancel the bout. How could this sporting event take place as if nothing was happening in Germany? The murderous evils of the Master Race were already being documented. Schmeling's Jewish-American manager, Joe Jacobs (no relation to Max), was urged to end his relationship with the fighter. The fact that the German government had disowned Schmeling as an Aryan hero ever since his loss to Max Baer further complicated the promoter's scheme. As columnist Westbrook Pegler put it, as far as Hitler was concerned, Schmeling "was absolutely on his own, because there seemed an excellent chance that having already been knocked out by a Jew, he would now be stretched in the resin at the feet of a cotton-field Negro."

Hitler didn't have to worry. After the Baer fight, Louis's life had become a party. He was twenty-two years old, unbeaten in all his professional fights, rich, handsome, and famous. He ran with the black superstars of his time—Duke Ellington, the great jazz composer; Bill "Bojangles" Robinson, the dancer and Hollywood star; singer Lena Horne; and Paul Robeson, one of America's greatest opera singers and a fighter for human rights. Louis didn't have time to train, and when he did show up at camp he brought his golf clubs along, which amused Grantland Rice but infuriated Blackburn. He was also newly married to Marva Trotter, a young black woman from a respectable middle-class family that fit Louis's packaged public image nicely.

Schmeling was not taking the bout lightly. "I've seen him spar," Schmeling told reporters. "I know how to beat him." The reporters did not believe him but they printed it to help build the gate.

They fought on the damp night of June 19, 1936. There were forty thousand people in the stands of Yankee Stadium and all seemed to be rooting for Louis to beat Schmeling and force Braddock to fight him. Louis was just a few punches away from becoming the champ. But, thinking about Braddock instead of Schmeling cost Louis the fight. Just before the bell, Blackburn reminded him, "Don't go for the knockout yet, keep your left high."

Louis told Chappie not to worry, that Schmeling was a "pushover."

At the bell, Schmeling waded out in a tight crouch, almost doubled over. Louis moved around him, popping his long jab down into Schmeling's eye, which soon swelled shut. The second round was like the first, with Schmeling getting tagged but staying down in his crouch. Louis dipped down to throw a left hook. Chappie had warned him to keep his left up but Joe felt confident. The hook landed.

So did Schmeling's counterpunch, a blistering right cross that sent Louis reeling. He never totally recovered. He was flustered as his upper-cuts bounced off Schmeling's rock-hard ribs, and Schmeling's rights kept looping in again and again, bludgeoning Louis's head. He went down and sprang right up, but in a way the fight was over. He had never been down as a pro before; never been hurt like this. He held on for another eight rounds, Schmeling's relentless beating actually holding him up.

Near the end of the twelfth round, Schmeling stepped back and Louis toppled to the canvas.

"I was sitting on the dressing table and crying like I don't think I ever did before," he said in his autobiography. "It seemed at that moment I would just die."

Louis was not the only one who cried that night. Americans found out how important he had become to some of them. Brokenhearted people sat numb beside their radios and wandered silent into the streets. Men stoned streetcars in Chicago. A girl in New York drank a bottle of poison and almost died.

Adam Clayton Powell Jr., later to become a powerful congressman, wrote in the weekly *New York Amsterdam News*: "Along came the Brown Bomber, Death in the Evening, and our racial morale took a sky high leap.... Then ... the Yankee Stadium fiasco.... Gone today is the jauntiness, the careless abandon, the spring in our stride—we're just shufflin' along."

Overnight Schmeling became the hero of Nazi Germany. Chancellor Adolph Hitler cabled Schmeling on "his splendid victory," Goebbels embraced it as a "splendid patriotic achievement," and the German press pronounced his triumph "as a great example of the new Youth and...a victory for Hitlerism." Nor did they forget that Schmeling's victory put him next in line for a title shot with Braddock.

On August 1, 1936, while Joe Louis licked his wounds and plotted his comeback, Hitler declared the Olympic Games underway. He had spent millions to transform Berlin into a sporting showcase for German rebirth, an international extravaganza of political theatre that shaped the Games for the next fifty years. As William L. Shirer has written, "Hitler, we who covered the Games had to concede, turned the Olympics into a dazzling propaganda success for his barbarian regime."

Besides Hitler there were two other big winners at those Olympics: Avery Brundage, who twenty-four years after finishing far behind Jim Thorpe in the decathlon had solidified his control of American amateur sports, and Jesse Owens, the Ohio State track star who won four gold medals. One of Owens's autobiographies is subtitled, not ironically, *The Man Who Outran Hitler*.

There had been strong opposition to sending a U.S. team to Berlin, not only from Jewish groups but from leaders of the Amateur Athletic Union who pointed out that non-Aryans had been systematically excluded from the German clubs that supplied Olympic athletes, a clear violation of the Olympic charter. But Brundage, president of the American Olympic Committee, manipulated votes, purged potential boycotters, and insinuated that Communists were behind a plot to keep the Americans at home. By a narrow vote, he prevailed.

Brundage, who died in 1975 after serving twenty years as president of the International Olympic Committee, has been called sexist, racist, and pro-Fascist, and after recent revelations about his sordid personal life, a self-righteous hypocrite as well. Yet, he was clearly a true believer of that flawed Olympic Ideal. In 1968, during an interview about the Black Power demonstrations at the Games in Mexico City, he made clear that the survival of the Games overrode any other consideration because they represented the "one place in this troubled world free from politics, from religion, from racial prejudice."

As Olympic "policeman," Brundage could wink at such systemic violations as commercialism, nationalism, and drug use when enforcement might upset the Games, and he could be incredibly petty. On the ocean crossing to Germany in 1936, the beautiful and feisty American swimmer, Eleanor Holm, had a glass of champagne with sportswriters. Brundage, who never much liked the idea of female athletes at the Games, threw her off the team and sent her home.

But the big news in American papers was the success of African-American athletes including Ralph Metcalfe, Mack Robinson (Jackie Robinson's older brother), Johnny Woodruff, Cornelius Johnson, and Jesse Owens who, according to Grantland Rice, had "easily, almost lazily, and minus any show of effort ... turned sport's greatest spectacle into the 'black parade of 1936.'"

Shades of the noble savage.

Obscured in the coverage was the last-minute decision to replace two Jewish-American runners, Marty Glickman and Sam Stoller, from the 400-meter relay, with Owens and Metcalfe. Glickman, who went on to become a leading sports broadcaster, still insists that Brundage ordered their removal to avoid embarrassing Hitler, whom Brundage admired.

The Germans called the African-American athletes "the Black auxiliaries" and could rationalize their victories as animals beating humans—but to have Jewish athletes on the victory stand would mock the dogma of the self-proclaimed Master Race.

Owens returned in triumph to a New York ticker-tape parade. Politicians from both major parties courted his endorsement, hoping it would win them black votes. A poor young man determined to cash in on his brief moment of glory, Jesse signed with an agent and gave exhibitions, even running against horses. He usually won, especially when given a head start or when the starter purposely fired his gun near the horse's ear, causing the horse to rear up.

"He was the quintessential example," according to sociologist Harry Edwards, the instigator of the 1968 Olympic Black Power demonstration, "of how America has historically utilized black athletes, black celebrities, in ways that were conducive to its broader political interests."

Broader political interests also helped Louis get his title shot. While Schmeling was the legitimate contender, American boxing officials and promoters didn't want to risk losing the title—and all the money that went with it—to Germany. They had a righteous political argument.

So suddenly a black heavyweight champion, especially such a humble, non-threatening one, didn't seem so scary.

Mike Jacobs swung into action, buttonholing and whispering. He found groups delighted to help him. The Non-Sectarian Anti-Nazi League, led by New York's mayor Fiorello La Guardia, threatened to mount a boycott of the proposed Braddock-Schmeling fight, determined, as one writer put it, to prevent Schmeling from "tak[ing] the title back to Germany and present[ing] it to Adolf Hitler for the German Museum."

Joe Gould, Braddock's manager, was worried about the loss of a big gate. Urged on by Mike Jacobs, he took advantage of the political controversy. Claiming concern over the boycott and of the possibility of a Nazi world champion, he reneged on his contract with Schmeling and made a better deal with Mike. Gould signed his fighter to a title defense against the Brown Bomber for a $500,000 guarantee from Jacobs, as well as ten percent of the net profits of all of Louis's heavyweight title fights for ten years should Louis defeat Braddock. Now the pie called Louis was being cut into many slices. But it still seemed worth it.

Braddock never had a chance, overwhelmed by a hailstorm of short punches. He tried Schmeling's strategy, crouching low to lure Louis into dropping his left, but Joe never made the same mistake twice. And this time he had trained hard, without golf clubs. In the eighth round he delivered his famous D.O.A., the Dead on Your Ass haymaker he had learned in the early days in Detroit. Braddock couldn't get up.

On June 22 1937, Louis became the first black heavyweight world champion since Jack Johnson.

In this time when most American sports are dominated by black superstars, it is hard to reconstruct Louis's significance. Louis was out there representing all black people in those bitter days when most colleges admitted few if any blacks, when college-educated blacks were lucky to get jobs as railroad waiters, when even the Army was segregated. There were no blacks in major league baseball. In Hollywood movies they mostly played servants.

And here was Louis, for all his public humility, breaking racial stereotypes by pounding white men into submission before segregated crowds.

In his 1964 book *Why We Can't Wait*, the late Rev. Dr. Martin Luther King Jr. tried to capture Louis's significance, describing "a young Negro" dying in the gas chamber of a Southern prison in the late 1930s and crying out, "Save me, Joe Louis. Save me, Joe Louis. Save me, Joe Louis..."

Those words, wrote Dr. King, revealed "the helplessness, the loneliness, and the profound despair of the Negroes in that period.... Not God, not government, not charitably minded white men, but a Negro who was the world's most expert fighter, in this last extremity, was the last hope."

Louis was one of the most active champions in history, fighting so often that opponents were dubbed "Bums of the Month." But his real certification would have to come from Schmeling, the only pro to defeat him. Before the contracts for their rematch were even signed, there were protests and petitions. By 1938, there was no denying the daily terror and death in Germany.

Now the promoters argued that this was just a prizefight, not a symbolic war. But Hitler gave Schmeling a hero's send-off and President Franklin Delano Roosevelt told Louis, "We're depending on those muscles for America."

The pressure was intense. In the weeks before the fight, uniformed American Nazis harassed Louis at his training camp. Picketers mocked

Schmeling with Nazi salutes and demanded he return to Germany. (Years later, it would be reported that not only had Schmeling been privately anti-Nazi, he had hidden the children of a Jewish friend during an early attack on Jews in Germany.)

None of this hurt the "steam-up." Writing in the *New York World-Telegram*, Joe Williams remarked that the political controversy surrounding the fight built the gate. "Those who view in Schmeling a political symbol will be desperately hopeful for his downfall. If they have the cash they'll come, because you can do your wishful thinking a lot better when you're on the scene."

Some 70,000 had the cash, nearly a million dollars, to be on the scene at Yankee Stadium that night of June 22, 1938, and they all seemed to expect an epic duel, the prelude to World War II.

It didn't last beyond the first round. Schmeling got off two punches before Louis swarmed all over him. Louis unleashed a barrage of combinations, and within seconds Schmeling was helpless, clinging to the ropes while being hammered to the canvas.

Schmeling went down, got up, and went down again. His manager threw in the towel but the referee ignored it. Two hooks and a classic Louis right to the jaw ended it. Schmeling lay broken. Joe stood in a neutral corner, his body quaking with adrenalin.

This time, when the bars and houses emptied, the streets were crowded with whites as well as blacks, with Americans of every color and ancestry. Louis had crossed the line from champion to idol, a hero of Democracy As one newspaper put it, "The Aryan idol, the unconquerable one had been beaten, the bright, shining symbol of race glory has been thumped in the dust. That noise you hear is Goebbels making for the storm cellar."

Obviously other events, from the Nuremberg Laws to the Anchluss, as well as Munich, "Kristallnacht," and Germany's invasion of Poland, were far more important in shaping an American consensus to resist Nazi Germany. Still, the Brown Bomber made his own contribution. Thinking about the fight at the close of World War II, Paul Gould, a correspondent for the *American Hebrew*, praised Louis's victory over

Schmeling as "a terrific blow to the theory of race supremacy." It was something that American Jews who battled anti-Semitism at home and suffered the death of six million European Jews at the hands of the Nazis could well appreciate.

Recalling the fight's importance to his own childhood, Art Buchwald remembers that he and his friends were sure of three things: "Franklin Roosevelt was going to save the economy ... Joe DiMaggio was going to beat Babe Ruth's record [and] Joe Louis was going to save us from the Germans."

Ironically, the savior was a man whose own people were still subject to lynchings, discrimination, and oppression. One southern paper put his victory in its own perspective. Although it applauded Schmeling's defeat as proof that the Germans were "stupor men" rather than "supermen," it reminded Louis that he was still a "colored boy."

But he was "the man" for most American blacks in the 1930s and the 1940s, even those with mixed feelings. Richard Wright thought the boxer was part of the problem, a "puppet" of the white capitalists who gave him the chance to perform. Yet he also thought that Louis was a blues hero and a man connected to a tradition that had survived through African culture and American slavery. In a breathtaking confluence of talent, Wright wrote the lyrics of "King Jo" to music by Count Basie. It was recorded in 1940 by Basie's band with Paul Robeson as vocalist.

> Black eye peas ask corn bread
> What makes you so strong?
> Corn bread say I come from
> Where Joe Louis was born.
> Rabbit says to the bee
> What makes you sting so deep?
> Bee says I sting like Joe
> And rock 'em all to sleep.

African-Americans young and old listened to the words and dreamed their own dreams of possibility and power. This bee was no Brer Rabbit, no animal trickster of slave folklore that offered black slaves the hope of the occasional opportunity to fool white masters.

He did so, not only for himself, but for his people and his country. Nine months before the Japanese bombed Pearl Harbor, Louis appeared on a national radio broadcast sponsored by the National Urban League to encourage the defense industry to hire blacks. "I've seen them do tougher things when they got the chance." Joe urged white Americans to "give Negroes a chance to work."

On January 10, 1942, he enlisted in the Army and traveled the country and Europe on morale-boosting tours, selling war bonds, giving talks, fighting exhibition matches, and successfully defending his championship twice—each time donating his share of the purse to the Navy and Army Relief Funds.

During his four-year tour of duty, Louis covered more than 70,000 miles, fought ninety-six exhibitions, and personally spent more than $100,000 buying dinners and gifts for soldiers he entertained. In 1944, he starred in *The Negro Soldier*, a short film directed by Frank Capra, designed to encourage black enlistments and enthusiasm for the war effort. Filled with footage of Louis and Schmeling, both in the ring and in military training, the film recalled Joe's symbolic triumph and announced that "in one minute and forty-nine seconds an American fist won a victory. But it wasn't the final victory. Now those two men who were matched in the ring that night are matched again. This time in a far greater arena and for far greater stakes." The fight now "was for the real championship of the world to determine which way of life shall survive."

Sportswriters such as Paul Gallico, who once described Louis as "a primitive puncher just emerging from the pit," now praised "Citizen Barrow" as "one of the most popular champions, cheered by black and white alike ... a simple, good American," who, like "every unsung youth who has shouldered a gun," has made a sacrifice in behalf of his country.

Louis's war time patriotism in a racially divided country made him a symbol of national unity and purpose. His line, "We're on God's side," became one of the most quoted of the war.

More than one million black men and women served in the armed forces during World War II, all in segregated units. Although Louis's fame and status did provide certain privileges, they did not exempt him from that reality, one he duly noted and fought against. Louis made it clear that he would not appear before segregated Army audiences because if "whites and blacks were all fighting the same war, why couldn't their morale be lifted at the same theater?"

Assigned to Fort Riley, Kansas, in 1942, Louis met a former All-American football player at UCLA who complained that the base commander would let him play on the camp football team but not on the baseball team. Louis used his influence to give Jackie Robinson the chance to hone his diamond skills even more. According to Robinson, Louis also intervened to get him into Officer's Candidate School.

As the saying would later go, "No Joe Louis, no Jackie Robinson."

Joe had his problems, too. While on tour with the "Parade of Champions," Louis and future welterweight and middleweight champion Sugar Ray Robinson found themselves at Camp Siebert, Alabama, waiting at the bus depot for a taxi. When an M.P. ordered them to sit on a bench reserved for blacks, they refused and were arrested. Brought before the camp's commanding officer, Louis said: "Listen, I'm an American, I'm fighting this war like anybody else, and I expect to be treated like anybody else." Joe let the story out, and, as he remembered, public outrage at how he was treated brought a change in U.S. Army policy. Happy about the outcome, Louis was also aware of its limited meaning: "If I was just an average black G.I., I would have wound up in the stockades."

Louis was not militant. It was not in his character nor in his training by Roxborough, Black, Blackburn, and Jacobs. But his efforts on behalf of black America, although often discounted later, especially in the Muhammad Ali era, did not go unnoticed in his own time. In 1945 he was a close second to another black idol, A. Philip Randolph, the great labor leader, in balloting for the NAACP's Spingarn Medal, awarded annually to the person who had made the most important contributions in the area of civil rights. That same year the army awarded him the Legion of Merit for his extraordinary service to the cause.

Louis was discharged from the army in 1945. Over the next six years, he fought 120 times, mostly four-round exhibitions, sometimes two in the same night. He successfully defended his title three times before announcing his retirement as undefeated champion of the world on March 1, 1949. None of the fights was particularly memorable. Nor was his return from retirement—an unsuccessful attempt to regain the title from Ezzard Charles in 1950 and, in 1951, a cruel thrashing from young, tough Rocky Marciano, who reflected America's feeling by crying for Louis when it was over.

Joe Louis Barrow Jr., a lawyer still known as "Punchie," thinks of his father in those years as similar to the main character in Arthur Miller's *Death of a Salesman*. Barrow said: "Wasn't Willie Loman a grand guy, just like my father, and then he started growing old and losing his customers? He was never really aware that he had lost his territory. That's the tragedy of it, just like my father."

In the play's elegy for the salesman, Charlie, the successful neighbor, could be speaking of the boxer, too, when he says, "No one dast blame or pity this man."

And Joe himself said, "Well, like the man said, 'If you dance you got to pay the piper.' Believe me, I danced, I paid the piper, and left him a big fat tip."

For those who want to label him "victim" or "Uncle Tom" or an example of America's penchant for destroying its heroes, there is plenty of grist in the later years. Deeply in debt to Mike Jacobs and the Internal Revenue Service, partly because of his own extravagance and partly because of greedy mismanagement, Louis could never pay off what he owed. He ended up in Las Vegas as an official "greeter," glad-handing customers on the golf course and in the casinos. Along the way he divorced and remarried Marva, divorced her again, and married two more times—his last to an attorney named Martha Malone Jefferson, who legally adopted Louis's children from his incessant philandering and valiantly kept him afloat during bouts with mental illness and cocaine addiction.

The Rev. Jesse Louis Jackson, named for the champion, delivered the eulogy for the Brown Bomber at his funeral on April 17, 1981, at the

Caesars Palace Sports Pavilion. "God sent Joe from the black race to represent the human race," Jackson said. "He was the answer to the sincere prayers of the disinherited and dispossessed. Joe made everybody somebody....We all feel bigger today because Joe came this way."

Louis's self-assessment was typically more modest.

"I think I just come along at a time when white people began to know that colored people wouldn't be terrorized no more," he said. "And the way I carried myself during that comin' up made some whites begin to look at colored people different."

CHAPTER EIGHT

JACKIE
ROBINSON

ON APRIL 15, 1947, A HANDSOME, INTELLIGENT, ARTICULATE, POISED, TWENTY-eight-year-old former U.S. Army officer, once the greatest all-round athlete in the history of the University of California at Los Angeles, walked out to first base in a baseball game in Brooklyn, New York, and the country held its breath. It was the most eagerly anticipated debut in the annals of the national pastime; it represented both the dream and the fear of equal opportunity, and it would change forever the complexion of the game and the attitudes of Americans.

Jackie Robinson's major league career was billed as "a noble experiment," and as patronizing as that now seems to describe this obvious overachiever in a child's game, it represented an enormous risk to those who saw him as surrogate and role model. America was still segregated by law and custom. This would be integration at its most visible and dramatic. If it worked.

Jesse Jackson would later capture the moment in a flight of rhetoric: "The fate of a race rode on his swing."

Comedian Dick Gregory would use humor: "It was the first time a

black man shook a stick at a white man and 50,000 white people cheered."

Ernest J. Gaines's fictional heroine, Miss Jane Pittman, said: "When times got really hard, really tough, He always send you somebody. In the Depression it was tough on everybody, but twice as hard on the colored, and He sent us Joe…after the war he sent us Jackie."

Athletically, Robinson's debut was a disappointment—in four at-bats he grounded out twice, once into a double play, flied out to left, and got on when his bunt was booted for an error. But his rookie season, by any measure, was a monumental success.

He was voted the first Rookie of the Year, for both leagues, and he led his team into the World Series.

Far more importantly, Jackie Robinson allowed America to feel good about itself.

The country had just come through a murderous war and, although it had defeated evil dictators with a stunning display of national purpose, individual courage, and technological muscle, some Americans were beginning to question their country in some basic ways.

Why should women go back to the kitchen? They had proven themselves as competent as men in the factory and the office, even as they continued their duties at home. They had been critical to the fighting war itself in overseas hospital and support units.

And what about the so-called American dilemma of race relations? How could America justify the segregation of Negroes when they had fought and died in the same war as whites, for the same cause?

And then Jack Roosevelt Robinson appeared, this grandson of a slave, son of a plantation sharecropper, this handsome, pigeon-toed, ebony fury, dancing off first base, drawing every eye in the stadium, making the pitcher crazy, giving the Dodgers the spirit that would make them a contender for years to come. He gave white players the chance to show they were tolerant (as had Babe Ruth, he put money in teammates' pockets and revived the game), and he gave black and white fans a chance to cheer together without making a larger commitment.

"By applauding Robinson," wrote Roger Kahn, who covered the era, "a man did not feel that he was taking a stand on school integration or on open housing. But for an instant he had accepted Robinson simply as a hometown ball player. To disregard color, even for an instant, is to step away from old prejudices, the old hatred. That is not a path on which many double back."

To prove his people's worth, Joe Louis needed to appear non-threatening to whites while he knocked white men unconscious. The pathway he opened for Jackie was even more complex; Robinson had to get along with white men in a collective effort to beat other white men.

If he could do it, there might be a future together: "There's nothing that moves our culture more toward multiculturalism on a daily basis," said Jesse Jackson, "than the expectation of whites and blacks winning together."

There are people who consider Robinson one of the great moral forces of the American century, and there are baseball historians who split the eras of the game into B.J. and A.J. His name has become shorthand for "the first" of anything Americans deem pioneering, ennobling, worthy. But there was more at work in his story than pure virtue.

"He was my hero," says the sociologist Harry Edwards, "but let's not forget that it was good business to bring the black ball player and all those black fans into the major leagues."

"And don't forget," counsels his widow, Rachel, "he was not a saint, he was a real man. He had a temper, he loved golf, he made mistakes. He chose Nixon over Kennedy because Kennedy wouldn't look him in the eye and his mother had always taught him not to trust anyone who doesn't look you in the eye. He was able to acknowledge in his lifetime that it was a misjudgment on his part.

"Jackie taught us that an individual can make a difference, a committed individual can have an impact. One of his favorite sayings was that a life is not important, except in the impact it has on other lives."

Hank Aaron remembers vividly the day in 1948 he cut high school classes to hear Jackie speak in a corner drugstore. The Dodgers were in Mobile, Alabama, for a spring training game, and Robinson never missed a chance to offer himself to local blacks, particularly youngsters.

"I can't remember exactly what he said, but I do know my mouth was wide open," said Aaron in a 1994 interview. "I was in the back, but I felt like I was hugging him, you know? Holding his hand. I saw a concerned citizen. He was saying something like, 'Hey, just give yourself a chance. If I can make it, all of you can make it. It may not be in sports, but it can be in something.'"

In his autobiography, *I Had A Hammer*, Aaron wrote: "That same day, I told my father I would be in the big leagues before Jackie retired. Jackie had that effect on all of us—he gave us our dreams.

"Before then, whenever I said I wanted to be a ball player, Daddy would set me straight. I remember sitting out on the back porch once when an airplane flew over, and I told Daddy I'd like to be a pilot when I grew up. He said, 'Ain't no colored pilots.' I said okay, then, I'll be a ball player. He said, 'Ain't no colored ball players.' But he never said that anymore after we sat in the colored section of Hartwell Field and watched Jackie Robinson."

For a black youngster who would never be a ball player, the impact was just as powerful. Robert Curvin, who became an editorial writer for *The New York Times*, grew up one of nine children in New Jersey. When his mother couldn't get work as a clothes presser, they went on welfare. There were no vacations, no dinners out, but when Robert was thirteen, his mother and some of her friends hired a car and went on a "pilgrimage" to Ebbets Field. They needed heroes.

"I felt proud. I felt inspired.... I know that my life was enriched by my attachment to him; the level of my expectations were raised by his example."

The restraint, resilience, dignity, and intelligence that Robinson exhibited made Curvin "more aware of the barriers America erected against blacks—and the need to strike them down...it was his courage that thrilled us, inspired us and held us to him even after he had moved on. His spirit had entered the bloodstream of a generation."

Jackie was the youngest of five children born to Mallie and Jerry Robinson, struggling Georgia sharecroppers, on January 31, 1919. Six months later, his father deserted the family, and a few months after that Mallie moved the family to Pasadena, California, in search of a better life.

Residents of that affluent Los Angeles suburb tended to regard blacks and other minorities who weren't waiting on them as "intruders." Robinson's mother supported the family by working as a domestic. When a welfare agency helped her purchase a house, neighbors petitioned the city to remove them.

Robinson remembered that he and his brothers "were in many a fight that started with a racial slur on the very street we lived on. We saw movies from segregated balconies, swam in the municipal pool only on Tuesdays, and were permitted in the YMCA only one night a week."

The Robinsons were not evicted from their house, and in 1936 a local judge ordered the city's pools to allow blacks to swim whenever they were open. In protest, the city government fired all of its black workers, including Robinson's brother, Mack.

By this time, Jackie was a local athletic celebrity. In grade school, classmates bribed him with their lunches to be on their teams. Inspired by Mack, who in 1936 had won an Olympic silver medal to Jesse Owens's gold in the 200-meter dash, Robinson became a football and track star in high school and then at Pasadena Junior College. In 1940 he enrolled at UCLA.

In two years there he established himself, according to one sportswriter, as "the Jim Thorpe of his race," the school's first four-letter man, in football, basketball, baseball, and track. An honorable mention All-American in football and basketball, he averaged eleven yards a carry as a halfback in his junior year and was the highest-scoring basketball player in the Pacific Coast Conference both years he played. His broad jump mark in 1940 was good enough to win the NCAA championship. Somehow he also found time to win the Pacific Coast intercollegiate golf championship and to compete successfully in swimming and tennis.

But he was never only a jock. That iron spine of self-righteousness that supported him through ten major league seasons showed itself early. When Robinson thought he was right, when he thought he was being treated unfairly, he would fight. As a kid on Pepper Street in Pasadena, he used his fists; as a high school and college athlete he became known for haranguing officials in his high-pitched, insistent voice.

Rachel Robinson met him in her first year at UCLA. He was already a senior and a campus hero. "He could have been arrogant or showy or flashy, and he was just the opposite. I think one of the first things I learned to love about him was his humility. And he was so sure of himself, of his commitments, to his family, to his race."

Rachel, now retired as a psychiatric nurse and teacher at Yale Medical School, closes her eyes and smiles. "He was gorgeous. Gorgeous. Those beautiful teeth, that wonderful smile. A way of carrying himself. Even the pigeon-toes were kind of fun to look at.

"He said he didn't want to go steady with anyone until he was sure that the person was interested in him as a person and not as an athlete. That impressed me a great deal."

Robinson did not graduate from UCLA. Having used up his athletic eligibility, "convinced that no amount of education would help a black man get a job" and that there was "no future in athletics," he left college to be an assistant athletic director for the National Youth Administration. He played football for the semipro, integrated, Los Angeles Bulldogs.

Robinson was coming of age at a critical moment for African-Americans; one that provided a mixed legacy of possibility and frustration. Thanks to the efforts of the National Association for the Advancement of Colored People, A. Philip Randolph, and other black activists, as well as the informal lobbying of First Lady Eleanor Roosevelt, the New Deal did offer some hope to black Americans. There was money for black colleges and for the construction of housing and public facilities in black neighborhoods under the auspices of the Public Works Administration. There was a substantial increase in the number of federal appointments given to African-Americans. There were opportunities to learn vocational skills in programs like the National Youth Administration. This is why so many blacks deserted the Republican Party and rallied around Frankin D. Roosevelt. But American society, North and South, remained highly segregated, one in which "separate but equal" translated into gross inequities between whites and blacks, affecting every aspect of life.

The engine of change went into high speed with World War II. In the spring of 1942, along with hundreds of thousands of other young American men, Robinson was drafted into the army.

Robinson's war was fought on stateside army bases against other Americans. With Joe Louis's help, he was able to get into Officer's Candidiate School after he and other black applicants were pushed aside.

As a second lieutenant at Fort Riley, Kansas, he made such waves about segregated post exchange seating that he soon found himself at Fort Hood, Texas, where he casually sat down next to a friend, the white wife of a fellow officer, on a base bus. The driver ordered him to the rear with the "colored." Robinson refused, citing the recent desegregation of base buses. He proclaimed his rights to the military policemen who were obviously waiting to make an example of this uppity officer. There was eventually a court-martial; but as Jules Tygiel recounts, thanks to able counsel and the weakness of the case against him, Jackie was found innocent.

Robinson's army experiences were downplayed at a time of intense patriotism, and he tended to give short shrift to his next job, a brief stint with the Kansas City Monarchs of the National Negro League. Although Jackie appreciated that he made good money—$400 a month in 1945—he recalled that "it turned out to be a pretty miserable way to make a buck."

For an educated Californian, an "officer and a gentleman" used to playing with whites, a nondrinker, the Negro Leagues may have seemed pretty miserable, but for several generations of black men they were a chance to make money playing a game and become celebrities.

"We had our good times," said Larry Doby, who played in the Negro Leagues before becoming the second black major leaguer. "The Negro League players were dedicated athletes playing a game they loved. There was laughter and songs in the bus, new people, fans in every town. When you come down to it, all the major leagues offered was more; more money, more bars, more women, more friends, more opportunities."

The Negro Leagues were a parallel world, almost a twilight zone of baseball as far as most of America was concerned. The great players of the Negro Leagues, like Josh Gibson, "Cool Papa" Bell, and Buck O'Neil, were referred to as the Black Babe Ruth or the Black Honus Wagner. It was a shadow identity.

Satchel Paige, the wondrous pitcher, was in a league of his own. He was an arrogant, self-absorbed, showboating superstar with an amazing assortment of pitches and a cracker-barrel shtick ("Don't look back; something might be gaining on you"). Paige was still effective when he finally got to the bigs at age forty-two in 1948.

But as far as most white sportswriters were concerned, black ball players were "invisible men." In his excellent book *Invisible Men*, Donn Rogosin wrote: "The importance of the Negro leagues transcended the world of sport. A small group of black men, gifted with remarkable skills, reached far above the menial and the mundane. In the process they became worldly, and some became wise.

"Scuffling to make a living playing the game that they loved, these men became symbols of competence and achievement for all black people. Because they provided joy and excitement in their often dramatic quest for victories and Negro League pennants, they enriched life in black America. When their baseball victories came against white opponents, they undermined segregation itself."

Baseball was only one of a number of institutions that flourished in Black America—including black churches, colleges, music, and a film industry—that would be stripped by integration to provide the enormous pool of black talent that often took white America by surprise.

But baseball seemed the least threatening; it was only a game, after all. The Negro Leagues flourished through World War II and reached their apogee in 1946, the same year Robinson broke the color-line in organized baseball by playing with the minor-league Montreal team. Doby and Monte Irvin led the Newark Eagles to victory over the Kansas City Monarchs in the seventh game of the Negro World Series, and there were two East-West Games, a high spot on the calendar of "registerites" or "exclusives," as the society pages of black newspapers called the bourgeoisie who paraded in fine clothes for the masses. Although the ball players certainly made more money than most of the people who came to see them, they were not of this "elite."

Their playing year began in February; a few days of "spring training," then barnstorming through the Deep South, picking up new young players along the way. By late April or early May, they would open the season with black high school bands, booster groups, and decorated floats. The first ball would be thrown out by Lena Horne or a liberal politician like New York's Mayor La Guardia, with Damon Runyon and Heywood Broun in box seats. They'd then go on a grueling tour that often included three games a day (the third, the so-called "twilight" game, went on until the ball could no longer be seen).

The game they played put a premium on stamina and finesse. There were brush-back pitches and high-spike slides, as well as the introduction of the batting helmet and the umpire's inside chest protector. There was a mercenary quality that would be appreciated today; players jumped from team to team as quickly as owners would buy and sell them. Loyalty was irrelevant in a game where teams appeared and disappeared. Owners were often racketeers whose scams and numbers banks could go out of business at the drop of a gun.

Black baseball was often a thoughtful game of bunting, running, stealing—the fundamental techniques of "inside" baseball that had been blasted away by the Babe Ruth big stick era. (Even though the Negro Leagues had their own Babe Ruth, Josh Gibson.) Negro League players talked about their game, long theoretical discussions that included the rookies they taught and broke in. The "each one teach one" ethic of the black community was included in baseball life.

Playing in the Negro Leagues was the pinnacle of the black sports experience in America. According to Rogosin, there were about two hundred playing jobs in the two Negro major leagues, and perhaps another two hundred on minor league and barnstorming teams. These men grew old at their positions. It would be the best job most would ever have, and more money, attention, fame, and adventure than most anyone else of their race could expect. In retrospect, they were not as bitter as one would expect. They had status. They married schoolteachers.

And they were role models, a responsibility many took seriously. They dressed with care and style on the road, behaved in public, and had table manners. They were professional men, and within their communities they were men of respect, no matter how invisible they might be to white America.

And they were never quite that invisible. They earned their meal tickets entertaining rural white America, sometimes clowning, often playing straight ball against local teams. The Negro Leaguers almost always won and usually held the score down if they expected to return the next year. There are tales of Negro League teams, enraged by insults, blowing some local whites off the field and then burning rubber out of the county. But for the most part it was good-natured baseball.

Often it was very good baseball, according to Babe Ruth, Ted Williams, Bob Feller, and other white stars who played against blacks. Were blacks kept out of the majors for so long purely because of racism or because the good old boys knew that many of them would lose their jobs? White owners were making money renting their stadiums to black teams when their own clubs were on the road. And there were plenty of black owners who didn't want to lose out.

"The noble experiment had less to do with brotherhood than it had to do with business," says Dr. Harry Edwards, the Berkeley sociologist. "World War II had decimated the ranks of professional baseball. It got so bad they brought in players with one arm, with one leg. There were women's leagues organized to sop up the interest in baseball.

"And finally it became clear there was all this Negro talent out there, all these Negro fans. If it had been about brotherhood, they'd have brought in Negro managers, Negro coaches, trainers, all these people were available in the Negro Leagues. But it was about business."

Ironically, the classic baseball of the Negro Leagues has been blurred by the comedy acts, teams called the Clowns, the Zulu Cannibal Giants, and the Tennessee Rats, baseball equivalents of basketball's Harlem Globetrotters. They were immensely popular, particularly with white audiences, and they were controversial in the black community where they were seen as racial stereotypes damaging to the professional image of the real ball players. Here were Gibson, Paige, Quincy Trouppe, and Chet Brewer trying to prove themselves as worthy as the white boys, while Spec Bebop, a dwarf, was cavorting with King Tut, a tall man in evening clothes and top hat, and catcher Pepper Bassett was behind the plate in a rocking chair. In 1935, when the Ethiopia-Italy war created a new awareness about Africa, the comedy teams appeared in grass skirts and painted faces.

Wendell Smith, considered the Jackie Robinson of sportswriting, wrote: "Negroes must realize the danger insisting that ball players paint their faces and go through minstrel show revues before each ball game. Every Negro in public life stands for something more than the role he is portraying. Every Negro in the theatrical and sports world is somewhat of an ambassador for the Negro race—whether he likes it or not."

Smith, then writing for the *Pittsburgh Courier*, a black newspaper, as well as Sam Lacy of the *Baltimore Afro-American*, Joe Bostic of the *New York People's Voice*, and Lester Rodney, the white sports editor of the communist *Daily Worker*, were the most persistent voices for major league integration. In 1942, Robinson and Nate Moreland, a Negro League pitcher, were given tryouts with the Chicago White Sox. A year later, Bill Veeck Jr.'s plan to purchase the Philadelphia Phillies and fill the roster with black players was stymied at the last minute by Kenesaw Mountain Landis. Baseball's first commissioner was a determined foe of integration.

That same year, Paul Robeson, appearing to soldout houses in a major Broadway production of Shakespeare's *Othello* with an otherwise all-white cast, urged baseball owners to catch up with changing racial attitudes and integrate the game.

Robeson was one of America's most fascinating characters, an all-American football player, a singer, actor, and international human rights advocate who seemed to combine the over-the-top flamboyance of Jack Johnson and the powerful beauty of Joe Louis with the mind of a concerned intellectual. He was simply a superior human being who happened to be black in a country still struggling to break loose from blatant white supremacy. Robinson would eventually be used in the anti-Communist campaign to bring Robeson down.

By March 1945, with Landis dead, the new baseball commissioner was Albert "Happy" Chandler, a former senator and governor from the segregated state of Kentucky. Nevertheless, regarding Negroes, Chandler declared, "If they can fight and die on Okinawa, Guadalcanal [and] in the South Pacific, they can play ball in America." But a year later baseball owners secretly voted, 15-1, to keep their sport white.

The dissenter, of course, was Branch Rickey, the principal owner and general manager of the Dodgers, a superb judge of baseball talent and a good administrator; he built the excellent farm systems of the St. Louis Cardinals and the Dodgers. He was also capable of befogging a room with his cigar smoke and pious rhetoric. Sportswriters called him "The Deacon" and "The Mahatma" because they couldn't quite figure him out; was he a cunning businessman who used his Methodist morality as justification, or was he simply a righteous man who did well by doing good? Robinson called him "tough, shrewd, and courageous."

To explain his own inner feelings about the integration of baseball, Rickey would pull out a story from 1904 when he coached the Ohio Wesleyan College baseball team. In South Bend, Indiana, for a game against Notre Dame, Rickey's star hitter, Charlie Thomas, was denied a room because he was black. Eventually, Rickey had a cot put in his own room. That night, he found Thomas weeping and rubbing his hands raw. "Black skin! Black skin!" cried Thomas. "If I could only make them white."

Rickey said that image of Thomas had haunted him for more than forty years. Rickey's boosters repeated the story to prove the man a saint. His critics wondered if it was true. In any case, Rickey understood that whoever tapped into the black talent pool would buy pennants for years. Other owners knew that, too, but none had the soul or the smarts—or the guts—to make it happen. Rickey also understood that "the first" had to be the best at more than just the fundamentals of baseball.

"We had a whole lot better ball players than Jackie," said Buck Leonard, the "Black Lou Gehrig," "but Jackie was chosen 'cause he had played with white boys."

The story of Robinson's first meeting with Rickey is an American legend. He was brought to Rickey's Brooklyn office by Clyde Sukeforth, who had scouted and approved him. Robinson apparently believed he was being recruited for the Brooklyn Brown Dodgers of the United States League, Rickey's proposed idea for a new Negro circuit with a major league affiliation. Rickey was always tricky with false fronts and subterfuge.

When Rickey asked Jackie if he thought he could play in the majors, Robinson, incredulous and thrilled, according to one of his autobiographies, choked out a "Yes."

"I know you're a good ball player," Rickey barked. "What I don't know is whether you have the guts."

For the next three hours, Rickey lectured and harangued, spoke loftily of social justice and pointedly of beanballs and spikings. This had to be done right; it was bigger than baseball. There would be constant assaults, verbal, psychological, physical, and Robinson would have to swallow it, turn the other cheek, and channel all his competitive fire onto the game itself. Could he control his temper?

Robinson wrote: "All my life back to the age of eight when a little neighbor girl called me nigger—I had believed in payback, retaliation. The most luxurious possession, the richest treasure anyone has is his personal dignity.

"'Mr. Rickey,' I asked, 'are you looking for a Negro who is afraid to fight back?'

"I never will forget the way he exploded.

"'Robinson,' he said, 'I am looking for a ball player with guts enough not to fight back.'"

"It's been reported a great deal that Rickey was paternalistic, in control of Jackie, and [he] dictated to him, but I didn't see it that way," says Rachel Robinson, who saw it all. "I saw them very much as partners, as being very interdependent. They couldn't do without each other, and they knew that. There was a lot of backroom planning. If something was going wrong, we'd get together with Mr. Rickey.

"And Jackie really suffered having to control all his natural impulses.

He was very stressed, being challenged all the time and not being able to fight back. Remember what an aggressive man he was, how outraged at injustice."

Rickey has been criticized for his overly elaborate precautions. He hired Wendell Smith to room with Robinson, to act as buffer and liaison with the black community. Rickey instructed black leaders to give Jackie breathing room, to avoid the banquets, parades, and role model demands that would dull his playing edge, and to be as restrained and orderly at the ballpark as the man they came to see lest they loosen white backlash and race riot.

In retrospect, much of that seems condescending and unnecessary. But until the spring of 1946, when Robinson appeared in Montreal as the starting second baseman for the Dodgers' top farm club, no one really had a handle on what might happen.

Montreal was the dress rehearsal for the Big Show. Rickey figured that a Canadian city with little history of black-white racial tensions (Indian-white or English-French was another story) would provide the Robinsons with a friendly hometown. And he was right. On the other hand, the Royals' manager, Clay Hopper, was from Mississippi; he told Rickey he didn't consider Negroes fully human and would be shamed back home to have one on his team.

By the end of that season, Hopper was one of Jackie's biggest boosters. Winning is a color of its own. Despite the beanballs, the racial slurs, the vicious bench-jockeying, Robinson led the International League with a .349 batting average and took the Royals to the championship of the minor leagues, scoring the winning run in the final game against Louisville of the American Association.

And he did it the way he had promised Rickey—thrilling fans with daring play while pretending to be above the abuse. At a game in Syracuse, opposing players threw a black cat on the field and yelled "here's your cousin."

At his next at-bat, Robinson doubled and scored. He sauntered past the Syracuse bench and said, "Guess my cousin's happy now."

One wonders if Robinson would have been a better player had he been able to concentrate entirely on the game; or did his mission enhance his strength, energy, and focus? The example he set of grace under pressure was inspirational. There have been better baseball players, but no one came close to performing as well carrying such a load of other people's hopes and fears.

And then the load grew heavier. In the winter of 1947 at training camp in Havana, Cuba, Rickey had Robinson moved from second to first base for the Royals. He instructed Dodger manager Leo Durocher to casually tell sportswriters that all the Dodgers needed to win a pennant was a good first-baseman. At that unsubtle clue, several Dodgers, led by the southerner Hugh Casey, threatened to quit if they had to play with a black man. Rickey said he would accept their resignations. They backed off, grumbling.

Trying to avoid racial friction, Rickey housed Robinson and several new black Montreal players, including future major leaguers Roy Campanella and Don Newcombe, in separate and very unequal quarters away from the comfortable digs of the white players. Robinson grumbled at that, but Rickey waved it off, telling him to concentrate on playing so boldly, so flat out spectacularly for the Royals in their games against the Dodgers, that sportswriters and fans would demand his promotion to the big leagues. The scheme included the fiery manager Durocher as Robinson's protector when things got rough.

But then Durocher was suspended from baseball for hanging out with gangsters, and Rickey, to smother that negative story, quickly announced that Robinson was Brooklyn-bound.

The St. Louis Cardinals secretly threatened to strike. Sports editor Stanley Woodward of the *New York Herald Tribune* found out and called Ford Frick, president of the National League.

Frick, once Babe Ruth's ghostwriter, asked Woodward what he was going to do with the story. Woodward said he would do nothing unless Frick confirmed it. Frick said, "I won't deny it," and Woodward's scoop blew up the Cardinals' plan.

That was just for starters. There was a barrage of hate mail and threats to kidnap and kill little Jackie Jr. and Rachel. Jackie Sr. began the season in a slump. Then the Phillies arrived with a sewer-storm of racial abuse from the dugout that shocked even the southern-born Dodgers. The ringleader was Philadelphia manager Ben Chapman who years before as a New York Yankee had been notorious for anti-Semitic remarks. In a way, Chapman helped the noble experiment enormously by uniting the Dodgers around Robinson and against a common enemy. By August, when Enos Slaughter of the Cardinals went out of his way to spike Jackie, it was Hugh Casey who led the Dodgers roaring out of their dugout.

Robinson himself seemed to think that Pee Wee Reese, a Kentucky-born shortstop highly respected by other ball players, was the key Dodger who clinched his acceptance. On several occasions when bench-jockeying or slurs from the stands became almost unbearably vicious, Reese would casually sling an arm over his black teammate's shoulder in a gesture of solidarity that bolstered Robinson and shut up the hecklers.

There were opponents who helped, too. Hank Greenberg, the great Detroit Tigers slugger, never forgot the anti-Jewish invective he had to endure. He was playing first base, closing out his career with Pittsburgh, when Robinson was intentionally hit by a Pirate pitcher.

"He stood beside me on first base with his chin up like a prince," Greenberg recalled. "I had a feeling for him because of the way I had been treated. I remember saying to him, 'Don't let them get you down. You're doing fine. Keep it up.'"

That first season, Jackie batted .297, was voted Rookie of the Year, and led the Dodgers to the first of six pennants in his career, and then into an exciting World Series in which they played well but lost to a great Yankee team.

More important to management, the Dodgers broke major league attendance records. Robinson was a box office sensation and paid back his $5,000 salary, the rookie minimum, at least a hundredfold. Robinson didn't do badly, either; the gifts, honoraria, and endorsement contracts (mostly for products marketed to blacks, including cigarettes which he did not smoke) made him one of the league's top earners. That winter, he attended so many banquets he arrived at spring training twenty-five pounds overweight. Durocher was back and sarcastically screamed him into shape.

Robinson had a somewhat romantic view of that first year. In his last autobiography, published the year he died, 1972, he wrote: "I had started the season as a lonely man, often feeling like a black Don Quixote tilting at white windmills. I ended it feeling like a member of a solid team. The Dodgers were a championship team because all of us had learned something. I had learned how to exercise self-control—to answer insults, violence, and injustice with silence—and I had learned how to earn the respect of my teammates. They had learned that it's not skin color but talent and ability that counts. Maybe even the bigots had learned that, too."

Maybe everyone had learned something. In a 1947 poll, Jackie was voted the second most popular man in the country, after the crooner Bing Crosby.

But the transformation of racial attitudes did not mean that American society—or even major league baseball—would be swiftly and peacefully integrated. Over the next few seasons, Don Newcombe, Roy Campanella, Joe Black, Sandy Amoros, Charlie Neal, and Jim "Junior" Gilliam joined Robinson to make the Dodgers the only truly integrated team in all of professional sport. By 1953, only six of the major leagues's sixteen teams carried a black player on their rosters. As late as 1960, there were only six black players in the entire American League. The Boston Red Sox signed their first black player, Pumpsie Green, in 1959, almost a decade after the Boston Celtics became the first team in the National Basketball Association to sign a black ball player.

In *Baseball's Great Experiment*, Jules Tygiel makes a strong case for the role that first wave of black major leaguers played in breaking southern prohibitions against interracial competition and by demanding equal treatment in hotels, restaurants, and Pullman cars.

Ultimately it took Supreme Court decisions, federal legislation, and the agitation, strategies, and sacrifice of civil rights activists to insure the legal end of segregation. But the most visible first steps were taken on the ball field.

"We were paying our dues long before the civil rights marches," said pitcher Don Newcombe, proudly recalling Dr. Martin Luther King Jr. telling him that "you'll never know what you and Jackie and Roy did to make it possible to do my job."

Roy Campanella was a jolly, light-skinned, part-Italian future Hall of Fame catcher who described himself as "not a crusader." He thus became the favorite of many sportswriters who began to resent the 1949 model Jackie Robinson who was no longer constrained to turn the other cheek, to be Rickey's "ball player with guts enough not to fight back" or to grin politely at their pontifications.

Robinson's natural inclination was always to fight back at any real or imagined injustice, and he quickly earned a reputation among umpires and opposing ball players as a hothead and troublemaker. Robinson insisted that the reputation reflected the prejudice of whites who could only accept him as the "humble Negro" and not, to use his words, as the "uppity nigger."

Rachel Robinson felt that Jackie was finally free in 1949 to be himself—the aggressive, romantic, exuberant, tender man with strong opinions that he loved to express. That was also the year he won the batting title (.342), led the league in stolen bases (37), and was voted Most Valuable Player. It was the first time a black man was National League MVP; in the next ten years, black men would win eight times, proof of the vein of talent that pool Rickey and Robinson had mined. In that same period, 1950–59, there were seven black National League Rookies of the Year.

The pastime was ahead of the rest of its nation. As Americans began to agitate for justice and equality outside the white lines, and for enforcement of the Supreme Court's 1954 ruling that segregated education was unconstitutional, there was a backlash—a revival of the Ku Klux Klan and more and more incidents of whites trying to intimidate blacks with Jim Crow laws and lynch mobs. In the summer of 1955, a fourteen-year-old from Chicago, Emmett Till, was drowned in Greenwood, Mississippi, for allegedly insulting a white woman. His killers were acquitted by a local jury. Later that year, in Montgomery, Alabama, forty-two-year-old Rosa Parks refused to give up her seat on a bus to a white man. At the next stop, she was arrested. The resulting bus boycott was led by a twenty-six-year-old minister, new to the city, named Martin Luther King Jr.

Robinson was an early supporter of Dr. King and a member of the NAACP. But to civil rights militants of the turbulent sixties, especially those who believed that history began with them, the politics of Jackie Robinson seemed middle-of-the-road, accommodating, or worse; after all, he supported Richard Nixon for a while, worked for New York's Republican Governor Nelson Rockefeller, and became a banker and an executive of one of the first fast-food chains, Chock Full O' Nuts. Robinson believed that the democrats "took black people for granted" and that true equality required economic power; thus his founding of Freedom National Bank in Harlem and his corporate involvement with a chain that hired mostly black workers. Jackie Robinson hewed no line but his own. While his rage for life was tempered by illness and tragedy, he never retreated or surrendered.

But he was willing to admit mistakes, or at least revise old opinions. In the middle of his 1949 MVP season, perhaps the height of his baseball glory, Robinson was called before the House Un-American Activities Committee (HUAC) to "give the lie" to statements Paul Robeson had reportedly made at an international peace conference in Paris.

Robeson had challenged America's cold war foreign policy and allegedly stated that it would be "unthinkable that American Negroes would go to war on behalf of those who have oppressed us for generations against the Soviet Union which in one generation has raised its people to full dignity."

While he may not have said that in Paris, those words certainly reflected his views. They were fighting words in the early days of America's battle with the Evil Empire and as threatening then as Muhammad Ali's "I ain't got nothing against them Vietcong" would be in 1966, when the Vietnam War divided America.

Other prominent African-Americans were recruited to denounce him and to pledge black allegiance to the anti-Communist crusade.

Robinson, in part, said:

I can't speak for any 15,000,000 people [Robinson's estimate of the number of American blacks] any more than any other person can, but I know that I've got too much invested for my wife and child and myself in the future of this country, and I and other Americans of many races and faiths have too much invested in our country's welfare, for any of us to throw it away because of a siren song sung in bass. But that doesn't mean that we're going to stop fighting race discrimination in this country until we've got it licked. It means that we're going to fight it all the harder because our stake in the future is so big. We can win the fight without the Communists and we don't want their help.

Most press reports omitted those sections of Robinson's prepared remarks that acknowledged Robeson's right to his own opinion while emphasizing the denunciation and implicit loyalty oath.

Robeson went on to denounce HUAC "as an insult to the Negro people" and to question its members' own loyalty because of their "ominous silence" about the lynchings of blacks. Robeson expressed his respect for Robinson and his right to his own opinion. Recognizing the pressure on him, Robeson insisted that Robinson was "the victim of this terror" and that he regarded him as a "brother." There was "no argument," he insisted, "between Jackie and me."

Robeson was unable to find work in America because of his radical political views, and his passport was revoked by the United States government for eight years. He was not silenced, but his volume was effectively turned down, and his example had a chilling effect on other outspoken dissenters.

Meanwhile, the 1952 Hollywood version of Robinson's story, in which he played himself, highlighted his HUAC performance in clear, calculated, anti-Communist, cold war terms.

Twenty years later, in his autobiography, Robinson stood by his 1949 testimony, but added: "I have grown wiser and closer to painful truths about America's destructiveness. And I do have an increased respect for Paul Robeson, who, over the span of that twenty years, sacrificed himself, his career, and the wealth and comfort he once enjoyed because, I believe, he was sincerely trying to help his people."

Robinson came to realize that their mission had not been completed. The brush-back pitches and verbal barbs the pioneer black players stood up to were not in the same league with the lynchings, beatings, and murders experienced by their brothers and sisters on the civil rights fronts.

There is a simple explanation for this: Baseball was only baseball—a sport in which the participant, black or white, was primarily a commodity and an entertainer who did not threaten the country's basic power relationships.

And even in sport the changes have come slowly. Five decades after Robinson became "the first," African-Americans are still primarily performers, a small minority among managers, coaches, referees, front-office personnel, journalists, and a token rarity among owners.

On the fortieth anniversary of Robinson's first major league game, an old Dodger friend, Al Campanis, told a national television audience that most blacks "lacked the necessities" to manage. Campanis was demonized and run out of baseball as if he was an aberration and not just parroting the conventional old white boy line.

Robinson died in 1972, at age fifty-three. His last years were hard ones; diabetes, perhaps caused or at least exacerbated by the stress of his playing days, had dimmed his vision and slowed him down. Jackie Jr., recovering from a heroin addiction acquired in Vietnam, was killed in a car crash in 1971 at age twenty-four.

Robinson has not always been afforded the attention and respect he deserves by later generations of players and fans. In a very real way, he died trying, still going for one more base, still trying to stretch a single into a double, pushing the edges of possibility. Robinson never quit, a man with the courage to take it when he had to, and then the courage to give it right back when he could.

Prickly and warm, smart and sentimental, he was among the most accessible of idols, among the most willing to put himself on the line, and to reach out. Ernie Banks remembers that when he first played for the Chicago Cubs, it was Robinson who took him aside and told him to lose the gold cap on his tooth. He was in the bigs now, a role model.

Credit Robinson for inspiring the African-American players who followed him, such fierce, bright, politically aware warriors as pitcher Bob Gibson; the first black manager, Frank Robinson; the broadcaster and National League president, Bill White; and Curt Flood, whose brave challenge to the reserve clause failed but opened the way for contract reforms for every player.

Every black athlete alive in the forties and fifties was nurtured by Robinson's example, and all acknowledge it. He helped Althea Gibson win tennis championships at both Wimbledon and Forest Hills in 1957 and 1958. He helped Wilma Rudolph win three gold medals in track at the 1960 Olympics. The great champions—Kareem Abdul-Jabbar, Jim Brown, Arthur Ashe—have all offered their public thanks. Even Joe Louis, who outlived him, said that Jackie Robinson and Paul Robeson were his heroes.

Jackie Robinson also lives on in ways other idols do not because of Rachel Robinson, the canny curator of his legend and the force behind The Jackie Robinson Foundation which, in her words, "helps young black men and women break through the barriers in the board rooms and businesses of America, not just the playing fields."

Jackie's ferocity as a "race man" never seemed to get in the way of his positive impact on whites, especially those who saw him play and understood him as a profile in courage for all.

Many years after Robinson's death, an exhibition commemorating his life toured the country. A person who saw it wrote Rachel one of the most touching letters she ever read: "If the guards in the museum tell you that an old white lady was standing in front of the cases crying, that was me."

PART IV

FAIRWAYS TO THE FUTURE

CHAPTER NINE

MICKEY MANTLE

HE ARRIVED IN THE SPRINGTIME OF THE AMERICAN DREAM, 1951, A GOLDEN teenager from the old Indian Territory. He had muscles in places where most people didn't have places. He had a country-fresh grin. He even had a name that made us smile.

Mickey Mantle was the fielder of dreams in a time that seemed to promise infinite possibility. He would be the new Babe Ruth in a new age of abundance, another post-war hero with a bat instead of a gun, a cowboy in the outfield.

The fifties in sports not only mirrored the optimism, growth, and consensus of the world beyond the white lines, it seemed free of that undercurrent of turbulence, the crabgrass in the lawn, the crack in the picture window that nagged at the happy days.

For all the talk of drab suburban conformity presided over by men in gray flannel suits, this was the decade of *Playboy*, Fidel Castro, Sputnik, Communist witch-hunts, the Beat Generation, the *Quiz Show* scandals, and the Pill.

It is also more in retrospect than reality that sports in the fifties was

mostly sun and games. There were fixes in college basketball, racial backlashes in baseball and football, and the betrayal of old rust-belt cities by club owners moving their baseball teams west. The fastest-growing sport, golf, wore a White Only sign and another that said, Women Some Days Only. Television would soon have its way, making sports no worthier than sitcoms or game shows as a vehicle for delivering consumers.

But for so many of the male baby boomers who toddled into fandom in the fifties, those days are still best remembered as a green and sunny romp over the most famous patch of lawn in America, center field in Yankee Stadium, with a fleet, muscular blond called "the Mick."

The measure of a baseball player's greatness has become his statistics, but Mantle's numbers—536 homeruns, sixteen all-star appearances, ten seasons batting more than .300—do not begin to suggest the hope that sprang forth every time he swaggered to the plate, batting lefty or righty.

Would he delicately drop a bunt and beat it out with sprinter's speed? Would he blast the ball into orbit, sending it farther than a ball had ever been hit before? Would he be walked by a pitcher afraid to challenge him? Would he strike out with such forceful abandon that we knew, we just knew, that next time he would absolutely crush the ball?

Mantle's power, energy, and youth reflected America: all things were possible when you had infinite resources and the will to win.

And like America in the fifties, he was burdened with a distant sense of doom. For America it was the threat of atomic attack by the Soviet Union. For Mantle it was the same dreaded Hodgkin's disease that killed most males in his family before the age of forty. The threats proved empty, but they dominated the psyche of the country and the center fielder, and gave each an urgency and a poignance that affected behavior in often destructive ways.

Could such a mushroom cloud of dread have been in the mind of seven-year-old Bob Costas on a day his father took him to Yankee Stadium? A New York City schoolboy in 1959, Costas's childhood was surely influenced by the rehearsals for war in every classroom. "Duck and cover!" the teachers would shout, and kids went bumping down under their desks to shield their bodies from the explosion. They covered their eyes against the blinding light of the blast. So little Bobby Costas had the fear. He also didn't have much of a relationship with his father, except through baseball, a fantasy world they could share without threat.

On the day in 1959 that Costas remembered in 1994, Mantle did not play. It was one of many games he missed because of injuries. In those days, when the game was over fans could walk across the playing field to leave by the center field gate. Mr. Costas took his son's hand, and they strolled with the crowd into the outfield. Costas remembers being overcome by the monuments beyond center field. He thought that Babe Ruth and Lou Gehrig were buried there and that someday Joe DiMaggio and Mantle would be buried there, too. Tears rolled down his cheeks.

"I turned and looked back toward home plate," said Costas, his eyes moistening thirty-five years later, "and from the perspective of a little seven year old I couldn't even see the plate because all I could see was the crest of the hill, which was the pitcher's mound. And I said to my father, 'Is this where Mickey Mantle stands? Could Mickey Mantle hit a ball this far? Did he run all the way back here to catch a ball?'

"And my father knew the answer or thought he did, and I thought he did, and I remember it like it was yesterday. My father and me. I don't care who says that's corny. I remember it like it was yesterday, and Mickey Mantle was at the heart of that."

Long before he became the premier baseball broadcaster of his time, an image-maker, a Grantland Rice of his time, Costas slipped a Mickey Mantle card into his wallet. It was there for years. It was there all the years that Costas, quintessential fan, didn't really know his icon, the years that "the Mick" roistered through the night with Whitey Ford and pulled Billy Martin out of barroom fights, the days Mantle got to the stadium hung over, the mornings after his retirement that he drank his "breakfast of champions": brandy, Kahlua, and cream.

And the card was there in 1994, when Mantle came out of the Betty Ford Clinic bearing an admission of alcoholism and of his own bleak, dark days in the sunshine, a shock for those to whom Mantle had been the beau ideal of fifties manhood, all those middle-aged men who smile still at the mention of his name.

Mantle at age sixty-two was wrinkled and worn, sober but grieving for his own life and for one of his four sons: Billy Mantle had just died at age thirty-six of a heart attack, at a drug treatment center, as if he were in Mickey's place.

"I've always felt I wasn't there for my kids like my dad was for me," said Mantle. He had missed their growing up and enlisted them as drinking partners as young men.

Costas's sensitive interview with Mantle after he checked out of the clinic was a memorable moment in both of their careers, and to Costas a way of paying back the Mick for touching his childhood. By the time Mantle said he felt "like I've let everybody down some way or other," everyone in the studio was crying.

It was not as if there hadn't been little cries of help along the way. But who really listened to Mantle in the seventies and eighties as he talked, often under the influence, sometimes remorsefully?

"My only regret is that I didn't take better care of myself," he would say, sipping at a drink. "People think that my legs and my injuries hampered me a lot; they did, but if I had taken better care of myself like Willie Mays and Stan Musial and Hank Aaron, the guys that are up in the record books, Pete Rose..." His voice trailed off and he looked wistful.

Mantle's picks were interesting: Musial, the forties' hero of Mickey's father, Mutt; Aaron, the man with a mission who stood for something and actually broke Babe Ruth's home run record; Rose, whom Mantle sarcastically called "Charlie Hustle" for his flat-out rookie play, almost an insult to the Mick's fifties cool. To some observers, Mays, Mantle's contemporary who played the same position, was a more complete ball player, but his prickly personality and black skin counted against him in the commercial marketplace.

Mantle still outsells them all. In late 1994 in a major memorabilia auction, the little Commerce, Oklahoma, house in which he grew up went for $60,000; the buyer planned to take the souvenir with him. And on that holiday season's list of authenticated signed baseballs, DiMaggio was tops ($349.95), followed by Ted Williams ($199.95), then Mantle ($119.95). Nobody else broke $100.

In a more important sweepstakes, in 1995, Mantle was bumped to the top of a transplant list to replace his ruined liver. At least one medical ethicist said he deserved special treatment as an American hero even if he had brought his problems on himself.

Mantle began drinking, he has said, after he came to New York, out of shyness, boredom, and pain. He could never admit neediness, and age would not help him. In true fifties fashion, his personal troubles were dismissed, ignored, rationalized, forgiven by others. By the eighties, even Mantle had a handle on the dark secrets of those years, although they were clothed in almost Freudian terms. He would recount a recurring dream:

"Well, first of all I take a cab to the ballpark, and I'm in my uniform and I've got a bat. And I get there and the game's going on, and I hear them say, 'Mickey Mantle hitting, number seven, Mickey Mantle.'

"But I'm not in the ballpark and the gates are closed. There's a hole that I can crawl under and halfway through the hole I get stuck, and I can still hear the guy saying, 'Now batting, number seven, Mickey Mantle.'

"And I can see Casey and Billy, Whitey, Hank Bauer, all the guys are looking around, like where's he at? And I'm stuck in the hole and they can't hear me and...

"And then I wake up. And I usually can't get back to sleep."

Mantle was a good example of the commodification of information; the press was locked into the fakelore it had created about a shy westerner, flawed with osteomyelitis in his knees, playing through pain to affirm the cult of masculinity demanded by the Cold War.

Mantle's binges, many of them highly publicized events with the explosive and unpredictable Billy Martin, were celebrations of male entitlement. John L. Sullivan would have enjoyed the nights out, this time in the service of America's anti-Communist crusade.

Mantle was portrayed as a devoted husband and father, providing home and material comforts. But the burden of raising his four children fell on his wife. He played baseball all spring, summer, and fall, and in the offseason went hunting and drinking with his pals. Mantle was a "real man," hard-driving, unafraid, determined, tough, and strong—the kind who could hit a baseball a mile, drink a buddy under the table, or kill a Commie without batting an eye—an urban cowboy like Mickey Spillane's Mike Hammer, the hard-boiled private eye who, in *One Lonely Night*, a 1951 bestseller that sold over three million copies, boasted about how he killed "reds" in ways quite similar to Frederic Remington's passionate outbursts about Indians and immigrants a half-century earlier: "I killed more people tonight than I have fingers on my hands. I shot them in cold blood and enjoyed every minute of it. I pumped slugs in the nastiest bunch of bastards you ever saw.... They were Commies.... They were red sons-of-bitches who should have died long ago.... They never thought there were people were people like me in this country. They figured us all to be soft as horse manure and just as stupid."

And just like Mike, the nineteen-year-old Mickey was white. Jackie Robinson still reigned supreme in Brooklyn, and Mays, also nineteen, had just come up with the New York Giants when Mantle joined an all-white team. The Yankees were still four years away from signing their first black ball player, Elston Howard, a competent catcher who enjoyed a long career as a player and coach. He was, however, slow afoot, which manager Casey Stengel noted when Howard first arrived: "Goddamn, we've finally got one and he has to be slow."

Stengel may have been joking, but the implicit racism suggests something of what went unstated in the minds of many white American males.

Mantle, as would Arnold Palmer and Vince Lombardi, provided a comfort zone for white middle-class Americans, even as they admired (and may have felt threatened by) the talent and courage of Robinson, Larry Doby, and the other black pioneers of baseball's integration. In 1951, the United States was still a highly segregated society. *Brown v. Board of Education* was still three years away, and the charged and often violent struggle for civil rights that it precipitated had yet to approach full steam. The prominence of white male sports heroes simply reaffirmed the fact that white men still dominated American society.

Mantle was a hero to his own teammates, who were in awe of his talent. They winced as he limped past them in the locker room, swathed in yards of tape.

"He was a God among his teammates," said Jim Bouton, the former Yankee pitcher. "I remember on payday, when the traveling secretary brought our checks to the clubhouse, guys would wave the checks and say, 'Thanks, Mick.'

"Players respond to money and muscles, and Mick had both. We were always thinking up ways to describe how strong he was. I think the winner was Dale Long who said, 'Mickey Mantle has muscles in his shit.'"

In his 1970 bestseller, *Ball Four*, Bouton portrayed the light and dark sides of Mantle. Bouton recalled his first Yankee victory, in 1962. "When the game was over I walked back into the clubhouse and there was a path of white towels from the door to my locker, and all the guys were standing there, and just as I opened the door Mickey was putting the last towel down in place. I'll never forget him for that.

"On the other hand, there were all those times when he'd push little kids aside when they wanted his autograph and the times when he was snotty to reporters, just about making them crawl and beg for a minute of his time. I've seen him close a bus window on kids trying to get his autograph."

In a new time of backyard leisure, the blossoming of baseball as what the poet Donald Hall has called "fathers playing catch with sons," Mantle was the symbolic son, star of the most successful team in all of sports, centered in the nation's media capital, a traditionally white team in the post–Jackie Robinson era, and one with the richest history. In 1936, a year after Babe Ruth lumbered off, in glided Joe DiMaggio, the son of a San Francisco fisherman. Tall, handsome, graceful yet powerful, DiMaggio was every bit as laconic as that cowboy archetype, the Virginian. No less than *Life* magazine stamped him U.S. Prime in a paragraph it would never print today: "Italians, bad at war, are well suited for milder competition.... Instead of olive oil or smelly bear grease, he keeps his hair slick with water. He never reeks of garlic."

DiMaggio was promoted as a first-generation American who didn't talk with his hands. Now that baseball was the establishment sport, it needed a cool gent. You could bring "Joltin' Joe" home to dinner. He could marry your daughter, which in fact he did; his brief, sad marriage to Marilyn Monroe seemed at first like a royal mating. DiMaggio has always been the curator of his own image, careful in interviews, wary of playing in old-timers' games lest his last image be that of a clown. He retired after the 1951 season—Mantle's rookie year—because he wasn't the Yankee Clipper anymore and he didn't want millions to see him in decline. The audiences for baseball games were suddenly counted in the millions, not thousands, thanks to television.

On May 17, 1939, Columbia played Princeton in baseball for fourth place in the Ivy League. NBC cameras transmitted pictures and Bill Stern's play-by-play to television sets in Manhattan (there were about four hundred). One reporter noted that the players looked like "white flies" and that the "ball was seldom seen except on bunts and other infield plays." He should have seen the future. Three hundred million people would someday watch the Super Bowl, making thirty-second commercials worth a million dollars to advertisers.

The future came in bursts. Fewer than a million families owned television sets in 1949. As late as 1950, most Americans had never seen a live professional baseball game. Only sixteen cities, located mostly in the Northeast and upper Midwest, fielded teams. Altogether, only forty-two franchises in the major professional team sports existed. Although Hank Greenberg became the first baseball player to sign a $100,000 contract, in 1947, the salaries of most professional athletes tended to be in the same league as many of their fans. Players in the American Basketball League in 1948 earned no more than seventy-five dollars a game.

By 1953, however, the total number of television sets topped twenty million. And by 1960, almost 90 percent of American households had a set, an enormous impact on the planning of sports events and the marketing of athletes. By 1971 the number of professional baseball, football, basketball, and hockey teams had swollen to eighty-seven; by 1980 to one hundred one. Over the past forty years, baseball has almost doubled the number of its franchises; the addition of the Colorado Rockies and the Florida Marlins in 1993 brought the total to twenty-eight. Five teams now play in California. Two even play America's national game in Canada.

In 1871, a franchise in baseball's first professional league cost ten dollars. In 1983 the going price for the Detroit Tigers was $50 million. In 1989, fifty-six million people came out to major league ballparks. Many more watched the game on television in cities which had been awarded franchises because of the size of their television market.

In 1959, the American Football League came into being only because the ABC television network agreed to broadcast its games for a five-year period for $2 million. It lasted just five more years because NBC was outbid by CBS for NFL rights and took second-best for $42 million. In 1967, some 575,000 fans attended pro-football games each week while over 11 million households watched the games on television. By 1980, a year in which an average of twenty-five hours of professional football broadcasting became available each week, 20 million households were hooked.

Players' salaries eventually rose, too. As late as 1975, the average salary for a major league baseball player was $46,000. Today, even journeymen major-leaguers are millionaires and professional football, basketball, and baseball rookies sign multimillion, multiyear contracts before the ink on their college diplomas—if they indeed earned one—is dry. The baseball and hockey strikes of 1994 were seen as logical extensions of the boom—an attempt by owners to cap their costs, by players to hold on to what they had long fought for.

The Mick, of course, did not grow up with television. But by the end of his career, it had made him a household word and an idol of the game.

Mantle was born on October 20, 1931, in Spavinaw, Oklahoma, in a two-room shack on a tenant farm. His father, christened Elvin but nicknamed Mutt, had lost his job grading county roads, and the same Great Depression had wrecked the market for the corn and wheat he tried to sell. He could become—à la John Steinbeck—a *Grapes of Wrath* "Okie" heading out of the dust bowl to California, or he could go down into the lead and zinc mines.

He opted for the mines, moving his family to Commerce, in the northeastern corner of the state, in a hardscrabble neighborhood surrounded by hills of chat—slag heaps of spent, leftover ore. Beyond the hills, Mantle recalled, were the reservoirs ringed by the beautiful summer homes of Tulsa's rich.

Mickey Charles (he was named for his father's favorite ball player, the Hall of Fame catcher Mickey Cochrane) was raised to climb over those hills of chat. Baseball would set him free. Mantle remembers a rural boyhood of sixteen cows to milk, a horse to ride to school, football with his brothers and sister, and Saturday matinees.

But baseball took precedence over everything. By the time Mantle was six months old, his mother had made him his first baseball cap, and before he was three he was walking around in a homemade baseball uniform cut down from one of his father's. Mutt would come home grimy from the mines, and before he washed up for dinner he would take little Mickey into the backyard, hand him a cupcake leftover from his lunch bucket, and a ball. Mutt was still a local semipro star but he poured his passion for the game into Mickey. He was a good coach and he knew tactics; he insisted Mickey learn to hit both right- and left-handed because he foresaw the days of two-platoon teams. "See that guy?" he once said to Mickey at a minor-league game. "He's going to be a major league star." It was Stan Musial.

Mantle trusted his dad when he said he could be a star, too. They talked baseball constantly, even down in the mines. Young Mickey worked part-time and summers as a "screen ape," pounding rocks with a sixteen-pound hammer until the pieces were small enough to pass through a screening sieve. Mantle credits his powerful upper body to those ape days.

In his sophomore year of high school, Mantle was kicked in the left shin during football practice. The leg swelled and his temperature shot up to 104 degrees. After two weeks in a local hospital, he was diagnosed as having osteomyelitis, an inflammatory disease of the bone. The prognosis was amputation.

His mother saved his leg, badgering a local lawyer to draw up papers transferring Mantle to the charity ward of a major hospital in Oklahoma City, one hundred seventy-five miles away, where doctors had a new drug, penicillin. A few days later, her son came home on two legs.

A Yankee scout, Tom Greenwade, spotted Mantle as the best prospect he had ever seen. He signed him dirt cheap to a minor league contract for a $1,100 bonus, citing the risk of bad legs. (The former governor of New York, Mario Cuomo, signed at about the same time for $2,000 with the Pittsburgh Pirates.) Mantle was granted a deferment from Korean War duty because of the disease. He spent two years in the bushes as a shortstop. In 1951, at Greenwade's urging, the Yankees brought the nineteen-year-old to a special pre–spring training instructional camp in Arizona. It was there that Stengel fell in love with Mantle's talent. He became Mantle's second father, and Mantle became the disappointment of his career.

Stengel, a former outfielder himself, moved Mantle to the outfield to make better use of his speed. Mantle was the fastest major leaguer sprinting to first, and at bat he hammered booming drives. He was willing to work on his fielding in the new position and on his erratic throwing. But something always kept him from totally applying himself, from mining his own talent. Mantle didn't react well to criticism, turning surly. He got down on himself. When he started off poorly in his rookie season, he withdrew into a shell. The crowds, reacting to his hype and his attitude, booed him. A columnist wondered in print how he could play the game when he wasn't healthy enough to fight for his country. Bleacher bums called him "draft dodger" and "coward" and, perhaps the worst epithet of the fifties, "Commie." That was the word that wrecked lives.

A year earlier, on February 9, 1950, Senator Joseph R. McCarthy of Wisconsin had proclaimed to the Women's Republican Club of Wheeling, West Virginia, that the State Department was rife with Communist sympathizers, fanning post-war, anti-Communist hysteria. It was part of a concerted effort to cast the Soviet Union as a mortal enemy in a grim struggle for global supremacy, and it lasted throughout Mantle's playing days.

Maybe it was being called a Commie or maybe he just got depressed after the Yankees sent him back to Oklahoma City for another draft physical. Didn't they believe he'd rather be playing baseball in Korea than have these unreliable knees? After the second exam, Mantle was once again classified 4F, unfit for service, but he was also dropping flies in the outfield and hitting only .269. In June, Stengel sent him down to the Yankees' minor-league team, Kansas City, to regain his confidence. But he still couldn't hit.

In a story he loves to tell, Mantle called his father at the mines and told him he was going to quit. Mutt ordered him to stay put, jumped in his car, and drove five hours to Kansas City. He burst into his son's hotel room.

As he tells it, Mantle said to his father, "Ah, Dad, listen, I tried as hard as I could. And what for? Where am I headed? I'm telling you it's no use, and that's all there is to it. Hey, what are you doing?"

His father was furiously throwing his son's clothes into his cardboard suitcase. "I'm taking you home. I thought I raised a man, not a coward."

Shocked, Mickey pleaded, "Give me another chance. I'll try, honest I will."

"What the hell. Why not?"

In the hotel coffee shop, Mutt told his son, "So you've had your slump. Everybody has them, even DiMaggio. Take my word, it'll come together."

And, of course, it did. Mickey stroked five hits in his next game, including two homers, and raised his minor-league batting average to .361. Stengel brought him back to the Yankees in August. A month later he was starting in right field in the opening game of the World Series against the New York Giants.

Stengel told him to cover the aging DiMaggio in center field. "Take everything you can get in center. The Dago's heel is hurting pretty bad."

In the second Series game, that other hot rookie of 1951, Willie Mays, hit a high fly to center. Mantle ran over from right, but when DiMaggio yelled, "I got it," Mickey stopped short and caught his spikes in the rubber cover of the drain hole buried in the outfield. His knee popped and he went down.

On his way to the doctor the next day, Mickey leaned on Mutt for support. His father collapsed. They watched the rest of the World Series together from adjoining hospital beds. Mutt was dying from Hodgkin's disease.

Mantle went home to Commerce that winter and bought his family a seven-room home. For the first time they had their own telephone. At his father's urging, he married Merlyn, a local girl he had dated. He rested his bad leg, but he didn't follow the prescribed exercise regimen. The muscles deteriorated and the knee remained vulnerable to injury for the rest of his career. As he is the first to admit, Mantle never took proper care of himself.

Mutt died without seeing his son explode as a performer. In 1953, Mickey hit .311 with 23 home runs. But if the knee was vulnerable, so was the psyche. He was sure of himself in the clubhouse where he was one of the boys, a joker, on his way to becoming a leader. But among fans and sportswriters he could be rude and abusive.

"I got into trouble with the press early because I was scared," said Mantle. "I was young when I came to New York and got misquoted, well, maybe not so much misquoted as it came out not sounding like me talking. I was scared and I didn't really know how to handle it, so if you misquoted me, I just wouldn't talk to anybody, which made the whole joint mad."

But not so mad they wouldn't continue to write about him. After all, the media were creating a superstar as much for themselves as for the Yankees and baseball. And Mantle was coming on. In 1956, he won the triple crown—batting .353, hitting 52 homers, and batting in 130 runs. It was the first of his three Most Valuable Player awards. And the Yankees beat the Dodgers in the World Series.

But fans and sportswriters considered that golden year a prelude—not a peak—and the pressure to do even better increased. He was sometimes booed for not hitting homers. Ironically, it was not until 1961, when it became clear that he would not be the next Babe Ruth, that Mantle began to feel the affection from the stands that he revels in today at old-timers' events, at card shows, in his Manhattan restaurant.

He was not quite thirty but already in his eleventh big league season when Mantle and his friend and teammate, Roger Maris, set off in tandem after Ruth's astounding 1927 record of 60 home runs. Baseball insiders thought Maris would be Mantle's pacer, goading him on and making it difficult for managers to pitch around Mickey, who would eventually win the race.

By the second week in September, Maris had 56 homers and Mantle 53 with 18 games remaining. Mantle had a bad head cold; he felt sore and stiff. An amphetamine injection caused an abscess on his hip. He was hospitalized and hit only one more homer that season. Maris hit five more.

"I couldn't do wrong after Roger beat me in the home run race in 1961," Mantle said in that sardonic tone he had acquired in the 1980s. "I became the underdog; they hated him and liked me. Everywhere I went I got standing ovations. All I had to do was walk out on the field. Hey, what the hell. It's a lot better than having them boo you."

As if he ever seemed to care. He never courted the crowd or the press. He was a man of the locker room and the barroom.

"When you were playing, especially if you were alone or if you struck out a couple of times, you'd say, 'What the hell's it all for anyway?' But if you hit a home run and your teammates jumped all over you, you knew what it was for.

"Somebody asked me how I would like to be remembered, and the first thing I thought of is that I really believe that all the players that played with me liked me. Sometimes I sit in my den at home and read stories about myself. Kids used to save whole scrapbooks on me. They get tired of 'em and mail 'em to me. I must have seventy-five or eighty. I'll go in there and read 'em and you know what? They might as well be about Musial or DiMaggio. It's like reading about somebody else."

Maybe for Mantle, but not for Costas or the baby boomers thrilled to pay $4,000 a week to attend Mantle's fantasy baseball camp and relive that Afternoon in America when they were young.

CHAPTER TEN

ARNOLD
PALMER

FLYING OVER AMERICA, YOU SEE THE ODD-SHAPED PATCHES OF GREEN SHIMMER-
ing on beige deserts, nestled among red-rock mountains, smack dab in
the middle of suburban tracts, alongside cities and lakes, even on cliffs
jutting over oceans and bays. These emeralds from the air are the
American dreamscapes, the fifteen thousand golf courses (more than two
million acres—bigger than Delaware, twice the size of Rhode Island) that
have been irrigated and fertilized and cosseted like English gardens. They
are the Arnold Palmer theme parks.

One can imagine Arnie's acolytes down there, wearing plaid polyester
Arnold Palmer clothes cleaned at Arnold Palmer laundries, wielding
Arnold Palmer irons, confident that if an errant shot beaned someone
their Arnold Palmer insurance policy would cover the claim as they
tried to find the swing they had learned in an Arnold Palmer Golf
Academy lesson that would bring their game closer to what they remember from an Arnold Palmer video.

Palmer has been called, in sportspeak shorthand, "the Babe Ruth of
Golf," and there are parallels: he, too, was a vibrant, powerhouse

performer whose inclusive personality gave new life to a game. But while Ruth served primarily to affirm the values of an era through a spectator sport, Palmer actually helped change behavior by democratizing an exclusive game with clubby conventions.

"There is something about golf that suggests Dad and granddad also played," says the commentator Heywood Hale Broun. "It's too expensive for most of us to own a yacht or race horses, but almost anyone can buy a set of clubs and move right into the middle class. The poor toss baskets and go to a vacant lot—if there is one—to play baseball, but the middle class play golf, which is a sort of super outdoor pinball."

Joe Louis loved golf. He lost to Max Schmeling because he was spending too much time whacking a little white ball instead of practicing to whack a big white man. Jackie Robinson loved golf and played whenever he could, although not at the country club near his Stamford, Connecticut, home, which did not admit Negroes to its membership. He woke up early to play on courses open to the public. Richard Bernstein, a *New York Times* book critic, remembers caddying for Robinson; he was enthusiastic, competitive and, no matter how well or poorly he was playing, unfailingly pleasant to caddies, waiters, cabbies. He tipped well above average.

Golf at the end of the twentieth century still has its pretensions and racism, yet it is also the sport of choice for so many ethnic and black entertainment stars and celebrity athletes that even one's own tournament does not carry much cachet unless it can draw the biggest rappers, actors, comics, and slam-dunkers.

What is it about golf? Its vestiges of WASPiness? Or the endless variations of the game itself. You can be alone or in a crowd, and you can make it a walk in the park or a stressful competition. The ball is not moving when you try to hit it, and no one is trying to hit you. But the undulating lawn (perhaps designed by Arnold Palmer's company) defies you to blast it through a corridor of trees, bloop it over a pond and a sandtrap, tap it across velvety grass into a hole. The game both drives people crazy and makes them happy.

And it sells billions of dollars worth of clothing, equipment, food, drinks, hotel rooms, airline tickets, gasoline, and television time.

The year that Arnold Palmer was born, 1929, there were over 5,000 golf courses in America, and most were private.

In his golden year, 1960, there were more than 6,000, with public and private courses almost evenly divided.

In Palmer's sixty-fifth year there were 14,648 courses, and more than half were open to the public. Palmer had helped make golf accessible to millions of Americans like himself, children of the working class carried upward by cold war prosperity and the leisure revolution. "Arnie's Army," as the gallery that trailed him over tournament golf courses was called, was more than a mob of fans; it was a new American class following its leader.

And what a leader to follow!—this grinning, swaggering, shoulder-rolling, chain-smoking, tousled-haired, muscular he-man, his shirt out and his tongue untied. He chatted up the gallery, promising a shot, groaning, then making fun of himself when he didn't make it, throwing up his hands in joy when he did. Palmer cared, he wanted to do well, he was hungry to win, and he gave fans permission to feel all of those emotions along with him.

"People are themselves winning through Palmer," Ernest Dichter, the father of motivational research, told the *Wall Street Journal*. "He looks and acts like a regular guy, and at the same time he does things others only wish they could do. His expressiveness makes spectators feel they're part of his game. He looks as though he needs their help, and they respond."

This was all new in the fifties, especially in a buttoned-up country club sport like golf. It was many years before athletes would routinely "act out," before tennis players tossed their rackets in the air or baseball players spat at the stands or football players danced and spiked or basketball players bumped chests and led their own cheers. Arnie kept hitching up his pants (because they didn't fit properly, sniffed one designer) in an American can-do gesture that had his generation following him up the fairway to the future.

"Trying to follow Palmer down the course," said George Plimpton, "was not unlike running before the bulls at Pamplona."

Palmer was a bull himself, a golfer with a fullback's chest, charging ahead, like America, and his gallery followed—brushing aside starchy volunteer officials, other tournament golfers, and each other to get closer to this sunny man who signed autographs and talked to them as he tossed his smoking cigarette on the grass to line up a putt, stroked, then picked up the cigarette and kept talking and walking, puffing along the track to the top.

For all this air of accessibility, though, Palmer is among the most private of sport's megastars, careful with his image, his money, and his inner thoughts. He is a multimillionaire of deeply conservative, even reactionary, views and a blue-collar hero. His early involvement with Mark McCormack's International Management Group (IMG), eventually the most powerful agent in sports, not only made him one of the top money-making athletes for most of the second half of the century, it eventually helped change the economic face of sports. And as amiable as Palmer is, he can become very angry when crossed; according to one biographer, he threatened to punch his former pilot when the man asked permission to write an insider's memoir.

Palmer has also remained, in the public mind, a squeaky clean family man, among the few sports superstars without a sexual or chemical blemish. His best-known transgressions are considered lovable hijinks; buzzing golf courses on his way home in his private plane, for example. Even his rare tears, at the dedication of a children's hospital or at his retirement from the regular PGA Tour, somehow seems macho, tears that even his hero, John Wayne, might have shed.

Here is a man who enjoys a drink or three, but in his world this is manly, too, especially since he seems in control of his health and looks; he starts the day with four glasses of water at room temperature, just like his grandpappy did. The only thing that really seems to scare him is lightning—he'll walk right off the course at the first glint in the sky. Well, naturally, the man has proper respect for the heavens, as well as the traditions of his game.

There were golf heroes before Arnie—Walter Hagen, Bobby Jones, Ben Hogan—but none claimed a populist army as they honed their expensive games on the costly, manicured grounds of racially, ethnically, and sex restricted country clubs.

His background was working class. Palmer's father, Milfred J. "Deacon" Palmer, was a construction worker on the nine-hole golf course that the Latrobe Electric Steel Company built for itself in Latrobe, Pennsylvania, a steel town of 12,000 set in the shadows of the Allegheny Mountains, thirty-five miles from Pittsburgh. After the course was finished, Arnie's "Pap" was kept on the grounds crew. He eventually became head groundskeeper, and during the Great Depression, after he had taught himself the game, took on the job of head pro as well.

The family lived on the edge of the course. Arnold was born on September 10, 1929, the oldest of four children. "Deac" seems to have been something of a drinker, and somewhat heavy-handed with the kids in the manner of the day. Palmer's publicized memories are fond. He had his own handmade golf clubs by the time he was three. He broke 100 at age seven. But he only played on the course in early morning or late evening after the members were finished. The golf pro was a servant in those days; while Arnie had a country club upbringing, he was never "of the club."

The measure of Arnie's American Dream to Palmer himself may be this: in 1971, several years after the Latrobe course had been expanded to eighteen holes, he bought it. When "Pap" died in 1976, Arnie scattered his ashes over the 18th green.

Golf seems to have dominated Palmer's life from childhood. After winning the Western Pennsylvania Junior championship three times, young Palmer received a golf scholarship to Wake Forest, in Winston-Salem, North Carolina, with his friend, Bud Worsham. When Worsham died in a car accident in 1950, Palmer quit college and joined the Coast Guard. He later returned to college but never graduated. With no desire to become a teaching pro himself, he tried selling paint for a brief time.

Then, in 1954, Palmer won the National Amateur Golf Championship, married Winnie, a Pennsylvania girl who wore an engagement ring he had bought with money hustled in a friendly round of golf and, like America, hit the road. Those first few years on the professional tour with Winnie beside him in a Ford hardtop were solid, if uneventful. He won the Canadian Open in 1955, a year in which golf's leading money winner earned a total of $63,122. Palmer pocketed a respectable $8,226 for his labors. In each of the next two years, he won four times, making close to $28,000 in 1957, good enough for fifth place right behind Slammin' Sammy Snead.

In 1958, Arnie won the Masters at Augusta National, but not too many people outside of golf paid much attention. In the mid-fifties, comedian Milton Berle, often in drag, received as much television time in a month as the professional golf tour did in a year.

But America was looking for manly heroes, although there was no consensus on who was manly and who was a hero. Kids went crazy over Davey Crockett, teeny-boppers went nuts for Elvis Presley, and Beatnik groupies found their role model in Jack Kerouac, whose novel *On the Road* captured a yearning identical to coonskin caps and "Love Me Tender." Senator McCarthy was history, although the dislocations of McCarthyism lingered for years. Richard Nixon and John F. Kennedy were heading toward the first presidential campaign promoted like a heavyweight title fight.

In this time of fervent anti-Communism, consensus, and conformity, the fuse of the social revolution of the 1960s was already burning. The war against Fascism had released two convulsive changes in American society that threatened white male dominance even as they had proved essential to Democracy's victory. Urged to join the fight to defeat a common foe, African-Americans had made important contributions to the war effort both at home and abroad. The status of Joe Louis as American hero, Jackie Robinson's breaking of baseball's color line, Harry Truman's integration of the Army, and the Supreme Court's 1954 decision to formally end segregation in schools stirred dreams of universal equality.

Women also derived new expectations from their war effort. "Rosie the Riveter" had built the planes and ships her husband and brothers and sons used to storm the beaches at Normandy. In those hours on the assembly line and in offices, women also built hopes of a post-war life outside the traditional hearths and homes.

But the end of World War II brought with it backlash for both groups. White men returned home and reclaimed jobs from African-Americans and women. Major league baseball players picked up their bats and gloves and the All-American Girls Baseball League folded. Blacks experienced an intensified wave of restriction and discrimination.

Neither group rolled over, however, although it would be years before the civil rights movement and the feminist movement burst free from the establishment's attempt to return America to "normalcy."

Palmer played an unconscious role in the attempt to push blacks and women back into their "place." He apparently shared the belief that blacks and whites would be happier in their own neighborhoods and that women belonged in the kitchen ("Stop hitting the ball like a woman," he was heard to mutter to himself after a mediocre shot). At the time, however, his energies were focused on becoming the King of Golf, the anti-Elvis, *Sports Illustrated* Sportsman of the Year for 1960—the quintessential hero for the quintessential fifties' sport, a consumer-oriented, television-made, white suburban businessman's kaffeeklatsch.

Palmer's victory at the 1960 Masters has become one of golf's Homeric idylls, a triumph witnessed by millions on national television. Nagged by a blister on his foot, he shoved a torn scorecard into his golf shoe and charged on. But when Palmer reached the seventeenth tee, Ken Venturi was already in the clubhouse, ahead by a stroke, savoring his victory.

Palmer needed birdies on the last two holes, which were also two of Augusta's most demanding. He grimaced, ran a big hand through his hair, tossed his cigarette to the grass, and attacked the course. His eight-iron shot on the seventeenth landed twenty-seven feet below the cup. Palmer twice walked away from the putt, waiting for the surging crowd to quiet down, before taking a breath that sucked the air out of the heavens. And then he stroked it in. His gallery roared as he jumped with joy.

Grinning, confident now, he strode to the next tee and blasted a long drive on the 420-yard par-4 eighteenth, dropping his approach shot five feet from the pin. As Palmer lined up his putt, a pro named Bob Rosburg, watching on television in the clubhouse, said: "I'll guarantee you he'll get it in the hole if he has to stare it in. The ball's scared of him." The scared ball dropped in, and Palmer won the second of his four Masters' green jackets.

It was that signature determination, so obvious on his deeply-tanned face—call it drive or aggression, the will to win no matter how long the odds, that go-for-broke risk taking—that captured the nation's fascination. And Palmer played it to the hilt. Two months later, he won his only U.S. Open in even more dramatic style. Seven shots down entering the final round, he birdied six of the first seven holes, completed the front nine in 30, and ended the day with a 65, then a record for the lowest final round ever in the Open. He won by a single stroke.

Describing Palmer's "last gasp heroics," the golf writer Herbert Warren Wind declared that author Burt Standish would have rejected the plot for one of his Frank Merriwell novels "on the ground of implausibility."

Some of Wind's *New Yorker* readers no doubt recognized the reference to the fictional hero of an earlier time when sport was emerging as a new frontier and characters like Merriwell, the Great John L., and the Babe replaced the gunslingers and "rough riders" of the mythical Old West as symbols of American masculinity. Palmer also shot from the hip, clubbing the land into submission, hole by hole.

Obviously, it wasn't all image. The man could play golf. Back-to-back victories in two major tournaments on television catapulted him into a prominence he maintained well into the sixties by compiling a remarkable record: 47 Professional Golf Association tour victories and 31 second-place finishes between 1955 and 1966, including 7 wins in golf's premier events—the Masters, the U.S. Open, and the British Open. But victories alone, even last round cavalry charges, didn't make Palmer into sport's first one-man corporate conglomerate. Without the values of Cold War America, color television, and a new consumer age that far surpassed the twenties, Michael Jordan would have had to look elsewhere for a forefather.

Palmer set the table for the sales-jocks to follow, especially in his ability to use television to turn himself into a marketable commodity. He had enormous help from McCormack, a Cleveland lawyer who became his manager in 1960. Their relationship also jump-started McCormack of IMG and made him the so-called "Big Daddy of Sport," head of a billion-dollar corporation with sixty-four offices in twenty-five countries that represents hundreds of high-profile clients from Joe Montana to Martina Navratilova, not to mention events such as Wimbledon and world tours for the Pope.

But golf and Palmer came first, and television delivered them to the world. In 1958, the year Palmer won his first Masters, the PGA switched most of its tournaments from match play, in which individuals knock each other off on the way to victory, to medal play, in which the top finishers stay alive round by round, because television executives wanted to keep marquee names playing longer to provide increased drama for viewers.

"Big money golf tournaments are not only proliferating in the U.S. today," observed *Life* in 1962, "but are capturing the interest of millions who were only foggily aware of their existence a few years ago."

The reasons were clear: Golf "attract[s] increasing hordes of people to whom sports cars, sportsclothes, and sports-oriented conversation have become passport to a new snobbery; television, meanwhile, has introduced the public at large to the leading players, the countermarching crowds which follow them ... and to the peculiarities and tensions of their quiet wars."

The most famous of them all was Palmer, "one of the best known, most easily recognized and most heavily breathed-upon public figures in the country."

McCormack offers two cultural clues to Palmer's popularity. Palmer, he tells us, "is a man of enormous simplicity, of steak and Bonanza ... a TV fanatic" whose favorite shows are "westerns."

He is also lucky, McCormack continues, to have married Winnie, "a remarkable hostess ... at ease entertaining ... the large assortment of people that are likely to come trooping into Latrobe with Arnold all but unannounced—writers, golfers, salesmen, promoters, and McCormack. There is always a pot of coffee ready, or sandwiches, or tea if you care for it, while you and Arnold plow ahead with matters that move the world."

Thus Winnie took her place in the age of June Cleaver and Harriet Nelson, and in a mindset about women and women athletes that haunts us today. The most successful women athletes of that time were the Russian "she-men" who regularly trounced American women in that televised athletic cold war, the Olympics. Even African-American women, who occasionally beat the Russians, did not alter conventional perceptions of a woman's place. They, too, were reported to be freaks of nature. When Wilma Rudolph won three gold medals at the 1960 Rome Olympics, her "long lissome legs and a pert charm" were noted by the press, but she was still a jungle animal, "the black gazelle."

Until Billie Jean King came along, the most popularly accepted female athlete in America was the "Million-dollar Mermaid," Esther Williams, Olympic swim team member (until the Games were canceled by World War II), cover girl, and star of wet Hollywood extravaganzas in which she always got her man and never smeared her makeup, in the pool or out.

If, as Babe Didrikson's story seemed to confirm, a woman couldn't be a "real woman" and an athlete at the same time, Palmer's story reinforced the notion that an athlete was, per se, a "real man." And Palmer was super-real, SportsWorld's version of fictional television's most popular men, a *Father Knows Best* kind of guy yet also a Marlboro Man with the will, daring, and determination of *Bonanza's* Ben Cartwright, *Gunsmoke's* Matt Dillon, and *Have Gun Will Travel's* Palladin—all frontier knights in shining armor who ruled the West with a firm, masculine hand, protecting civilization and women and destroying evil as they came upon it.

With trusty Winnie tending the hearth and providing sanctuary for real men to do the world's work, Palmer, too, readied himself to lead his Army as they turned wilderness into lawn, reveling in the kind of leisure world of golf, camaraderie, and consumption that only a capitalist democracy can provide. A cold war mentality of domino theory, massive retaliation and "containment" required resurrection of the nineteenth-century frontier values that defined women as homemakers and wives, providing "havens in a heartless world" for their men who prepared to do battle against the new "red" menace—be it on battlefields, board-rooms, bookstores, or movie screens, where little tolerance existed for any dissent from a belief in American exceptionalism or the evils of Communism.

In such a world, one patriotic entrepreneur suggested that Palmer endorse a combination golf course-fallout shelter, using federal funds to build shelters into the "naturally hilly terrain on the golf course" where food and necessities could be stored in the event that a Russian nuclear attack forced Americans underground. Although he turned down the proposition, it's not surprising that Palmer was approached. In an era when everything seemed political, even celebrating American materialism proved a person's commitment to anti-Communism. Playing a leisurely round of golf decked out with all the appropriate equipment and clothing became a patriotic act, one that more and more Americans were able to do, just like Palmer, the new Apostle of Abundance.

Commenting on the state of the American economy in 1956, an article in *Fortune* titled "What a Country!" exclaimed, "Never has a whole people spent so much money on as many expensive things in such an easy way as Americans are doing today."

Americans who had saved their money during World War II were now ready to spend it. Industrial plants retooled for peacetime. New industries—from plastics to electronics—churned out gadgets and products "guaranteed" to provide pleasure and comfort such as drip-dry clothing, alligator shirts, polyester plaids, electric golf carts, and hi-fi stereos. More than $10 billion a year was spent annually on advertising to persuade people to consume for the pleasure of it, whether or not they needed the product or had the ready cash.

The bellwether of the U.S. economy was the automobile. Between

1950 and 1960, as David Halberstam points out in *The Fifties*, the number of cars registered in the United States increased from 49 to 74 million, powerful new cars with souped-up V-8 engines, ostentatiously finned and ornamented, altered slightly each season to lure buyers back year after year. As the head of styling at Ford put it: "The 1957 Ford was great, but right away we had to bury it and start another. We design a car, and the minute it's done we hate it—we've got to do another one. We design a car to make a man unhappy with his 1957 Ford 'long about the end of 1958."

Cars became both a status symbol and a necessity. How else would it be possible to get to the golf course or to enjoy the American suburban dream, the Levittowns of identical one-family homes with a Bendix washer and seven-inch Admiral television set? By 1970, more Americans lived in the suburbs than in America's big cities. Many, like Palmer, commuted to work.

Palmer left Winnie and his two young daughters at home as he flew—often piloting his own jet—to tournaments and appearances and deal meetings. McCormack described two typical weeks in 1966: Palmer finishes third at the Philadelphia Golf Classic and flies into New York, spending nine hours the next day filming commercials for Noxzema, which hopes to put out a new line of products called "Swing;" then off to Shawnee, Pennsylvania, to help open a frozen-food factory owned by his father-in-law; back to New York the next morning to pick up four executives from the U.S. Banknote Corporation, which he represents, and fly them back home to Latrobe for a round of golf; on Thursday some public relations work with executives from a company whose lawn equipment he endorses. Two days at home, then he's off for a day of promotional work in Winchester, Kentucky, before returning for two days of meetings with fourteen executives from various corporations under the Arnold Palmer Enterprises umbrella; on Wednesday it's off to Toronto—a golf outing and banquet with people introducing his sportswear line to Canadian markets; in Latrobe the next night, Palmer works on his golf clubs while Winnie prepares a birthday surprise for the next day—an intimate dinner with the chairman of the board of Chrysler and America's First Golfer, former president Dwight D. Eisenhower, and his wife, Mamie.

It was Ike, after all, who made the Free World safe for golf in 1944 as Commander-in-Chief of D-Day and turned the White House lawn into a putting green in the late fifties, thus making himself the real general of Arnie's Army.

By the late 1960s, McCormack felt confident enough to tell the *Wall Street Journal* that Arnie did not have to win another tournament to make big money, which is pretty much what happened. He won his last Grand Slam tournament in 1964, and his most exciting hard charges after that were racing across airports in Hertz commercials, often with O. J. Simpson. Oh, yes, Palmer's auto dealerships supplied cars to Hertz.

Incredibly, in 1994, thirty years after that last Masters victory, in the year that he became sixty-five, Palmer was No. 4 on *Forbes* magazine's annual list of top money-earning athletes. Michael Jordan was No. 1 for the third year in a row, with $30.1 million, and Shaquille O'Neal was No. 2 with $16.7 million. Palmer's take was $13.6 million. Only about $100,000 of that was prize money, mostly from PGA Senior Tour events. The rest was from Cadillac, Rolex, Pennzoil, and all the Palmer subsidiaries.

If there was a cloud that could rain on the Palmer umbrella logo in this sunny golfer's sky, it was the corporation controlled by No. 3 on the list, Jack Nicklaus. Eleven years younger than Palmer, his rival and stalker for a generation, Nicklaus earned $14.8 million, mostly from his business ventures and endorsements. For most of a generation, Palmer had beaten Nicklaus on the dollar scoreboard but not always on the course. A disciplined technician where Arnie had been a swashbuckler, Jack was considered by many experts to be the better golfer, but he had never come close in popularity. When the Golden Bear (his logo) first appeared on the national golf scene in 1962, he looked like what he was, an overweight, well-to-do Ohio State frat boy whose genius for the game was not matched by accessible good looks or an easy amiability with his public.

Golf's civilized veneer has obscured the intensity of the Palmer-Nicklaus rivalry, but *Orlando Sentinel* columnist Larry Guest writes of Palmer walking up to people wearing Nicklaus's polo shirts, pinching the embroidered Golden Bear and the flesh underneath and saying, "Whatcha doin' wearing that pig on your shirt?"

After a heavy meal, according to Guest, Palmer has been known to stand up and say, "Well, time to take my Nicklaus."

This is about as "up close and personal" as most people will ever get to Palmer who, according to authorized biographer Thomas Hauser, can be enormously charming to a stranger for a minute but increasingly chilly if more is required.

"In terms of world view and appeal, Arnold is cut from the same cloth as Ronald Reagan," says Hauser. "People see what they want to see in him. I've never met anyone whose image has been so carefully cultivated that the public thinks they really know him. There's substance to the man, he's smart, he's gracious, but people react to the image.

"He's an American icon. There was talk in the seventies about his running for governor of Pennsylvania, and I think he would have won. I think he could have been president. I think he didn't do it because he wanted to play golf."

Hauser included in the book some mild rebukes by the late Arthur Ashe and others of Palmer's seeming insensitivity to the world outside the country club and his lack of concern at playing at segregated golf clubs. Palmer has never used his enormous influence and appeal to reach out to the marginalized and excluded. But that, of course, has been part of his appeal to the members of the club and to those who hope to join and pull the drawbridge up behind them.

Even his critics call him a "decent" man; home on the golf range, it is very hard to hear a discouraging word about Palmer. Nancy Lopez, a Mexican-American and the most celebrated female golfer of her time, and Jim Thorpe (no relation to the idol), one of the few African-American golf pros, suffered discrimination on their way up yet have nothing but praise for Palmer.

"When I think of golf I think of Palmer," says Lopez, who was a rookie sensation in 1978, at age twenty-one. Her father, who owned an auto body shop, was a Palmer fan (although he didn't get to meet him until his daughter was famous) and taught her the game on public courses in New Mexico.

Lopez is thrilled when people say she has done for the Ladies Professional Golf Association tour what Arnie did for the men's. The T-shirts she sells read, "Nancy's Navy." And in her favorite Palmer story, her husband, former major league baseball player Ray Knight, was asked, after playing a round with Palmer, "What's it like playing with the King of Golf?"

"No big deal," replied Knight. "I sleep with the queen."

But for all her breeziness, Lopez understands how much harder her trudge up the fairway has been than Palmer's. It took a female civil liberties lawyer to get Nancy on her high school golf team. The women's tour employs an "image" consultant to advise athletes on cosmetics, clothes, and hairstyles to enhance their appeal to sponsors—mostly men.

Part of Lopez's appeal is her comforting persona—she is a wife and mother who often takes her daughters on tour. And there are no vacations, she admits; in the off-season, Ray goes hunting. The queen stays home with the kids.

Thorpe's father, like Palmer's, was a greenskeeper who started his son playing early. In 1994, Thorpe was the only African-American on the tour. He admitted concern at the lack of minority involvement in the sport; the next black hope, Tiger Woods, was twenty-seven years younger than Thorpe, who was then forty-five. But his mood brightened perceptibly when he talked about his hero and his father's hero.

"I played with Arnold Palmer at his tournament, the Bay Hill Classic," said Thorpe, "and he was having a terrible day, shooting 80, 81, for him just a bad round of golf, and as we left the scorers' tent on the eighteenth hole, there was a man standing there holding a little crippled girl.

"And Arnold fought his way through maybe five hundred people who wanted to speak with him, shake his hand, get his autograph, to talk to that little girl, no cameras, no nothing, just out of the kindness of his heart.

"He hugged her, put her on his knee, gave her some hope and inspiration. And knowing what a golfer goes through when they're having a bad round, you just want to hide in a corner and beat yourself up, and here he was and that's why he's the people's champion. He gives back."

CHAPTER ELEVEN

VINCE LOMBARDI

ONE RAINY DAY AT THE GREEN BAY PACKERS' TRAINING CAMP, ACCORDING TO Henry Jordan, the Coach looked up at the sky and roared, "Stop raining, goddamn it."

As Jordan, the five-time All-Pro defensive tackle, has told audiences ever since: "There was a flash of lightning, some thunder, and then it stops. Coach looks at me and I look at him. Well, I've been eating fish on Fridays ever since, and I'm a Methodist."

Jokes involving Vince Lombardi and super powers were sports banquet standards by the early sixties. The squat, brusque, former high school science teacher with the picket-fence smile became the symbol of professional football at a time when it seemed to be replacing baseball as the national pastime—at least for the young and restless technojocks, those Wall Street whizkids, computer programmers, and corporate middle-managers who rode the fifties' boom into the sixties.

Why football?

It was about Social Darwinism, claimed New York Jets wide receiver George Sauer Jr., who saw the values of football reflecting current

thought: "The way to do anything in the world, the way to get ahead, is to aggress against somebody, try to dominate, try to overcome, work your way up the ladder, and in so doing you have to judge and be judged as what you want to be in relation to somebody else all the time."

It was about fear of female equality, claimed college and pro basketball player Mariah Burton Nelson, who titled her book on the subject, *The Stronger Women Get, The More Men Love Football*.

It was about spirituality, claimed theologian Michael Novak: "He who has not drunk deep of the virtues of football has missed one of the closest brushes with transcendence that humans are allowed."

It was about the pleasures of violence, claimed the National Football League itself, in an official press release referring to its game as "vicarious warfare nurtured by the technology that is this land's hallmark."

Of course, it was not vicarious down on the field, where the ethnic and black sons of the working class, swollen with steroids and pumped up by amphetamines, slammed into each other in spiraling crescendos of brutality packaged by the League in special "Crunch" video highlights.

Unlike baseball, which is diminished by television, football was perfect for television; the brief explosions of the blitz, the bomb, the hit, were enhanced on the small screen. All the game needed was a little offside commentary; with the exception of a few promotable characters like Joe Namath, the heavily masked and padded players seemed like toy figures on the screen, crews of G.I. Joes kept in check by a powerful father-sergeant-foreman figure who told them how to play and how to live, meting out both reward and punishment. Howard Cosell became the commentator and Vince Lombardi the father figure. No women need apply.

And if there was any truth to all the commentaries that called football America's new religion, then Lombardi was the father, Namath the son, and Cosell the holy ghost.

One wintry night in Green Bay, Wisconsin, so the story goes, the Coach's wife turned in bed and said, "God, your feet are cold."

"You can call me Vince," the Coach said.

Lombardi's fame came late in life, but his timing was perfect. The same year Arnold Palmer won his first Masters—1958—the Baltimore Colts beat the New York Giants for the NFL championship in a sudden-death overtime that ended what some consider pro football's greatest game. Lombardi was pacing the sidelines at Yankee Stadium that day as a Giants assistant coach.

The game was seen by thirty million television viewers and is often credited with putting the pro game on the mainstream stage alongside baseball.

Within a few years, Lombardi's role as a molder of men and winning teams put him on the mainstream stage with Mickey and Arnie in that mythical House All-American Activities Committee of athletic idols who offered their own testimonies of masculine virtue in a time of political, racial, and sexual tensions and challenges.

Lombardi arrived in Green Bay in 1959. He was forty-six. He stayed nine years, won 98 games, lost 30, tied 4, and took the Packers to 5 National Football League titles and the first two Super Bowl championships. After the 1967 season, he stepped down as coach but stayed on as general manager. In 1969 he moved to Washington to coach the Redskins to a 7-5-2 record. He became sick in June 1970; colon cancer was raging through his body. Unlike Babe Didrikson, Lombardi never made it back for an encore. He was dead at fifty-seven.

The stats in his bio don't begin to tell his story. By all accounts an authoritarian and master pyschologist, Lombardi, *Time* magazine noted in its obituary, "was an unrelenting tyrant...screaming blasphemous exhortations through his gapped front teeth as the cold Wisconsin sun glinted off his thick glasses." Coach's "histrionics would have embarrassed Knute Rockne: he raved, he cried, he prayed in the locker room. It was pure schmaltz, but it worked."

And while America was losing a war for the first time, a man who could win contained little wars was more than a football coach. For the conservative *National Review*'s Victor Gold, "the Lombardi legend" deserved to be pulled "off the Sunday afternoon screen and project[ed]...onto the larger canvas it deserves: A Coach, yes, but in the no-win seasons of the sixties, a vintage American winner; in the autumns of indecision, a man to reassure us that our doleful intellectual compatriots are wrong—that given faith, pride, discipline, loyalty, inspiration, second effort...all things are possible. "In the America of Vince Lombardi's vision," Gold concluded, "everything was there for the obtaining."

But Lombardi's vision was open to interpretation. And he may never have uttered his most famous line—"Winning isn't everything, it's the only thing;" he certainly did not believe that the end always justifies the means, that dirty tricks are permissible in the course of a quest, be they crackback blocks to win a game or illegal bombings to win a war.

Lombardi was a basically moral man who was packaged and sold by the NFL and its house sportswriters as a teacher of life, a prophet of piety and patriotism, and a social engineer who could control the most vicious forces on earth (like the middle linebacker Ray Nitschke), the most undisciplined artists (the running back Paul Hornung, Notre Dame's Golden Boy from the Golden Dome) and harness them to a productivity that would make any corporation proud. He was vain and egoistic enough to go along with most anything that promoted him.

Lombardi was powerfully built without being particularly large, and so aggressively unattractive that he made handsome coaches look insincere. He had a single-minded vision for success and would let nothing get in its way. He once was asked to comment on a statement made by his famous, bestselling offensive lineman, Jerry Kramer, that the Packers were a little flat this particular season because of a new league alignment that would bring them less challenging competition.

"Kramer who?" snapped Lombardi, pushing the reporter back with his glare.

"Your guard. Jerry."

"He didn't say that."

"But I heard him on the radio."

Lombardi's chest swelled, he bared his teeth and snarled, "Don't come in here and tell me things like that."

Lombardi was born in Brooklyn's Sheepshead Bay on June 11, 1913, the first of Harry and Matilda Lombardi's five children. They lived in a solid, lower middle-class neighborhood overseen by extended families and the Catholic church. When Lombardi was fifteen, he switched from public school to Cathedral Prep, a pre-seminary high school for boys who wanted to become priests. Although he remained devoutly religious all his life (in Green Bay he attended Mass daily), three years later he transferred to St. Francis Prep, his mind now set on a college football scholarship.

Like Mickey and Arnie, Vince had a strong father. By high school he resembled the short, stocky, thickly-muscled butcher described by one biographer as an intimidating, volatile, brusque man with a heart of gold who worked hard and demanded respect and obedience from his children.

"Before you can exist as an individual," Harry Lombardi told them, "the first thing you have to accept is duty, the second thing is respect for authority, and the third...is to develop a strong mental discipline."

It was a similar message that Lombardi imparted to his own Packer "boys;" nor did he treat them much differently. Dismissing the harsh, at times physical, discipline he received at his father's hand, Lombardi recalled that when "there was one of those violent scenes" his father "was not one to remember it any more than I am when I chew out a boy and fifteen minutes later can't tell you who it was."

Lombardi entered Fordham on a football scholarship in 1933, the same year that Jim Crowley, one of Rockne's "Four Horsemen," became head coach. Crowley grew up in Green Bay and had played high school ball for Curly Lambeau, founder and coach of the Green Bay Packers, who himself had played briefly for Rockne at Notre Dame. Assisting Crowley were former "Fighting Irish" stars, none more important than Frank Leahy, who taught Lombardi how to tackle and block.

"His terrible temper occasionally frightened us before he learned to control it," said Leahy, who later coached Notre Dame.

Surrounded by these ghosts and mentors who foreshadowed his future, Lombardi struggled to find a place on a team moving towards the big time. Finally, as a senior, he became part of Fordham's own football legend, a tough, hard-nosed guard on the "Seven Blocks of

Granite" defense that allowed only thirty-three points in eight games.

Lombardi's path to becoming his era's most celebrated football coach was far longer and more tortuous than Rockne's. After graduating from Fordham in 1937, Lombardi played semipro football, tried law school for a semester, then took a job as an assistant football coach at St. Cecilia High School in Englewood, New Jersey. He tried to enlist in the navy, but poor eyesight kept him out of World War II. He eventually became head coach at St. Cecilia, taught physics and chemistry (although he was never as good a student as Rockne), and married Marie, his college sweetheart.

In 1947, Lombardi returned to Fordham as an assistant coach, then moved on to a similar position under Colonel Earl "Red" Blaik at West Point. He stayed at the academy for five years, weathered its cheating scandal, and then moved up to the pros as offensive coach for the Giants in 1954.

Lombardi learned something at every stop, reinforcing his beliefs that discipline, respect for authority, and giving 110 percent at all times were the keys to success. "Be a hard loser," he would tell communion breakfasts and Lions Club luncheons and Packer backer dinners. "If he does not quit or curl up he has the right stuff in him...that is the measure of the man."

Like Rockne, Lombardi believed that nothing taught a boy to be a man better than football. And according to Lombardi, nobody taught football better than Red Blaik, who taught him how to organize efficient practices and study films of each opponent—techniques that became Lombardi hallmarks at Green Bay. Blaik (who once called his assistant a "thoroughbred with a vile temper") was a hard-driving, relentless commander-in-chief consumed by the game. He brooked no disagreement and demanded perfection. He became Lombardi's role model.

Football was full of "physical, mental, and moral challenges," Blaik insisted in his book, *You Have to Pay the Price*. "In its sacrifices, selflessness and courage, a game beyond any invented by man...closest to war."

This may have been appropriate rhetoric for a coach at West Point, especially in the midst of the cold war. But it wasn't quite enough for thirty-seven football players, including Blaik's own son, expelled from West Point along with sixty-three other cadets on August 3, 1951, for violating the school's honor code by cheating on a common examination.

Blaik defended his players, challenged charges that they had instigated the scandal, and dismissed claims that "Blaik's boys" received preferential treatment because they were football players. Good soldiers to the end, Blaik and Lombardi picked up the pieces of a shattered football program.

"Next to me," Blaik later observed, "Vince was probably the most deeply affected person. He was terribly, terribly broken up."

It was not an isolated incident. Six months earlier, three members of the City College of New York's (CCNY) basketball team were arrested for conspiring to fix their games for small amounts of cash. That scandal eventually involved thirty-two players from seven different colleges, including New York University, Kentucky, and Bradley. CCNY coach Nat Holman's boys came from different backgrounds than Blaik's predominately white, Protestant "Black Knights of the Hudson." They were mostly Jewish and black kids from New York City streets who, in 1950, became the only college basketball team to win both the NCAA and National Invitation Tournament in the same season.

There were calls for reforming college sport, similar to the charges and demands of the 1929 Carnegie Commission that raked Rockne's Fighting Irish over the coals. At a time when Sen. Joseph McCarthy was claiming that Communists had infiltrated the State Department and undermined the fabric of American life, some observers even suggested that the cause of corruption had less to do with the business of big-time college sport than with the erosion of American morality at a time of national crisis.

Frank Hogan, the Manhattan District Attorney who broke the CCNY case, told one reporter how "disagreeable and sickening" the whole investigation had been. "It just makes you wonder what has happened to our moral values."

Although Holman admitted that lax recruiting and admission standards were part of the problem, he took himself off the hook by blaming the scandal on "a relaxation of morals in the country." Claiming that he constantly warned his boys about gambling and point shaving, Holman insisted that "when they were asked the big question, they were not quite strong enough. They needed toughness!"

In the end, Holman and Blaik hung on to their jobs while players at both institutions paid the price. CCNY basketball and Army football were de-emphasized; scholarships were reduced, recruiting scaled back. Contests against local schools with smaller programs replaced games against national powers.

The NCAA was given more power by its members to impose sanctions on colleges that violated rules. But in the long run, big-time college sport remained untouched by both scandals. Once television and shoe company megabucks appeared, what happened at West Point and CCNY became quaint old tales. Division I basketball and football today often seem like minor-league apprentice programs of the NBA and NFL.

The scandals and the cynicism they engendered among fans worked enormously to pro football's advantage in the fifties. In prior years, sportswriters had sneered at pro athletes as "those play for pay boys." True sport was amateur sport, the purists pontificated, filled with truth and beauty. After the scandals, when love and money were less distinguishable, pro sports suddenly seemed cleaner—or at least less hypocritical.

Lombardi ultimately profited, too. He was unable to get a college head coaching position (he wondered if his Italian heritage was part of the problem) and so settled for the Giants job, which put him in the ballpark at The Creation, December 28, 1958, the day that professional football tackled the attention of the nation.

Both the Colts and Giants had finished the season with 9-3 won-lost records, but the similarities ended there. The Colts had clinched their division in early December. Well-rested and ready, they featured the league's most potent offense and a rock-solid defense, second only to the Giants, whose defensive coach, Tom Landry, would eventually inherit Vince's mantle as America's Coach in Dallas with the Cowboys. Although playing before a sold-out Yankee Stadium crowd full of

Giants faithful, the Colts were odds-on favorites to win their first NFL title.

More than thirty million people watched New York's quarterback Charlie Conerly and ball-carrier Frank Gifford square off against their Baltimore counterparts, Johnny Unitas and end Raymond Berry. The Colts outclassed the home team in the first half and went into the locker room leading 14-3.

Lombardi came up with a new strategy. The Colts had keyed on Gifford, stifling him and the Giants' offense. Why not use him as a decoy and run counterplays?

Sam Huff, the Giants' fierce middle linebacker, offered his own contribution. "Stop fucking it up," he told the offense, "and we'll bring you their fucking heads."

They almost did. The Giants shut out the Colts, scored two touchdowns, and led 17-14 with two minutes to go. Baltimore had one last chance to win or tie. Starting on his own fourteen, Unitas marched his team down the field. With seven seconds to go, Steve Myrha kicked a twenty-yard field goal to tie the game. For the first time in NFL history, the championship game went into sudden-death overtime.

The Giants received the kickoff but couldn't move the ball. Baltimore took over on its own twenty and rolled down to the Giant one. When Alan Ameche busted over right tackle and into the end zone, the Colts had won their first title and professional football was major league.

But it was television that really made the difference; league owners understood that by 1950, when the Los Angeles Rams televised their home games and attendance decreased almost 50 percent from the previous season. The next season, the Rams "blacked out" home games and attendance doubled. In 1952, the owners agreed that Bert Bell, one-time owner of the Philadelphia Eagles and now league commissioner, would negotiate television contracts for the entire league.

Called before the federal courts by the Department of Justice for violations of the Sherman Anti-Trust Act, the league fared almost as well as professional baseball had thirty years earlier. In 1953, the same year the Supreme Court renewed baseball's exclusion from federal regulation, a federal judge ruled that professional football was a "unique kind of business" that required special dispensation in order to survive. Although the court refused to allow the commissioner to dictate television policy for all teams, it permitted individual franchises to black out home games and prohibit the telecast of other games into their city when they were playing at home. By 1961, the National Sports Broadcasting Act gave the NFL and other professional leagues all that Bell had dreamed of—the right of a professional sports league to negotiate a contract for the entire league with the networks. By then Lombardi had already led Green Bay to its first Western Conference title.

Lombardi spent only one more year in New York after the epic Giants-Colts game before taking over at Green Bay, America's only publicly-owned professional sports franchise. It was also the only original NFL team still playing in the same city where it began (in 1919, as the Indian Packing Company's team). But the club had fallen on hard times. It had won its last title in 1944. Its last winning season had been in 1947. The 1958 Packers finished with a 1-10-1 record, the worst in club history.

From his very first day, Lombardi guaranteed he would turn things around. With a five-year contract as coach and general manager, he informed the team's stockholders that there would be no interference with his authority or tactics. "You will be proud of this team because I will be proud of this team," he told them. They were thrilled at his take-charge style.

To his players, Lombardi was even more direct. On the eve of their first practice, he told them: "Gentlemen, we're going to have a good ball team. We are going to win some games. Do you know why? Because you are going to have confidence in me and my system.... By being alert you are going to make fewer mistakes than your opponents. By working harder you are going to outexecute, outblock, outtackle every team that comes your way.

"I've never been a losing coach, and I don't intend to start here. There is nobody big enough to think he's got the team made or can do what he wants. Trains and planes are going in and coming out of Green Bay every day, and he'll be on one of them. I won't. I'm going to find thirty-six men who have the pride to make any sacrifice to win. There are such men. If they're not here, I'll get them. If you are not one...you might as well leave right now."

Carefully planned practices ran on "Lombardi time" (if you showed up at the announced time, you were fifteen minutes late) and emphasized basic skills (blocking, tackling, sharp execution of the run and the pass). Lombardi was the toughest taskmaster football had seen since Rockne. Henry Jordan put it this way: "Coach Lombardi is very fair. He treats us all the same—like dogs."

Which was not entirely true. With Paul Hornung and Max McGee—roommates, roisterers, the skill players that every football team covets—Lombardi could be as forgiving as Rockne ever was with George Gipp. Boys will be boys. Lombardi forgave Hornung for betting on professional football games, even when the NFL suspended him for a year. After a succession of fines failed to keep McGee from breaking curfew, an angry Lombardi called out his wide receiver in front of the entire team. "Max, that's five hundred bucks...if you go again, it'll cost you a thousand." According to one account, as Lombardi calmed down, he grinned and said, "Max, if you can find anything worth sneaking out for, for a thousand bucks, hell, call me and I'll go with you."

The players loved it—at least those who stuck it out and enjoyed the success that followed the hard work. Bob Long, a wide receiver who played for Lombardi at Green Bay between 1964 and 1967 and then joined him in Washington, told writer Tom Dowling that "playing for Vince Lombardi and the Green Bay Packers was the greatest thing that ever happened to me. Even the injuries and pain were great.

"Like I had a bad knee up there, a torn cartilage, and I played on that bum knee for six weeks, and one day I made a cut and the leg gave way, just dropped away, and down I went. He came running out and screaming and hollering, and he says, 'Long, get up, run on that leg, there's no pain in that leg.' Two days later they operate, and the doctor says it's one of the worst torn cartilages he's ever seen."

Although advised not to play anymore that season, Long was back on the practice field two weeks later, running patterns, when his leg gave out again. "Down I went and here he comes again. You know that voice of his. He says, 'Get up! Run on that leg. There's nothing left in that god-damn leg to hurt!'"

Jerry Kramer's *Instant Replay*, an account written with Dick Schaap of one year in the life of the Packers by its perennial All-Pro pulling guard, also celebrated the macho joy in pain and humiliation that paid off in victory. "I loved Vince," Kramer wrote. "I knew how much he had done for us, and I knew how much he cared for us. He is a beautiful man ... his whippings, cussings, and his driving will fade; his good qualities will endure."

The reverent praise is understandable; Lombardi had made them the best in their business, a business becoming increasingly lucrative to players, owners, and corporate America.

"When I became commissioner of the League in 1960, the office was in Philadelphia, and there was a staff of two guys and an eighty-year-old Kelly girl," recalled Pete Rozelle, the public relations man who moved the NFL to resplendent quarters on New York's Park Avenue and negotiated the television contracts that put it over the top. By 1995, the Super Bowl attracted over 300 million viewers worldwide, while corporate America paid $1 million for each thirty seconds of advertising on the telecast.

Lombardi's role was more symbolic but no less important. As a public relations wizard like Rozelle knew better than anyone, the image of the product is as important as its substance. Pro football seemingly offered America a model of sobriety, discipline, traditional patriotism, old-fashioned manhood, and work ethic during the rise of militant feminists, anti-war protesters, radical civil rights activists, and a youth culture of drugs and free love with the "Coach Head," Timothy Leary, calling the plays. No wonder Head Coach Lombardi was celebrated beyond the white lines; the Packers were the imagined blocks of granite between conservative white America and the hippie hordes.

Of course, those challenging the status quo denounced his dedication to winning as an example of creeping fascism, especially as the Vietnam War escalated. By the time Richard Nixon, a bona fide football fan, was president, the St. Louis Cardinals linebacker Dave Meggysey could write: "Politics and pro football are the most grotesque extremes in the theatric of a dying empire. It's no accident that the most repressive political regime in the history of this country is ruled by a football freak."

That kind of intensity—which seems wild-eyed in retrospect—grew naturally out of the passions of the day and the passionate nature of the game; football had always been violent, it had always been a sanctuary in which men could bond, even express their love for each other without fear of ridicule, but it had never been so socially accepted, promoted, and held up as a metaphor for real life.

Eager for the attention and money that came with it, Lombardi went public, offering his views on everything from business management to long-haired hippies—often in the same set speech, always applying the lessons of football as the solution to all problems. Speaking to the American Management Association in New York in 1967, he told more than one thousand corporate executives that the game he loved was "a symbol... of what this country's best attributes are; namely courage, stamina, and coordinated efficiency. It is a Spartan game, and I mean by that, it requires Spartanlike qualities in order to play it, and I am speaking of the Spartan qualities of sacrifice and self-denial rather than that other Spartan quality of leaving the weak to die."

Lombardi insisted that too much freedom and lack of respect for authority challenged traditional American values and produced chaos. "The prevailing sentiment seems to be that if you don't like the rule, break it."

He went on: "It is increasingly difficult to be tolerant of a society which seems to have sympathy only for the misfits, only for the maladjusted, only for the criminal, only for the loser. Have sympathy for them, yes; but I think it is also time for us to cheer for, to stand up for, to stand behind the doer, the achiever, the one who recognizes a problem and does something about it, the one who looks for something to do for his country; the winner, the leader.... [W]e fail miserably in our obligation, unless we preserve what has always been an American zeal, and that is to be first in regardless what we do and to win and to win and to win."

Shades of the Rock!

Shake down the thunder from the sky!

Gene Ward of the *New York Daily News*, the country's largest newspaper, wrote of Lombardi that "there is no more famous football man anywhere…his ideas are applicable to all the people and all the problems in this trouble-wracked world. He cuts to the heart of things that twist humans and nations. He deals in proven basics."

On the occasion of Lombardi's posthumous induction into the Professional Football Hall of Fame in 1971, President Nixon implored: "Let's always try to be number one. In the spirit of American football at its best, let's be for the team. Let's be for our country."

The Watergate conspirators interpreted Lombardi's message in their own way. Hanging on the wall in the room where the Committee to Re-Elect the President met to plan its "dirty tricks" during the 1972 Presidential campaign was a sign that said: "WINNING IN POLITICS ISN'T EVERYTHING, IT'S THE ONLY THING."

Lombardi was dead by then, but one can assume he would have been appalled by the way in which his conservative beliefs could be twisted to harmful and illegal purpose, by political plotters or by high school and college coaches who physically and psychologically damaged young men by insisting on a win-at-all-costs mentality.

Lombardi died just before the start of the 1970 season, the first season of Monday Night Football, starring Howard Cosell, and the sixth season of Joe Willie Namath as quarterback of the New York Jets. Lombardi and Cosell were two traditionalists who understood each other, but Lombardi was put off by Broadway Joe's appearance and his reputation as a free-spirited, drinking, wenching braggart who disrespected tradition and authority.

"Namath set back the image of football twenty years," Lombardi told one reporter. Lombardi was wrong. Namath carried football into the Swinging Sixties. And the roots of his traditionalism were as strong as Lombardi's.

Namath was the symbol of football's economic spurt. His signing in 1965, for a then amazing $400,000, positioned the sport in the glamorous interlocking worlds of show business, television, and advertising, and forced the merger of the new American Football League with the establishment NFL.

After Namath boldly predicted the Jets' 1969 Super Bowl triumph over the Baltimore Colts, the Day of the Underdog was declared, although one of the Jets' principal owners was Leon Hess, the billionaire oilman.

Lombardi's worries were in vain. He was simply out of touch. Namath was a kind of straw dude for moralists. Namath, after all, was no Jim Brown. The great Cleveland Browns running back who retired from football in 1966 to be a movie star was the true radical; Brown was politically aware, and he had advanced progressive theories about the role blacks should play in the administration and economics of football. (As it turned out, he also had prehistoric attitudes about the treatment of women.)

Namath, meanwhile, was a second generation Hungarian from the steel mills of Beaver Falls, Pennsylvania, whose solid work ethic, brave willingness to play hurt, and grace under discipline had been refined by Bear Bryant of Alabama, one of those "legendary" coaches whose authority (as long as he wins) is never questioned by state legislatures—much less by athletes on scholarship.

Even as pro football hyped Lombardi and itself as paragons of patriotism, it cashed in on Joe Willie's false image as a hippie in a helmet.

Take Joe Willie's trademark white shoes, for example. If they had any meaning at all beyond fashion, perhaps they were warning signals to opposition linemen; break these legs at your peril, they're putting money in your pocket. Namath's own explanation rings true: in college he had wound white tape for added support around his standard black football shoes, inspiring a Jets official to present him with special-order white shoes before his first game. (He wound tape around them too.)

But that wasn't good enough at the time for sports editors as hungry as NFL public relations flacks to make a connection to the younger fan. Better for business if those white shoes were a personal statement, a symbol of the counterculture, a finger up the Power Structure's nose, a

Yeah, Yeah, Yeah, to the Beatles. Lombardi was not the only one who seemed to have missed the point.

Namath was a man of his times, while his contemporaries, Muhammad Ali and Billie Jean King, were actual shapers of their times. Namath wore his hair long because, as he said in 1965 and repeated in 1994, "the ladies liked it." It took almost thirty years before the simple explanation was believed. When the Jets' coach, Weeb Ewbank, asked him why he defied orders to get a haircut, Namath said he couldn't find a union barber, and his father and uncles back in Beaver Falls had raised him union to the core. The crew-cut coach, his own face saved, backed off.

When Namath grew a beard, provoking sportswriters and coaches to predict the breakdown of discipline in America, his response was that "the Only Perfect Man who ever lived had a beard and long hair and didn't wear shoes and slept in barns and didn't hold a regular job and never put on a tie. I'm not comparing myself to Him—I'm just trying to stack up against Bart Starr—but I'm just saying that you don't judge a man by the way he cuts his hair."

In the Age of Aquarius, with the musical *Hair* a hit on Broadway, high school and college coaches—men paid to persuade boys to work for free—had apparently decided to make a last stand on the hair issue. It became a "political football."

Addressing a gathering of athletic directors and coaches in 1969, Max Rafferty, California State Superintendent of Public Instruction and a former high school football coach, told the cautionary tale of Dee Andros, Oregon State football coach, who for "twenty-one years...had an invariable rule that his gridiron gladiators look the part.... In other words, if you want to play for me, fellows, no girlish necklaces and cutesy medallions, no Iroquois scalplocks, no hair-mattress beards, no Fu Manchu mustaches. You can sport these execrable excrescences and still go to Oregon State, but you [can't] play football for Dee Andros."

As Rafferty told it, one player grew a beard and challenged his coach. "Shave it or shove off," said the coach, but the player refused to leave and claimed his civil rights were being violated. A special commission on human rights appointed by the university's president found for the student and censured Andros for showing "insufficient sensitivity."

Rafferty urged his audience to hang tough against such assaults on the absolute authority required by coaches. He invoked the Football Gods: "Can you imagine the expression on gruff old Knute Rockne's face if some cap-and-gowned buffoon had called him 'insufficiently sensitive.'"

As Namath moved through beards, fur coats, whiskey, endorsements for casual sex, and his ownership of Bachelors III, an alleged gamblers' hangout, he introduced open talk about what Schaap has called "the three silent Bs of the sports world—broads, booze, and betting." It may have been Namath's greatest contribution. Yet he always played by the rules.

When Commissioner Rozelle ruled in 1969 that Namath either quit football or sell his interest in the bar, Namath cried on TV. He said it was unfair. And he sold out.

The mustache. That liberating Fu Manchu was shaved to film a television commercial for a supposed $100,000. And just when everyone else was sniffing, smoking, and shooting up, Namath came out for Johnny Walker Red, in moderation, as a pregame tranquilizer and a postgame painkiller.

By 1970, even some fans attending football games refused to stand during the playing of the national anthem as a silent protest against Nixon, the War in Vietnam, and racial injustice. Not Joe Willie. According to Dave Anderson of *The New York Times*, he said, "I liked it played. Every time I hear it before a game, it reminds me of where we are in the world, in life. I kind of thank God that we're in this country. When I hear it, I get a chill. It's a thrill to me. I can't understand why people are thinking about not playing it."

Yet several months later, Namath's name appeared on the Nixon White House "enemies list" as "Joe Namath, New York Giants; businessman, actor." Wrong team, wrong politics. Even Washington misread him.

Namath happened to be available just when SportsWorld needed a pop star, a big, dark, sexy-looking quarterback who could lift a league and a network into a position to challenge the early settlers, break open the territory, and spread the gold. He succeeded beyond their wildest hopes, primarily because he was a white, native-born ethnic, a Pennsylvania "good old boy" who could be merchandised as a "rebel" when he was actually a throwback to those mythic athletes of the so-called Golden Age whose supposed dedication to the team, responsibility to performance, and loyalty to family have been preached as sport's standards by every athletic evangelist from Pop Warner to Knute Rockne to Vince Lombardi. To Howard Cosell.

Yes, Howard Cosell. As the memory of that nasal accent with its idiosyncratic rhythms fades, as impressionists no longer include it in their repertoires, as athletes' faces no longer light up at his approach, it gets harder to recall the impact he made on sports in the sixties and seventies. You have to go back to the old videotapes and see what Roone Arledge saw when that boy wonder of television was using sports to help take the Almost Broadcasting System to the ABC of today.

"His voice was so funny on radio I thought it was an actor," Arledge recalled, "and he was not a traditionally attractive person. But I noticed how all these athletes admired him, respected him, wanted to be on his program. He brought an added dimension to sports. Despite some excesses, what he was doing was not really that different from what any good sports columnist was doing. It was just in a different environment, and people weren't used to it."

Arledge put him on the air for boxing and baseball, and later for the Olympics. Cosell helped shape events into personal stories of tragedy, triumph, and hubris that could sell even a dull game. Cosell's interviews with Muhammad Ali were journalistic and entertainment classics, especially in the late sixties after the fighter's title had been taken away unconstitutionally, as Cosell, a lawyer, correctly pointed out.

But Arledge's greatest triumph was putting Cosell on *Monday Night Football*; he admits now that one reason was to show Pete Rozelle that ABC, not the NFL, had announcer approval. The teaming of Cosell as the skeptical, needling know-it-all with such popular ex-athletes as

Dandy Don Meredith, Frank Gifford, O. J. Simpson, and Namath created a sitcom in the booth whenever the drama on the field couldn't hold its own. Spectators didn't have to worry that a dull game meant a dull evening. And the controversy over Cosell (one year he was voted both most liked and most disliked sportscaster) assured constant publicity for the broadcast and a sense that ABC was offering more than a game.

For all the carping—mostly by sportswriters—Cosell was wildly popular both with the stereotypical Joe Sixpack audience, who heard in him the voice of a fan, and with the athletes, because he took their work seriously. "I believe in all the clichés," he said. "I'm a sports fan."

Not surprisingly, Cosell, who died in 1995 at seventy-seven, got along well with both Namath and Lombardi. All three of them, intentionally or not, became part of the hype that made football America's new national game during a time of social and cultural upheaval.

PART V

THE WHOLE WORLD

IS WATCHING

CHAPTER TWELVE

MUHAMMAD ALI

THE SIXTIES AND SPORTS COLLIDED ON FEBRUARY 18, 1964, IN A SHABBY OLD upstairs gym on the south end of Miami Beach. The Beatles, on their first American tour, had come to meet Cassius Clay.

Clay was late for his daily workout and the $1-a-head fight fans were impatient. Few of them knew who these smallish, long-haired boys were. In their white, terry cloth cabana jackets, they looked like bunny rabbits, rare fauna in this hardcore gym. But they didn't sound soft. One of the Beatles said, "Where th' fuck's Clay?" and another said, "Let's get the fuck outta here."

But the promoter needed them for publicity pictures, and two massive state troopers blocked their way, then actually herded them into a small dressing room where they were imprisoned for another six or seven minutes. Clay finally burst into the gym, brandishing a cane, and roared, "Hello there, Beatles. We oughta do some road shows together, we'll get rich."

The Beatles gaped, as did others seeing Clay for the first time. Nobody was prepared for his size. He was 6-feet, 3-inches and about 210 pounds. Because he was beautifully proportioned, he always seemed smaller and

more compact in photographs and on television. But the surprise of Clay's size was just for starters; no one was prepared for his physical and mental quickness, his unerring instinct for publicity, his genius as a boxer and, eventually, his dedication to principle.

Cassius Clay had come to Miami Beach to fight for Sonny Liston's heavyweight championship of the world, and very few people thought he had a chance against Terrible Sonny, a thug with a heart of chat. The title was the richest single prize in all of sports, the blood-soaked mantle of the Great John L., of Jack Johnson and Joe Louis, and this cute Clay, this fresh-faced twenty-two-year-old with only nineteen pro fights, did not seem, well, manly enough. The boxing commissioners and sporting press expected Clay to be beaten badly—he was a 7-1 underdog—but no one raised too strong an objection to the supposed mismatch because it was flowering into a great payday, another in a newly profitable string of closed-circuit television spectaculars.

Even if his fists and chin were suspect, Clay was box office. Dubbed "The Louisville Lip," he had already been on the cover of *Time*, performed his doggerel ("Me. Wheeeeee!") in a Greenwich Village coffee house, and played himself in a movie (*Requiem for a Heavyweight*, starring Anthony Quinn.) His showmanship was amazing. Within minutes of meeting the Beatles, he led them into the ring and began clowning. They squared off and boxed. In a routine so neat it looked rehearsed, the musicians lined up, Clay pretended to punch the first one, and they all collapsed like dominoes. Exit Beatles laughing.

Then Clay worked out, not only the regular bag-banging, rope-skipping, and sparring, but a yelling session with his assistant trainer/spiritual adviser, Drew "Bundini" Brown, in which they repeated their slogan, "Float like a butterfly, sting like a bee, rumble, young man, rumble."

Afterward, Clay held a press conference in the dressing room as he got a rubdown. The steam from open shower stalls was curling the pages of reporters' notebooks when a columnist from Los Angeles asked, "But what if you lose, Cassius, what happens then?"

"So beautiful," he murmured at a fogged mirror. "Your publicity has overshadowed your talent. You are the double-greatest."

"Let's be serious for a minute," insisted a sportswriter from Boston, a city that seems to breed tough and testy sportswriters. "What if the champ beats you?"

Clay, on the rubbing table, laughed into the fists propping his chin. "I won't feel bad. I'll have tricked all the people into coming to the fight to pay $250 for a ticket when they wouldn't have paid $100 without my talk."

"So this whole act," said the Boston man, "is just a con job, eh?"

"People ain't gonna give you nothing no way, you gotta go get it." Clay pushed up on the table, and his eyes sparkled. "I'm making money, the popcorn man making money, and the beer man, and you got something to write about." His eyes danced over them. "Your papers let you come down to Miami Beach where it's warm."

The L.A. columnist chuckled, but the Boston man got angry. "Exactly what are you going to do when Sonny Liston beats you after all your big talk?"

"If Liston beats me, the next day I'll be on the sidewalk hollering, 'No man ever beat me twice.' I'll be screaming for a rematch." The big brown body relaxed and seemed to melt into the rubbing table. The voice dropped to a whisper. "Or maybe I'll quit the ring for good. I'm twenty-two years old now." He closed his eyes. "I think I'm getting tired of fighting."

The week leading up to a heavyweight title fight is always filled with false reports, staged non-events, and odd characters, but this one may have been the juiciest. Joe Louis was in Liston's camp, "Evil Eye" Finkel was placing a hex, and there were constant rumors of a fix.

And somewhere on Miami Beach, keeping a low profile, was Malcolm X, who had been one of Clay's main counselors within the Nation of Islam, a Muslim sect of which the white community knew little. It was led by the Honorable Elijah Muhammad, who claimed to be the messenger of Allah. He preached the credo of black separatism which scared many whites in those critical years of the civil rights movement. Not only did he say that black was beautiful, he called whites the blue-eyed devil and predicted an Armageddon in which tall black men now circling the earth in spaceships would land to save the faithful.

After President John F. Kennedy was assassinated in Dallas on November 22, 1963, Malcolm X characterized his death as "chickens coming home to roost," another chapter of American violence. Elijah silenced Malcolm X for that, in what some observers saw as an internal power struggle.

Malcolm X had become a kind of big brother to Clay, but their relationship was complicated by the politics of the Nation of Islam; Clay's loyalty was to Elijah. Meanwhile, the fight's promoters, concerned that tickets were moving slowly (who wants to pay $250 to see Liston thrash Clay in one round?), put pressure on Clay to renounce his religious affiliation, lest it hurt the box office.

Right up until he stepped into the ring on the night of February 25, 1964, there were rumors that Clay, fearing for his life, had fled the country. That morning, he had turned the routine weigh-in ceremony into a wild, mad scene, ranting and raging, lunging at Liston while Bundini Brown pretended to be struggling to hold him back. One boxing commission doctor diagnosed Clay as being "scared to death."

When Clay couldn't be found in his dressing room an hour before the fight, reports swept the city that he was headed toward the airport. Actually, he was standing quietly in a corner of the arena, watching his younger brother, Rudy, win his first pro fight.

Then Clay got dressed and taped and went out to "whup the big ugly bear." Reporters at ringside were surprised at the disparity in size between the fighters. They had believed their own David and Goliath stories. Clay was much larger.

He was in control from the opening bell, dancing easily away from Liston's powerful left hook, peppering the champion's head with lightning jabs and straight rights. In the third round, he opened a nasty gash under Liston's left eye that would later require six stitches.

Clay was in trouble only once. His eyes began to burn before the start of the fifth round; apparently some liniment had gotten on Liston's gloves and dripped into his eyes. Clay thought he was being poisoned into blindness. He screamed, "Cut the gloves off."

But his cool trainer, Angelo Dundee, said, "Daddy, this is the big one.

This is for the title. Get in there." Angelo pushed him out, and Clay danced until his eyes cleared and his confidence returned. Liston melted under the barrage of blows. He apparently injured his left shoulder swinging and missing. He didn't answer the bell for the seventh round. He quit and slumped on his stool.

And Clay, the new champion, leaned over the ropes to shout at reporters, "Eat your words. I am the greatest. I...am...the...greatest."

Terrible Sonny was actually charming at the next morning's standard post-fight press conference. He passed off the loss of his title as "one of those little things that can happen to you." Smiling, he said that the loss made him "feel like when the president got shot."

The medical reports on his injured left shoulder were vague, something between tennis elbow and torn muscles. Liston claimed to have thrown out the arm in the very first round. The press exchanged rumors: the so-called Black Muslims had threatened to kill Liston if he didn't dump the fight; Liston had bet his purse on Clay; Liston had quit because a return-bout clause in the contract assured him a rematch and an even bigger payday against Clay. None seemed so wild when Liston ended the session with an uncharacteristically cheery, "Thanks, fellas," and the suggestion of a wave with the slung arm.

Clay's press conference was also out of recent character. He spoke softly. "I'm through talking, all I have to do is be a nice, clean gentleman." He recapitulated the fight, said he would defend against all ranking contenders, and displayed such an even, mild temperament that hundreds left the hall to catch planes home or file stories on "the new Clay" before someone asked him if he was a "card-carrying member of the Black Muslims."

"Card-carrying," he snapped, "what does that mean? I go to a Black Muslim meeting and what do I see? I see that there's no smoking and no drinking and no fornicating and their women wear dresses down to the floor. And then I come out on the street and you tell me I shouldn't go in there. Well, there must be something in there if you don't want me to go in there.

"In the jungle," continued Clay, in rote speech that would become familiar in the years to come, "lions are with lions and tigers with tigers and redbirds stay with redbirds and bluebirds with bluebirds. That's human nature, too, to be with your own kind. I don't want to go where I'm not wanted."

Journalists trotted out civil rights arguments and citizenship arguments. They invoked Jackie Robinson as a sports idol who was also a hero of integration. Clay suddenly said, "I don't have to be what you want me to be, I'm free to be who I want."

It was all very simple, but at that time, coming from a brand-new heavyweight champion of the world, it was profound and revolutionary, an athletic declaration of independence: *I don't have to be what you want me to be, I'm free to be who I want.*

In the following months, Clay fulfilled that declaration beyond any reporter's imagination. He called himself Cassius X—like all Black Muslims he had dropped his "slave name." He visited heads of state in Africa and returned to announce that "I'm not no American, I'm a black man." He renounced his parents' Christianity in the same certain terms in which he had renounced integration.

He unveiled a new name awarded by Elijah: Muhammad Ali, he said, meant "worthy of all praise most high."

It would be a long time before most newspapers and magazines would call him by his new name. Reporters avoided the issue by calling him "Champ." Many wrote that he was "ungrateful" to a system that had made him rich and famous, at the least "misguided," certainly "brainwashed" by the Muslims.

The nationally syndicated Hearst columnist, Jimmy Cannon, a throwback to the Rice-Gallico era, called Ali's membership in Islam "the dirtiest in American sports since the Nazis were shilling for Max Schmeling as representative of their vile theories of blood." (This was the sportswriter who had written the line, "Joe Louis is a credit to his race, the human race.")

A heavyweight champion turning his back on mainstream religion, politics, and commerce was a particularly powerful statement in the historical swirl of the early sixties, that time of race riots sweeping American cities, of the Mississippi murders of voter-registration workers

Chaney, Goodman, and Schwerner, and of the Gulf of Tonkin "retaliation" that widened and deepened our involvement in Vietnam. Heavyweight champions had always been grateful cheerleaders for democracy and capitalism; even Jack Johnson only wanted the same piece of the American pie that the Great John L. Sullivan had enjoyed. If Mr. Man, the symbol of masculinity, wasn't satisfied with the status quo, either something was wrong with him or with the system.

The movie, record, and endorsement contracts offered to Clay if he should somehow survive the fight with Liston were not fulfilled by the champion Muhammad Ali. In some cases the entertainment companies and the advertising agencies were reflecting white America's distress over a Muslim champion, in others, the product or vehicle was no longer appropriate for a man professing religious beliefs that precluded selling or condoning booze, flashy clothes, frivolous entertainments, unmarried sex. In fact, Black Muslims were forbidden to perform in public, especially in sports, a rule that was obviously bent for the most famous member. In any case, Ali's continued membership in the sect was costing him a great deal of money. The press and its readers were beginning to realize he was "sincere." And some of them, black and white, felt threatened.

The Muslims were hard, healthy, disciplined, devout, separatist, and violent. There were scare stories envisioning Elijah galvanizing black America into a super Mau-Mau. There were rumors that the Nation of Islam was financed by, variously, the Ku Klux Klan, Texas oil, the Arab Legion, the Central Intelligence Agency. Some white supremacists applauded the group as fellow separatists. Black and white civil rights organizations had mixed feelings—the Muslims might upset integrationist programs, yet they might also push the government towards more "moderate" blacks like themselves.

Between black civil rights activists who presented themselves to "the white power structure" as the lesser of two evils in regard to the Muslims, and black writers and academics who were busy creating for themselves areas of expertise, Elijah's influence and membership were inflated on paper beyond his apparent reach.

Meanwhile, Ali went into training for his rematch with Liston and began to display the delicious inconsistencies that would make him a fascinating subject for many years to come. Just a few months after confiding that he was looking for "a virgin girl ain't no one touched" to be his wife, he suddenly married Sonji Roi, a sexy Chicago model, a divorced mother a few years older than he, a non-Muslim with a mind of her own and a wardrobe to match.

Ali hired as a camp follower the black movie comedian Lincoln Perry, whose screen name, Stepin Fetchit, had come into the language to characterize the lazy, dumb, cowardly black stereotype. The seventy-two-year-old Perry would lounge on the ring apron in a rubber skullcap and white turtleneck sweater. Once when the phrase "Uncle Tom" was brought up at a press conference by a reporter, Fetchit began yelling, "Uncle Tom was not an inferior Negro. He was a white man's child. His real name was MacPherson, and he lived near Harriet Beecher Stowe. Tom was the first of the Negro social reformers and integrationists. The inferior Negro was Sambo."

Fetchit was on hand for the rematch with Liston, which was delayed by yet another Congressional investigation into boxing, by Ali's hernia operation, and by politicians who ran the match out of Boston to rural Lewiston, Maine. By that time, Malcolm X had broken from the Nation of Islam. On February 21, 1965, he was shot to death while speaking in a Harlem ballroom, by members of the Nation.

Ali had distanced himself from Malcolm X after he left the group. Malcolm apparently made no attempt to bring the young fighter out with him but was very hurt when Ali snubbed him when their paths crossed coincidentally in Africa. After Malcolm X's death, there was a fire in Ali's apartment in Chicago. Arson was suspected.

On fight night, May 25, 1965, there were rumors that a carload of gunmen were on their way from New York to avenge Malcolm's murder by shooting Ali in the ring. While reporters, police officers, and fans in Maine were jittery, the closed-circuit television promoters were thrilled; they thought more theater tickets would be sold if audiences anticipated both a title fight and an assassination. The promoters may have planted the rumor. They inflated the hype further by taking out a one night, one million dollar life insurance policy on Ali.

The carload of gunmen either never arrived or arrived too late; early in the first round, Ali hit Liston with a short right that put him down for the count. Some people called it "the phantom punch" because they never saw it.

Stepin Fetchit called it "the anchor punch." He said he had taught it to Ali. And he had learned it from Jack Johnson. It was a history lesson, of sorts, and revived interest in Papa Jack.

Ali, by now, was considered a worthy subject of historical digging, too. The first white reporter to prospect deeply in Muhammad Ali's background, Jack Olsen of *Sports Illustrated*, found the black Clays of Louisville, Kentucky, an accomplished, active family of teachers, musicians, artists, and craftsmen. Cassius Marcellus Clay Sr., the boxer's father, was a handsome, unstable, smart, frustrated dreamer who had filled his sons' heads with grandiose visions and earthly dreads. Cassius Sr. wanted to be an artist but ended up a house painter. He blamed his failures on the white man. He often talked at home about Marcus Garvey and other black nationalists. Cassius Sr. drank a lot, and there was a sense of violence about him; rumors and police reports point to the possibility of abuse in the household.

When young Cassius began boxing he was no construction site brawler like John L., no sensitive boy sent back by his mom to beat the schoolyard bully, like Papa Jack. Someone had stolen twelve-year-old Cassius Clay's brand-new sixty-dollar bicycle—an expensive toy in 1954—and Cassius, righteously angry, went to tell the nearest policeman, who turned out to be coaching boxers at a downtown gym. Cassius was game from the start, quick, smart, dedicated, and gifted at publicizing the local youth boxing show on television on which he soon starred.

When he was fifteen, he heard that the famous trainer, Angelo Dundee, was in Louisville with Willie Pastrano, the light-heavyweight champion. Clay ran to their hotel and called upstairs: "This is Cassius Clay, the next heavyweight champion talking. I'm gonna win the Olympics and be heavyweight champ. Can I come up?"

Amused, they invited him up. Dundee remembers the flurry of questions about training techniques, food, running, trade secrets, ring lore. Within a few years, Pastrano would be his pal and Dundee his trainer.

For all Clay's ambition, intelligence, and willingness to work hard, education—public, segregated—failed him; years later his high school reported his IQ as 78, his only satisfactory subjects art and gym. Because he was an amateur boxing champion, he graduated. He was never taught to read properly; years later, he confided that he had never read a book in his life, not the autobiographies on which he cooperated, not even the Koran, although he reread certain pages dozens of times, he said. He memorized his poems and speeches, laboriously.

Other than boxing, Clay did not seem too interested in sports. Asked if he had ever played football, he said, "Just once, that's all. They gave me the ball and tackled me. My helmet hit the ground. POW. No, sir. You got to get hit in that game, too rough. You don't have to get hit in boxing, people don't understand that."

In boxing, Clay found the perfect expression for both his need for constant recognition and his enormous physical energy. Yet he would never have stayed with it if he hadn't been able to develop a style based on speed and conditioning; in the beginning, he was rarely hit hard and almost never hit often. The heavy toll would come later.

In boxing, too, he found the kind of stable male guidance he never received at home. The truly dedicated boxer, at least early in his career, delivers his body and soul to his trainer. For six years, Joe Martin, a white policeman, directed Clay along the main path of his life, one hundred-odd amateur bouts. Martin's last act for Clay was to persuade him to "gamble your life" and go to Rome with the 1960 U.S. Olympic team. Clay had an almost pathological fear of flying, but he also knew that a boxing gold medalist comes home a contender.

In Rome, Clay was everything the sports diplomats could have hoped for—a big, beautiful, brown, youthful, exuberant glad-hander who not only won the light-heavyweight medal but answered a Russian reporter's questions about racial prejudice with the perfect fifties reply: "Tell your readers we got qualified people working on that, and I'm not worried about the outcome. To me, the U.S.A. is still the best country in the world, counting yours. It may be hard to get something to eat sometimes, but anyhow I ain't fighting alligators and living in a mud hut."

In the first year of the sit-ins, such grateful patriotism would be rewarded. Although he still couldn't get served in many Louisville restaurants when he came home with his gold medal, he did sign with a local group of white whiskey, steel, tobacco, oil, newspaper, television, advertising, and real estate millionaires, men who, Cassius said, "have the connections and complexions to give me good directions." They turned him over to Dundee, an excellent trainer with matchmaking connections, and let the media hype their boy into a star.

Clay was the best sports copy of the century—accessible, funny, always up to something new. He wrote reporters' leads for them, often in verse:

This is the story about a man
With iron fists and beautiful tan
He talks a lot and boasts indeed
Of a power punch and blinding speed.

He predicted his victories ("This is no jive, Cooper will go in five") and bragged incessantly. Younger people gearing up for the sixties found this a delightful "put on" while older traditionalists were put off. *Time* wrote: "Cassius Clay is Hercules, struggling through the twelve labors. He is Jason, chasing the Golden Fleece. He is Galahad, Cyrano, D'Artagnan. When he scowls, strong men shudder, and when he smiles, women swoon. The mysteries of the universe are his Tinker Toys."

For all this hype of Clay as the "new man," he was, like Joe Namath, a product of the romantic male fantasies of the fifties. In mellow moments before he won the title, he would often spin out a daydream:

"When I get that championship I'm gonna put on my old jeans and get an old hat and grow a beard and I'm gonna walk down an old country road where nobody knows me till I find a pretty little fox who don't know my name who just loves me for what I am.

"Then I'm gonna take her back to my $250,000 house overlooking my $1 million housing development and I'll show her all my Cadillacs and the indoor pool in case it rains and and I'll tell her, 'This is yours, honey, 'cause you love me for what I am.'"

Yet he also flashed a certain "mack" or street hustler sensibility, according to Nelson George and other commentators; the constant reference to his own "prettiness," his unmarked light skin and good teeth combined with his put-down of darker African-American males with thicker lips and wider noses—most noticed in the buildup to fights with Liston and Joe Frazier—evoked the bragging of pimps.

Clay's sensibilities were also nurtured by his father's rage, the plantation atmosphere of Louisville, and current events. Clay was thirteen in 1955, when the fourteen-year-old Emmett Till was murdered while visiting cousins in Mississippi for whistling at a white woman. Ali has said that the photograph of the dead boy's smashed, swollen face in *Life* haunted him for years.

That image may have been another reason that he was receptive, at seventeen, to the Muslim speaker who "fished" him off a street corner in Atlanta and took him to a meeting where he heard that Christianity's "spooks and ghosts" were a white man's trick to enslave the black man on earth with a promise of "pie in the sky when you die by and by." Clay was told to get his "down on the ground while you're still around."

But for all his new religious beliefs, the champion Muhammad Ali still kept his faith in the American system. "Well, one good thing about America," he would say, "you stand up for your rights and people will eventually adjust to it. Like my name."

That would take a while. His first new challenger was Floyd Patterson, the decent, sensible former champion who said: "The image of a Black Muslim as the world heavyweight champion disgraces the sport and the nation. Cassius Clay must be beaten and the Black Muslims' scourge removed from boxing."

Ali replied: "I'm certainly not going to attack his religion. How can I attack all these Catholic people, the Pope, and those wonderful people who run hospitals and help little children. Why should I attack them for the sake of one fool?"

But other former champions seemed to agree with Patterson. Joe Louis was offended by Ali, or at least Louis was told that Ali should offend him, and the old champ turned up in the opposition camp nearly every time Ali was preparing for a title bout. Louis was paid "walking around money," and at least once a week, for the benefit of photographers, a "spy" from Ali's camp would be found in the gym, watching Liston or Patterson or whoever train, and Louis would give him the "bum's rush" out. Spectators, photographers, and even the spy seemed to enjoy the flurry, but Louis sweated and seemed to take it seriously.

Rocky Marciano was outspoken about Ali. He thought the new champ was bad for business; Ali demeaned the grandeur of the title. "It's a very bad situation now," said Marciano, "because there is a lack of respect for the present champion and that creates a lack of respect for all past champions. Nobody questions my fights—they were all tough ones—but people just don't treat you the same way since he came along. And just look around these days, where are all the books and movies about boxing? I got interested myself because of colorful writing, Hype Igoe and Jack London, and all those Johnny Garfield movies."

Ali, in turn, expressed contempt for Louis and Marciano—they were too small, too slow, too ugly, he said—although Ali seemed disappointed that Louis never gave him his due as a boxer. Louis, after all, had been his childhood hero.

"One time Joe Louis came to Louisville," Ali once said, "and he leaned against a telephone pole on my street. Didn't mean nothing to him, how many poles you think he leaned on? But my momma never forgot. She still can't pass that telephone pole without telling us Joe Louis leaned on it."

The Patterson fight, on the second anniversary of Kennedy's assassination, November 22, 1965, in Las Vegas, was a turning point in Ali's relationship with the sports press and boxing establishment. It was promoted as a Holy War, the good crusading Christian integrationist versus the evil Saracen separatist.

Patterson never had a chance. Ali had promised to "chastise Floyd" for not calling him by his proper name, and then, like a little boy pulling off the wings of a butterfly piecemeal, Ali mocked and humiliated and punished him for almost twelve rounds. Ali was in total control, and after an old back injury flared in midfight, Floyd was hunched and wobbly. Ali kept up an infight commentary, "No contest, get me a contender.... Boop, boop, boop...watch it, Floyd." The referee halted the bout because the challenger was "outclassed."

Afterward, Ali patronized Patterson and stuffed him down America's throat. "Floyd, you should get honors and medals the spot you was on, a good, clean American boy fighting for America. All those movie stars behind you, they should make sure you never have to work another day in your life. It would be a disgrace on the government if you had to end up scuffling somewhere."

Patterson had been the "white hope" of both the boxing industry and U.S. government, but for different reasons. Boxing was concerned about the possible control of the heavyweight title by a new group without old loyalties. Meanwhile, the government, stepping up its troop commitments in Vietnam, was concerned about an anti-establishment sports hero, especially one that Black Panther Eldridge Cleaver called the "autonomous" black, in his own fanciful assessment of Ali.

It was around this time that Ali began to be compared to Jack Johnson, the free-standing, free-thinking "bad nigger" breaking loose of his plantation chains. Some of that comparison was at Patterson's expense—he was put down as an "accommodating Negro" like Louis. Such conceits are almost always interesting and usually unfair to whoever is out of favor at the moment. Poor Patterson had failed both the counter-culture and the establishment; looking at the roster of contenders that were left, it was clear that Ali would have to be beaten outside the ring.

On February 17, 1966, the Senate Foreign Relations Committee was holding televised hearings on the war in Vietnam. On that day, General Maxwell Taylor said the administration intended to wage only a "limited" war, but he refused to be pinned down further. There was a sharp exchange between General Taylor and Senator Wayne Morse, who said he thought that before too long the American people "will repudiate our war in Southeast Asia."

Taylor snapped back, "That, of course, is good news to Hanoi, Senator."

The two men then set the lines on dissent as treachery or loyalty that would mark so many of the alliances, attitudes, public postures, and private actions of the following years.

Senator Morse said, "I know that is the smear…you militarists give to those of us who have honest differences of opinion, but I don't intend to get down in the gutter with you and engage in that kind of debate.

"All I am asking is that if the people decided that this war should be stopped in Southeast Asia, are you going to take the position that is weakness on the home front in a democracy?"

General Taylor, becoming angry, replied, "I would feel that our people were badly misguided and did not understand the consequence of such a disaster."

Senator Morse replied, "Well, we agree on one thing, that they can be badly misguided, and you and the President, in my judgment, have been misguiding them for a long time in this war."

The committee chairman, Senator J. William Fulbright, pounded his gavel to silence the applause and restore order.

On that day, of all days, Ali's draft board announced it had reclassified him 1A—in fighting shape for Vietnam.

Ali was training in Miami for a fight with Ernie Terrell that the boxing establishment was trying to stop for financial reasons; Jim Brown, the football star and head of the Negro Economic Union, was fronting a new promotional group that included several white closed-circuit promoters and two high-ranking Muslim officials. Ali's Louisville Sponsoring Group, its contract expired, was being squeezed out. It was a new version of the old story of Mike Jacobs, Joe Louis, and the Hearst Milk Fund. But the Vietnam War gave it all a much harder edge.

Ali had been originally classified 1Y during a period of higher Army standards and retested when public clamor over the draft touched such deferred athletic stars as Ali and Namath, who was classified 4F because of his bad knees. Ali apparently flunked the mental test the second time, too, which many people found hard to believe. Anyone who could remember all that doggerel could follow Army orders.

Some felt that the local draft board may have slipped Ali, then Clay, a 1Y as a gift to the Louisville Sponsoring Group, much the same as his high school diploma and the disappearance of a juvenile arrest entry for a minor street misunderstanding were hero's perks from the local board of education and local police department.

It always seemed strange that Ali was reclassified 1A when it was most convenient for the Sponsoring Group, for boxing, and for the country. And for their purposes, his reaction could not have been better or better-timed, on that day when General Taylor and Senator Morse were choosing up sides.

Ali got the news from a wire service reporter who called the house in Miami he was renting. He was playing with local children when one of the three Muslim women who cooked for him called him inside to the telephone. When he came out, he was angry and bewildered.

"Why me? I can't understand it. How did they do this to me—the heavyweight champion of the world?"

Soon, television trucks pulled up at the house. Interview followed interview on the patch of lawn in front of the gray cement house.

"I've got a question," Ali would scream back. "For two years the government caused me international embarrassment, letting people think I was a nut. Sure it bothered me, and my mother and father suffered, and now they jump up and make 1A without even an official notification or a test. Why did they let me be considered a nut, an illiterate, for two years?"

There was very little hard information beyond the announcement of the new classification itself, but some interviewers suggested Ali might be called up within weeks, and he became wilder.

"How can they do this without another test to see if I'm any wiser or worser than last time? Why are they so anxious, why are they gunning for me? All those thousands of young men who are 1A in Louisville, and I don't think they need but thirty, and they have to go into two-year-old files to seek me out."

Between interviews he sat on the lawn chair incongruously humming "Blowin' in the Wind," while Muslim bodyguards and friends chuckled at how the white devils were doin' Ali, proof of everything the Messenger ever said. They chipped in stories of their own about about racial discrimination in the army during World War II and Korea. Oh, brother, one might say, there are fat cracker sergeants just waiting to get you on the hand-grenade range, Muhammad Ali.

Ali would be set off again.

"I'm fighting for the government every day. Why are they so anxious to pay me $80 a month when the government is in trouble financially? I think it costs them $12 million a day to stay in Vietnam, and I buy a lot of bullets, at least three jet bombers a year, and pay the salary of 50,000 fighting men with the money they take [from] me after my fights."

After a while there were no more rest periods between rounds with the press, television, radio, neighbors, friends, or promoters, and his lawn became a worldwide dumping ground for questions, answers, advice, gossip, rumors, stories of death and dismemberment, accusations, anxieties, injustices, and always the interviewers—What do you think about...? How do you think...? Why did the...?

The Muslims were almost antic at this proof they were not paranoids but chosen people. Somewhere along the way a newsman asked for the fiftieth time what Ali thought about the war in Vietnam, and he shrugged, and the newsman asked, "Do you know where Vietnam is?"

"Sure," said Ali.

"Where?"

Ali shrugged.

"Well, what do you think about the Vietcong?"

And Ali, tired, exasperated, angry, betrayed, certainly without thought, carved his eternally famous quote on the facade of history: "I ain't got nothing against them Vietcong."

The media's response was immediate and overwhelmingly negative. The circumstances under which he made the remark was rarely reported after the first day. The older, more traditional columnists went on the attack.

Red Smith wrote: "Squealing over the possibility that the military may call him up, Cassius makes himself as sorry a spectacle as those unwashed punks who picket and demonstrate against the war."

Jimmy Cannon wrote: "Clay is part of the Beatle movement...the boys with their long dirty hair and the girls with the unwashed look and the college kids dancing naked at secret proms held in apartments...."

While the anti-youth fury of the middle-aged white writers was not surprising, their historical amnesia was; these men knew about the persecution of Jack Johnson, the secret life of Joe Louis, and the trials of Paul Robeson and Jackie Robinson. Perhaps they were genuine in their hawkishness; there were people who believed that if America didn't stop the commies in Saigon they'd be fighting them in San Diego. More than 5,000 Americans had already died in Vietnam, and there were 400,000 American troops in that country, the total disproportionately black. Or perhaps the columnists were just careful to echo the safe national line to protect their national syndication deals.

Not everyone echoed that line. On his daily shows over the ABC radio network, Howard Cosell, who never let you forget he had been a lawyer, defended Ali's constitutional right of free expression. Such younger columnists as Sandy Padwe, Larry Merchant, and Stan Isaacs were willing to cover Ali clear-eyed and in the context of his times.

But the fix was in. Under pressure from the federal government and veterans' groups, state boxing commissions would not license Ali's fights; his next four title defenses were against foreign fighters in Toronto, London, and Frankfurt, where Ali's political education truly began. He seemed to become more philosophical—and posturing—in overseas hotel rooms and gyms.

"All great men have to suffer," he would say. "Many people want Lyndon Johnson's position. He's worried, tense. You can't hold a high office or position and not have pressure. I'm living at a time when we have 22 million of our people struggling. I'm the top athlete in the world, my word means something, and I'm not wanting to follow the path of people beaten and killed. I'm taking a different path, a more difficult path; I'm giving 100 percent, not just donating some money, making one or two appearances for CORE, NAACP.

"A big Negro movie star called me up, 'You're showing us that we're not free either.' Another big Negro calls up, 'You're doing something we don't have the courage to do.'

"I'm run out of my own country, it makes me bigger. I always knew I was meant for something. It's taking shape, a divine destiny.

"Jesus was condemned, Moses, Noah, Elijah, Martin Luther King. To be great, you suffer, you have to pay the price. Why are so many powers on me? People just have to see this man the politicians are against. Who is this man they hold the meetings about?

"'I want to see him,' the people cry.

"Nobody asks me how many miles I run this morning. Nobody asks me how's my left hook. You can't rank me with no fighter.

"I'm in a class of my own. I'm a jet compared to props. I'm cruising at 650 miles per hour, at 35,000 feet, and the prop is 450 miles per hour at 20,000 feet. You never be happy in a prop again, once you been in a jet.

"What you gonna say about a fighter? He smells a flower, it's his favorite pastime. He went to the hospital and visited some sick people. His double uppercut is sharp. What does a housewife know about that? But people talk to me like a congressman."

In a Toronto hotel room, the stereo on the bureau playing Carla Thomas's "Comfort Me," Ali, stretched out on a bed surrounded by boxing gear, jockstraps, sweat clothes, and underwear, held court for several foreign newsmen.

"The Americans are envious," said a Dutchman, "because you speak the truth."

"Let other people defend me," said Ali with a wave too grand for the small room, "because to defend myself would be cheapening." He turned to a Turk. "Am I well known in your country?"

"You are beloved," said the Turk. "On the streets of Istanbul, children wear pictures of you on their shirts and cry 'I am the Greatest.'"

"They do, really?"

"Yes."

"Tell your people," said Ali, "that I will visit Turkey right after this fight with George Chuvalo."

In America, facing hostility, he might be moved to snap back, "I get booed and this makes me strong. If everybody said, 'Oh, champ, you is wonderful,' I'd just lay back. But if a guy says, 'Son of a bitch, I hope you get your ass whipped,' I got to beat him and everybody else."

But overseas Ali could explain softly to African and Indian students that those who were against him "don't like me because I'm free. The Negro has always sold himself out for money or women, but I give up everything for what I believe. I'm a free man, I don't belong to nobody."

He was a superb guest. In England he was constantly thanking "you Lords and you common market everyday people" for inviting him, and he praised British heavyweights so earnestly that people forgot that the term "British heavyweight" is generically derisive in boxing.

There was even some grumbling in the press when the prime minister canceled a date with Ali and his first British opponent, Henry Cooper, apparently at the behest of the American Embassy, which had pointedly ignored Ali's presence because he had just applied for a conscientious-objector deferment.

"It's somewhat disparaging when we are trying to present the image of a unified nation," an Embassy spokesman said.

The foreign fights themselves were not so satisfying. Chuvalo, a local last-minute substitute when Terrell dropped out of the Toronto fight, threw more than a hundred low blows, which Ali stoically absorbed to prove he could "take it" before jabbing George's face into raw meat and winning a decision.

Ali split open Cooper's papery skin with snake-lick jabs, then tried to dodge the torrents of blood until the referee stopped the fight, Britain's first heavyweight title match in more than a half-century. Despite the outcome, the British invited him back less than three months later to knockout Brian London, in three rounds.

He went on to Frankfurt, where he knocked out Karl Mildenberger in twelve. It seemed likely that Ali carried the German so that more commercials might be shoehorned into the home telecast, assuring its financial success and sponsor receptivity to the next Ali match.

By leaving America, Ali also enhanced his celebrity among Americans. His fights were usually replayed on the ABC television network, and he often discussed them by voice-over with Cosell before going on to a "controversial" interview that showed off both men at their bantering best.

By late 1966, the forces that had kept Ali from fighting in America allowed him back; perhaps they felt he was gaining too positive an image abroad, perhaps they didn't want to risk his running away from an imminent showdown with his Selective Service board. He fought three times in America against competent, uninspired heavyweights, whom he played like remedial instruments: Cleveland Williams, Ernie Terrell, Zora Foley.

By now, such black leaders as Dr. Martin Luther King Jr., Rep. Adam Clayton Powell, who would soon be denied his seat in Congress, and Julian Bond, barred from his seat in the Georgia legislature for his anti-war stand until the Supreme Court ruled the action unconstitutional, were citing Ali as symbolic of black manhood courageously refusing to knuckle under to an illegal and immoral system.

Another hotel, this one in Chicago. Ali had just closed up an apartment and stored a Cadillac. In the morning he would fly to Houston to face the draft board. He was sitting in the coffee shop, eating lunch, watching a spring storm lash the waters of Lake Michigan.

"I don't want to go to jail, but I've got to live the life my conscience and my God tell me to. What does it profit me to be the wellest-liked man in America who sold out everybody?"

A newsman at the table, Nicholas Von Hoffman, asked, "What about just playing the game like other big-time athletes? You wouldn't be sent to the front lines. You could give exhibitions and teach physical fitness."

"What can you give me, America, for turning down my religion? You want me to do what the white man says and go fight a war against some people I don't know nothing about, get some freedom for some other people when my own can't get theirs here?"

Then his eyes softened and his voice deepened and dropped.

"Ah-lee will return. My ghost will haunt all arenas. The people will watch the fights and they will whisper, Hey, Ali could whip that guy.... You think so?... Sure.... No, he couldn't.... Wish he'd come out of retirement....

"Twenty-five years old now. Make my comeback at twenty-eight. That's not old. Whip 'em all—if I get good food in jail.

"Allah okays the Adversary to try us. That's how he sees if you're a true believer.

"All a man has got to show for his time here on earth is what kind of a name he had. Jesus. Columbus. Daniel Boone. Now, Wyatt Earp... who would have told him when he was fighting crooks and standing up for his principles that there'd be a television show about him? That kids on the street would say, 'I'm Wyatt Earp. *Reach*.'"

Two days later, on April 28, 1967, Ali refused to take one step forward, thus fulfilling legal technicalities that made his case eligible for a civil trial before a federal judge. In one sense, the non-step was a non-event; after all, nothing really happened and probably wouldn't for some time. There were many legal bridges yet to cross. Two days earlier, one of the Beach Boys had finally been arrested by the FBI, nearly four months after he refused to step forward.

Yet in another sense, the feeling on that cold, drizzly day in Houston was that something quite extraordinary was happening, that Ali was not only confirming himself, not only authenticating his credo, "I don't have to be what you want me to be, I'm free to be who I want," but giving strength to all who had passionate political convictions—particularly antiwar protestors, civil rights activists, and feminists. Here was a man willing to give up the rewards of the heavyweight championship of the world for something as abstract as religious principle. Who else had as much to lose?

Ali had little to say that day. He had been grimly laconic at breakfast, silent after five hours in the armed forces processing station. There was little activity outside the station until a television crew staged a demonstration; they promised a dozen rubbernecking black secretaries and students time on the tube if they would whip up some black power posters and march in front of the Custom House steps. By shooting close, the cameramen were able to create the illusion of a sizable demonstration while the television reporters provoked loud and angry answers and shouts of "Burn, Baby, Burn" by asking deliberately insulting questions. It looked very exciting that night on the news.

Boxing commissioners responded to Ali's refusal to be drafted by either withdrawing their recognition of him as champion or refusing to license him to fight in their states. Once indicted and released on bail, Ali was not permitted to leave the country. Thus, he was stripped of his livelihood long before he was ever convicted of any crime.

Although Ali made several appearances at civil rights meetings and peace demonstrations, most notably for CORE and Dr. King, he showed no inclination to become involved in the growing antiwar, antiadministration movements, actions that would have brought him into conflict not only with Elijah's philosophy of divorcement from white politics but with his lawyers' advice that he keep a low profile while legal proceedings continued. Ali specifically declared that he had no intention of becoming "a Negro leader," usually citing the hypocrisies and compromises necessary to become one.

It looked as though Ali had been boxed and shelved for the duration, and in a sense he had been; but Ali as a symbol had been set free to inspire the so-called Athletic Revolution. He was appropriated—as are all idols—as a champion of causes he may not have fully supported or even understood.

The Athletic Revolution was really more of a mood than a revolution. The gladiators never attacked the stands, and there were surprisingly few instances of either physical intimidation or extortion in which athletes threatened at the last minute not to play unless specific demands were met. In general, athletes did not know what they wanted beyond an end to "dehumanization" or "racism" or "exploitation," newly acquired abstracts with which most sports fans showed impatience since they thought athletes had it made in the shade.

There were, however, justified complaints, particularly among black athletes in the so-called "revenue producing" sports of football and basketball. As the Rev. Jesse Jackson, a "scholar-athlete" himself for a football season at the University of Illinois, would put it, "We went from picking cotton balls to picking footballs, baseballs and basketballs."

There were few black coaches (other than assistants who recruited blacks), and the practice known as "stacking" classified certain positions as black (running back, defensive back; the "body" or instinctual positions) or white (quarterback, center; the "head" or decision-making positions).

Black athletes felt marooned on predominately white campuses with few black women to date (they were often prohibited from dating white women) and discrimination in nearby towns. Crew-cut coaches gave them grief over Afro hair, clothing, and speech.

Through the sixties, especially as athletes became involved with more politically-attuned nonathletes, there were fights and flare-ups and suspensions. Jack Scott, then a young Berkeley instructor, and Phil Shinnick, a former Olympian, were among the pioneers of athletic protest, and with rare exceptions, the mainstream media could not—or would not—get a handle on it.

As late as 1971, *Sports Illustrated* could print this editorial: "In recent years sports has opened some very special doors. Every male black child, however he might be discouraged from a career with a Wall Street brokerage firm or other occupational choices, knows he has a sporting chance in baseball, boxing, basketball, or track.... The black youngster has something real to aspire to when he picks up a bat or dribbles a basketball."

One of the shining examples of this "sporting chance," Arthur Ashe, would eventually become one of its most vociferous critics, campaigning among black parents to make their children put down the ball and pick up the book, to storm the libraries as relentlessly as they did the fields; it would give them a far more sporting chance to avoid being marginalized.

The struggle that Ashe and Billie Jean King helped lead against the phony amateurism in tennis was part of this athletic mood, as well as the outspoken books, manifestoes really, by football players Gary Shaw (*Meat on the Hoof*) and Dave Meggysey (*Out of Their League*).

Somehow, Jim Bouton's racy valentine to baseball, *Ball Four*, was perceived also as an expression of militancy. This may have had to do more with Bouton than the book; he was an early supporter of progressive causes, including the antiapartheid movement, which was unusual among athletes. Bouton thinks the baseball establishment hated the book because he revealed that baseball salaries were low and owners were cheap and devious; he urged players to ask for more money.

The first and most dramatic upheaval of the new athletic mood was in amateur sports, particularly in track and field, and the most dramatic leader was Harry Edwards, a twenty-five-year-old San Jose State instructor.

Actively supported by Floyd McKissick of the Congress of Racial Equality (CORE) and Dr. King, Edwards called for a black boycott of the 1968 Olympic Games unless certain demands were met, including the reinstatement of Muhammad Ali's title; the ouster of Avery Brundage, by now president of the International Olympic Committee; the desegregation of the New York Athletic Club; the banning from Olympic competition of South Africa and Rhodesia, and the placement of black coaches and officials on the U.S. team.

Edwards had struck a nerve. College athletic directors, amateur officials, sportswriters, and congressmen attacked him as a Communist riotmonger. His pet dogs were murdered. Athletes were pressured through their college scholarships, their club expense money, and their professional aspirations to reject Edwards; the sports establishment correctly sensed the danger.

"If there is a religion in this country, it is athletics," Edwards said in the fall of 1967. "On Saturdays from one to six o'clock you know where you can find a substantial portion of the country: in the stadium or in front of the television set. We want to get to those people, to affect them, to wake them up to what's happening in this country, because otherwise they won't care."

Edwards had been born in East St. Louis, Illinois, deserted by his mother early and raised by a father who worked as a laborer. He did poorly in school and ran the streets. But he also grew to be 6-feet, 8-inches, and 240 pounds, well-coordinated and brutally aggressive. A blue-chipper.

In high school he starred in track and field and football. Given an athletic scholarship to San Jose State, he was captain of the basketball team and set a school record for the discuss. He was big enough and tough enough to attract several pro football offers, but by the time he was ready to graduate, he had discovered academic scholarship. He went to Cornell University on a Woodrow Wilson Fellowship and came back to San Jose to teach sociology and say:

"We're not just talking about the 1968 Olympics, we're talking about the survival of society. What value is it to a black man to win a medal if he returns to be relegated to the hell of Harlem? And what does society gain by some Negro winning a medal while other Negroes back home are burning down the country?

"We have to use whatever means are available to wake up the country. It would be insane to pass up any means to avoid destruction and to gain human rights.

"It seems as though the only way we can reach a lot of the people is by showing them that all is not well in the locker room. No one attempts to change anything he's not in love with, and the Negro loves his country, fights for it in war, and runs for it. The tragedy here is that the country the Negro loves doesn't love him back."

A few months later, now supported by the black power activist H. Rap Brown, who casually suggested that athletes "blow Madison Square Garden up," Edwards led the boycott of the New York Athletic Club's 100th anniversary indoor track and field games, one of sport's glittering winter galas.

There were fierce press conferences in Harlem, bomb scares, and roaring mobs of demonstrators in black combat boots and dark glasses surging around the Garden, brandishing bullhorns and nightsticks—"cause" groupies screaming for murder in the February night. Sports fans had never seen anything like this before and couldn't seem to understand why it was happening.

Dialogue between NYAC members and demonstrators went nowhere. Club members pointed out how many great athletes had come out of their teams to star in national championships and in the Olympics; the NYAC was an important training ground.

Exactly, replied the demonstrators; the club's traditional policy of discrimination against blacks and Jews had, in effect, kept many promising athletes out of the elite competition they needed to progress.

The 1968 Mexico City Olympic Games were almost anticlimactic. Presidential candidate Eugene McCarthy called 1968 the "hard year"— Senator Robert F. Kennedy and the Rev. Martin Luther King Jr. were murdered, and antiwar protestors were gassed and clubbed outside the Democratic National Convention in Chicago.

Outside the United States, the Vietcong launched their Tet offensive, an anti-Soviet uprising was crushed in Czechoslovakia, and Mexican students were machine-gunned in the pre-Olympic "clean-up." No wonder the black power demonstrations were scaled down.

One early plan had been for all black athletes to wear black athletic shoes to signify solidarity. But many athletes were being secretly paid to wear Adidas or Puma shoes, distinguishable on television by their color and design. It was the early stirring of the "Just Do It" commercialism that would be raised to new heights by the Magic/Michael Dream Team at the Barcelona Olympics in 1992.

In 1968, athletes discussed different modes of demonstrating but were fragmented by varying levels of radicalism, sophistication, and intelligence. In some cases, athletes who thought they might be picked in the coming pro football draft were afraid of being labeled troublemakers, as were those athletes with government or college athletic jobs lined up.

Under the circumstances, the simple raising of black-gloved fists on the victory stand by Tommie Smith and John Carlos, two of Edwards's disciples, was at once a courageous personal gesture and the mildest, most reasonable display of black power that year. Both were summarily thrown off the team and hustled out of the Olympic Village.

In that same Olympics, after George Foreman beat a Russian to win the heavyweight boxing gold medal, a trainer thrust a small American flag into his glove. He waved it and instantly became a hero of the establishment and a pariah in the black, youth, and antiwar communities. Foreman was touted by the establishment as a future heavyweight champion of the world.

He was also doing, in a way, what Ali had done eight years earlier in dismissing the provocative questions of a Russian reporter about racism in America. By now, the cold war stakes were even higher with a bloody and unpopular war raging.

And the cold war was playing even better on sports television. Until Nike and Adidas became the East and West of the nineties, the symbolic struggle between America and the Evil Empire was the box office bonanza. As ABC's Roone Arledge would say years later, "We could have put on a canoe race, and if it was between the U.S. and Russia, we would have gotten an audience."

While Foreman was waving the flag, Ali was learning to flex his mind. The three and a half years of Ali's exile from boxing were probably the most intellectually enriching of his life. He traveled extensively throughout the country (the government wouldn't let him travel overseas) for court appearances, Muslim meetings, and college lectures, where his most fervent fans—young men who didn't want to be drafted and their girlfriends—educated him through questions and comments. There were rough moments—his antimarijuana jokes and his putdowns of interracial dating were booed—but he could always snatch back the audience with a bit of doggerel or the quickstep of the Ali shuffle.

Ali was convicted of draft evasion despite his claim of conscientious objection, and as his case dragged on he collaborated on an autobiography, *The Greatest*, which would eventually become a movie starring the greatest; appeared in a Broadway musical, *Buck White*; gave speeches; and tried to make money in various real estate and food franchise schemes.

Meanwhile, Smokin' Joe Frazier, a hard nut of a southern farmboy willing to absorb punishment for the chance to dish it out, became heavyweight champion of a changing world. Once, the simple, down-home values of this honest workman would have been appreciated; but as the seventies began he was regarded, especially outside the boxing industry, as a pretender to Ali's rightful throne.

Ali, the king in exile, *was* haunting all arenas; more and more people now saw him as the spirit of protest incarnate—against the Vietnam War, against racism, against sexism. As his case made its way to the Supreme Court, there was a growing feeling that Ali's conviction would be overturned on constitutional grounds.

It was in this new climate that the emerging black politicians of the New South were able to license a fight in Atlanta between Ali and Jerry Quarry, a journeyman heavyweight whose greatest appeal may have been his thin, white skin; another white hope who cut easily. After three and a half years without serious training, proper nutrition, or competition, Ali would need a warm-up before he met Frazier.

The Quarry fight, on October 26, 1970, did not last long enough to determine how much Ali had lost during his exile from the ring. Ali knocked out Quarry in the third round as Bundini Brown shouted, "Jack Johnson's heah. Ghost in the house!"

So were some very live celebrities. Diana Ross and Coretta King were waiting for him outside the ropes, along with the Rev. Jesse Jackson, Sidney Poitier, Andrew Young, Bill Cosby, Julian Bond, and Hank Aaron. The Reverend Ralph Abernathy used the postfight press conference to present Ali with the annual Dr. Martin Luther King Jr. medal and call him "a living example of soul power, the March on Washington all in two fists."

He would need all of that for Frazier.

"The Fight"—as it was rightly called—was held on March 8, 1971, in Madison Square Garden. The "steam-up" was intense. Here were two undefeated heavyweights fighting for a title that transcended boxing. Take your pick, it was the dancer against the slugger, the draft dodger against the patriot, the loudmouthed child of television against the softspoken laborer, Muslim against Baptist. Each would get $2.5 million.

"Joe Frazier is too ugly to be champ," said Ali, who nickamed his opponent "the Gorilla," which Frazier considered a racial slur, especially hypocritical from someone who dared to exclaim, "Anybody black who thinks Frazier can whup me is an Uncle Tom."

"He can keep that pretty head," said Frazier. "I don't want it. What I'm gonna try to do is pull them kidneys out."

He wasn't kidding. It was a brutal fifteen-round war in which both men were probably damaged for life. The twenty-seven-year-old Frazier, as expected, never backed up, never stopped marching forward, taking punches, throwing punches.

But the twenty-nine-year-old Ali, expected to jab and run, to dance his slower opponent dizzy, chose to stand toe-to-toe and slug, to exchange pain, to take whatever Frazier had to offer as if that would prove his manhood, his worthiness, to anyone in the world who doubted the sincerity of his convictions.

Ali's basic strategy was to stand against the ropes and let Frazier bang away at his arms and shoulders, to let Frazier burn himself out. But he underestimated Frazier's conditioning and strength—those blows eventually deadened Ali's arms. By the late rounds, Ali had no punches left to throw. In the fifteenth, Frazier knocked Ali down. Ali got right up, but the unanimous decision went to Frazier.

Both men won. Frazier was finally the undisputed champion, and Ali had underscored in the ring what he had proven outside it. He was willing to sacrifice, to pay the price. He had heart and principles. He was tough.

The next morning, Ali was saying: "Just lost a fight, that's all.... More important things to worry about in life.... Probably be a better man for it. News don't last too long. Plane crash, ninety people die, it's not news no more a day after. My losing not so important as ninety people dying.

"Presidents get assassinated, civil rights leaders assassinated, you don't hear so much about that no more. World go on, you got children to feed and bills to pay, got other things to worry about. You all be writing about something else soon. I had my day. You lose, you lose. You don't shoot yourself."

The public seemed to embrace Ali after his defeat, and there was little carping on June 28, 1971, when the U.S. Supreme Court, in a narrow and close 5-4 decision, reversed his conviction. He was finally free. As surely as he had predicted the outcome of so many of his fights, Ali had also foreseen his ultimate rehabilitation among so many of those who had attacked him.

Had he not said, years ago, "One good thing about America, you stand up for your rights and people will eventually adjust to it"?

"Black people have always understood," says Harry Edwards, "that I don't care how big you are, white America can bring you down. White America brought down Paul Robeson and Jack Johnson. The thing about Ali that was so amazing was that he was willing to pay the price, to walk away from all of the riches, all of the fame, all of the fortune, all of the prestige because of his commitment to his own personal dignity and integrity.

"The reality is that most people are not prepared to pay the price. And when you combine that with the emergence of the narcissistic Me Generation you have a combination of factors where you're not going to have any more heroes in sports, political or otherwise."

For the next three years after the Supreme Court lifted the threat of imprisonment, Ali was a fixture on television, fighting fourteen times, always chatting with Cosell afterward. There were knockouts over Quarry and Patterson, and a decision over Frazier.

Ali made more than $5 million, an enormous sum in those days for someone who was not the champion. Coasting on his image as a prince of principle, a family man, and a religionist, he also began to indulge in the kind of extracurricular pleasures from which sportswriters, even in those days, still averted their gaze. His appetites were Ruthian.

With seemingly equal enthusiasm, Ali posed for photographs, signed autographs, and granted carnal audiences. Seeing several women a day in private was not unusual, and he was not especially selective. He said that he tried not to ejaculate until the last one, so that none would be disappointed; his explanation that he wanted to leave as many as possible with the memory of an appointment with history seemed no more unusual than he was.

Such generosity, however, would lead to the breakup of his second marriage and probably his third. It also didn't seem like the best training technique. But then, after Frazier lost his title to George Foreman, there seemed little likelihood that Ali would ever be champion again. He might as well enjoy himself. Foreman the flag-waver had become a surly brute in the Liston mode. And unlike Liston, he was seven years younger than Ali, and bigger.

But to paraphrase Malcolm X, the chickens of the sixties—Ali's time—were coming home to roost. The Watergate scandal brought down Nixon's presidency. State laws against abortion were struck down in the Supreme Court's *Roe v. Wade* decision. Billie Jean King beat Bobby Riggs in a tennis battle of the sexes, and Frank Robinson became major league baseball's first black manager. Why wouldn't The Greatest once again float like a butterfly and sting like a bee?

Thus Ali went to Africa to meet Foreman in "The Rumble in the Jungle."

That fight, on October 30, 1974, in Kinshasa, Zaire, ranked with the first Liston fight and the first Frazier fight as highlights in a mythic career; Beowulf against Grendel's mother, St. George versus the Dragon.

It was also realpolitik. This was the first title fight in Africa. It affirmed and publicized a corrupt regime needing foreign investment. It was Don King's breakthrough coup in his rise from Cleveland ex-con to boxing boss. And it was possible because Ali, though expected to lose, was the only fighter with the worldwide box office appeal to put it over. Each fighter was guaranteed $5 million.

Ali was at his Louisville Lip best in the days leading up to the fight. He talked of being in his "ancestral home," of the world being "a black shirt with a few white buttons." And then he would laugh and say, "This is just another boxing match between a colored boy from Kentucky and a colored boy from Houston."

When he met the twenty-five-year-old Foreman in the ring, he whispered, "You have heard of me since you were young. You've been following me since you were a little boy. Now you must meet me, your master."

It was all true, of course. Twenty years later, when Foreman, now a shrewd, lovable television actor and pitchman, became the oldest man to regain the title, he was quick to admit how much of a hero Ali had been in his youth. But it was probably the famous "rope-a-dope" tactic that defeated Foreman more than the stars in his eyes.

Ali leaned on the ropes, as he had with Frazier, but this time he was able to absorb and deflect the thunderous blows off his elbows and shoulders without losing the strength in his own arms.

He was soon punching back faster than Foreman, taunting him, "You are just an amateur, George."

By the eighth round, Foreman was frustrated...and exhausted...and vulnerable. He was too young and inexperienced to figure out how to combat the Ali rope-a-dope. It might have been a relief when Ali finally burst off the ropes to fire three good rights, a left, and a sledgehammer right. Foreman leaned forward from the the waist, then pitched to the canvas.

Ali was champion again. He would lose it, then regain it a third time and, like almost every other fighter, he would stay in the ring too long. His friends would beg him to quit, his fans would watch, wincing, as he absorbed punches that thickened his speech and stiffened his gait.

No one can ever tell an idol that their time is up.

As Ali shuffled through middle age moon-faced and whispery, he became a nonthreatening holy child distributing Korans, a nostalgic comfort to his aging fans. His magical youth was clearly still alive deep within the prison of a body stiffened and diminished by what was called Parkinson's Syndrome and variously attributed to chemical fumes and too many punches.

There were still contradictions, schemes, silly jokes, magic tricks, out-of-the-blue charitable donations, and quick-buck fast-foods like Muhammad Ali potato chips in Sweet Chili, Sweet Hot, Sour Cream and Onion. He seemed financially comfortable, although nowhere as rich as he might have been. Millions had been squandered, given away, perhaps stolen.

But Ali was in good hands now. His fourth wife, Lonnie, was smart and protective; their mothers had been friends in Louisville: he may have once even baby-sat for her. His best friend and Sancho Panza, the photographer Howard Bingham, was often at his side.

And yet Ali was still vain, this man who once would not wear a protective cup because it made his backside look too large.

Once, after a *Today Show* appearance in which Bryant Gumbel smoothly moved him through conversational shoals like a tugboat guiding an ocean liner, Ali watched the tape with disgust. He pointed out how his hands shook on the screen, how his face seemed frozen.

"Shouldn't of done it," he said. "If I was a fan I'd be shocked. That man is in bad shape."

"You know I tell the truth," said Lonnie. "That man is shaking, but he can be understood."

"That man is dying," said Ali.

When the segment was over, he turned back to a visitor. "Answer quick. What color's sky?"

"Blue."

"Grass."

"Green."

"What's S-I-L-K."

"Silk."

"What do cows drink?"

"Milk."

"Drink water," he said triumphantly. "Mind control. I got it, you don't."

More than any other idol, Ali can still draw a crowd anywhere in the world, and for those of certain generations, still draw a smile.

Even Foreman is still humbled by him. Once asked if he felt any guilt for Ali's present condition, Foreman smiled and said:

"When you look at Muhammad Ali, you think about veterans of World War II, the big war. It was really a great war, fought for something special. And when you're sitting in an office with them and they happen to take off a leg and say, 'Look what happened to me,' or take out an eye, 'Look what happened to me in that war,' it's a thing of pride. Muhammad felt like he did something more than box. He made a lot of people feel good about themselves."

He can always do that.

One fine day in New York, Ali was the star, naturally, of a garden party at the mayor's mansion for the Joe Louis scholarship fund. Among the invited guests was Chuck Wepner, once known as the Bayonne Bleeder, a tall, tough white fighter from the New Jersey docks who was proud that he was never knocked down. Literally thin-skinned, he usually lost when his fights were stopped because of cuts. In 1975, in a fight he lost to Ali, Wepner knocked the champ down by deliberately stepping on his foot, and shoving him.

Wepner's career inspired Sylvester Stallone to create the Rocky Balboa character, which had its own enormous affect on boxing. The first Rocky movie came out in 1976, but this garden party was in 1991 and Wepner, who arrived late and alone and obviously nervous, wondered if Ali would recognize him. It wasn't only a matter of being snubbed but of dealing with Ali's reduced mental and physical circumstances.

Wepner passed Ali in a circle of admirers, once, twice, his eyes flicking sideways, too proud or shy to wave or shout for Ali's attention. The crowd around Ali stiffened, too. Had Ali seen Wepner, would he recognize him, would a greeting be coaxed out of that damaged body?

At the very last instant, just before Wepner was gone, Ali snatched the moment.

He burst out of the circle, lurched at Wepner, and, laughing, deliberately stepped on his foot.

CHAPTER THIRTEEN

BILLIE JEAN KING

BILLIE JEAN KING HAD NEVER WANTED TO PLAY BOBBY RIGGS IN THE SO-CALLED "Battle of the Sexes." It was silly, it was demeaning, and she had more important causes to promote in 1973—a new women's pro tennis tour, a women's sports magazine, and a women's sports foundation, as well as a vision of bringing her game to the people in a national recreational league grandly named World Team Tennis.

She was also in great demand as a spokeswoman for Title IX, that part of a new federal law mandating an equal share of the playing field for women. The feminist movement was a force in the early seventies, and Billie Jean was its most visible muscle.

But Riggs dogged her for three years, popping up at tournaments and press conferences and cocktail parties to say, "Hey, Billie, let's go and make some money."

She would brush him off. "Leave me alone, Bobby, I'm trying to make the women's tour happen."

King had never been so busy. In the late sixties, she had helped lead tennis out of "shamateurism," the long tradition of under-the-table

payments, and into the Open era of respectable professionalism. And when the new male pros squeezed their female colleagues out, she played a leading role in organizing the women's Virginia Slims tour.

There was no time for a no-win stunt; why should the Number One women's tennis player in the world, a twenty-nine-year-old athlete in top shape, play against a fifty-five-year-old has-been, a joke-a-stroke hustler? Even if King won, Riggs's age and character would smudge the victory.

But then Riggs talked the Australian star, Margaret Court, into a match. On Mother's Day, 1973, Riggs beat her badly. Court was over-whelmed as much by the media circus as Riggs's repertoire of junk shots. Riggs declared that the battle of the sexes was over, and that men had won. Or, in the rhetoric of the day, which he was pleased to parrot, the "chauvinist pigs" were triumphant, and the "girls" should go back to the bedroom and the kitchen where they belonged.

Whereupon the call went out for a Joan of Ace to lead the feminist revolution in sports. Billie Jean heard the voices.

"I was in Japan when she was playing Bobby," recalled King more than twenty years later. "I remember stepping from the jet way to the air-plane in Tokyo, just having lockjaw I was so angry that Margaret had lost. Absolutely annihilated her. I knew I had to play him.

"I thought it would set us back fifty years if I didn't win that match," she said. "It would ruin the women's tour and affect all women's self esteem. I took it very seriously. For eight weeks I went into total training, situps, weights, I must have hit three hundred-fifty overhead smashes a day with a training pro, Pete Collins, down at Hilton Head.

"I would meditate, thinking about the match emotionally and men-tally every single day. I tried to think of every possible thing that could go wrong, yet still find a way to stay in the solution and win."

She paused, an exuberant fifty-year-old with sparkling eyes, and sighed, "You know, I still wake up some mornings thinking I haven't played the match yet."

King played it on September 20, 1973, two months before her thirti-eth birthday. As Billie Jean dressed for her date with destiny, in the bow-els of Houston's Astrodome, she stood as close as she could to a cubicle in the visiting team's locker room that her kid brother, Randy Moffitt, had used when he pitched for the San Francisco Giants. She remembered all the nights that she and Randy had sat on the floor of their parents' house in Long Beach, California, and daydreamed out loud to each other. She would bang the strings of her racquet against her palm and talk about being the most famous tennis player in the world, and he would pound a baseball into his glove and talk about playing in the major leagues.

In 1954, the year of Babe Didrikson's great comeback from cancer to win the U.S. Women's Open golf tournament by twelve strokes, Sissie Moffitt, as Billie Jean was then known, was already a star, the ten-year-old shortstop and youngest member of the girls' softball team that won the Long Beach, California, public parks championship.

She was big for her age, faster and stronger than the boys and girls she beat in town foot races or knocked over while running for a touchdown. Her best sport was softball; forty years later she would still get excited recalling the game in which she made a running catch at her shoetops, whirled, and threw out a runner at third base to win a game. She loved the way her teammates and fans hugged her.

It was, of course, considered a passing phase. Despite the long history of women's softball and basketball, team sports for women were rarely considered "appropriate" after girlhood, especially in the fifties when Rosie the Riveter and her sisters were being herded back into the house.

In those places where the games flourished, they were considered idiosyncratic. Iowa girls' high school basketball, for example, which often outdrew boys' games in those days, was played with six young women to a team playing "girls' rules," which included far less movement and contact than boys' basketball.

And when women softball players got too good (read, better than boys), they were often labelled "dykes." Although there was some truth to the stereotype—softball did become important to lesbians both athletically and socially—it was an example of the lid placed on women's athletic possibilities. So long as big money was not involved, so long as male entitlement was not threatened, women could play in their own corners of SportsWorld, unobserved and left alone.

Didrikson's L.P.G.A. was still struggling, and women's track and field had yet to take off; it would be another six years before the graceful, willowy Wilma Rudolph won three gold medals in the 1960 Olympics to become a female role model that did not threaten men.

While boys were learning through team sports to network and cooperate as preparation for the business world, girls were isolated, directed into noncompetitive activities or individual sports that prepared them to be healthy housewives alone all day until the kids came home from school. It was a fifties' mentality that the Moffitts—white Protestants who believed in hard work, discipline, and stereotypical sex roles—could easily buy into. Betty Moffitt was a homemaker and sometime Avon Lady. Bill Moffitt was a fireman. They encouraged Sissie and Randy to play sports. Bill started coaching her to run, jump, and throw when she was four years old. He carved her first baseball bat. She could play with little boys only as long as she was a little girl.

The softball championship was just about the highlight—and twilight—of Sissie's baseball and football careers, which her parents declared "not ladylike." She was given the choice of tennis, golf, or swimming, none of which was immediately appealing. But her father said, "You run a lot and you hit a ball, I think you'd like tennis," at about the same time a new friend at school tipped her to the free lessons being given at the municipal park by a retired man in his sixties. Clyde Walker was delighted with this large—5-foot, 4-inch, 125 pound—enthusiastic, strong, "hungry" girl who loved to run and belt the ball.

"I knew after my first lesson that I had found my destiny. It was so clear. I couldn't wait for my mom to pick me up, and I remember jumping into this green DeSoto that we had, fluid drive, and jumping up and down on the seat saying, 'Mom, mom, I found what I want to do with my life. This is it.'

"And she's going, 'That's fine, but you've got homework and your piano lessons,' and I said, 'No, Mom, you don't get it. This is it. Let's go home and tell Randy and Dad.'"

Critical in her parents' support, says King now, was their insistence that both children play for themselves, for the love of the game and not for them; they did not need to live their lives through their kids' lives.

It was assumed that if Randy was good enough, he'd become a pro baseball player, and that if Sissie was good enough, she'd have some nice tennis experiences and some travel but would never be able to make a living as an athlete.

Somewhere around age twelve, said Billie Jean at age fifty, she began to doubt such conventional wisdom. She would become the best in the world and she would change the world, and she would make money at it.

"You know, I remember sitting at the Los Angeles Tennis Club, watching the sunset on the grass, and I knew I wanted to change tennis. I wanted to be number one and I wanted to take it to the people, this sport where you can run and hit a ball and have to be able to think and use your mind.

"The ball never comes over the net the same way twice. Not ever in a lifetime. You have to be in the solution, you have to identify problems, and you have to know, like in a chess game, how to develop a point. Of course, I couldn't articulate all that back then."

It is unclear at what age King was able to articulate her more visceral take on tennis at its best: "After I hit a perfect shot, my heart pounds, my eyes get damp, and my ears feel like they're wiggling, but it's also just totally peaceful. It's almost like having an orgasm—it's exactly like that."

King's almost mystical sense of destiny, along with the support of her parents and a municipal park system in Long Beach that encouraged youth athletics, created a rare starting block. She was also helped along the way by the Long Beach Tennis Patrons, a local group that subsidized some of the travel expenses and entrance fees of youngsters who needed to hone their games at tournaments.

At age fifteen, Billie Jean had the unusual opportunity to take free weekly lessons for three months from a former champion, Alice Marble, who had won the 1939 Wimbledon mixed doubles with none other than Bobby Riggs. Marble was a cultivated woman who had herself been No. 1 in the world when that world demanded at least a facade of gentility from its female athletes. Beneath the facade, of course, had to be a steely will. Marble was as much inspiration as teacher; to be so close to a champion, learning how to act, what to expect, lifted King's horizons as much as her ranking.

Even hurdles seemed to help King. Like golf, tennis was a genteel (Sissie would use the word "snobby") country club sport, and this exuberant, hustling, working-class youngster was clearly not to the clubhouse born. She still is stung, as much for her mother as for herself, at being kept out of a group picture of the Southern California Lawn Tennis Association because she didn't have a "proper" tennis dress. The white blouse and shorts her mother had made for her were not good enough.

"It was always on my mind," she says. "I didn't like injustice, I didn't like being discounted because of my gender or my family."

While such a thought may have put her ahead of her time, King was still stuck in the fifties. She moved steadily up the regional, national, and international rankings. But even after she and Karen Hantze, on a diet of Mars candy bars and Wimpyburgers, unexpectedly won the 1961 Wimbledon doubles title, she came back home, graduated from high school, and dutifully tried to live a conventional life.

From 1961 until 1964, King took courses at Los Angeles State College, worked part-time, played tennis part-time, and dated another student, Larry King, who seemed as directed as she was scattered. Later she would call him "brilliant and irresponsible," but at the time she was attracted by his focus. He was a tennis player, too, and together they concocted World Team Tennis, a kind of mass bowling league for recreational tennis players, both grass roots and anti-country club in concept.

The Moffitts were a little cool to Larry at first but relieved in the early sixties that Billie Jean wasn't dating outside her religion or race. Her father had threatened to "disown" her if she ever dated a "colored boy." He was hardly out of tune with his times; in fact, his support of her passion for tennis was progressive. A 1961 *Mademoiselle* article on skiing—it was atypical at the time for women's magazines to deal with sports at all—focused on what a woman should wear apres-ski. The title was

"Ten Ways to Score with a Man." Feminine hygiene ads in women's magazines typically depicted housewives swooning over their ironing boards, reminding them of their weak physical condition at that time of month. (Ten years later, the ads in those magazines had women with a tampon in one hand, a tennis racket in the other—the menstrual period now barely punctuation at all.)

Betty Friedan's *The Feminine Mystique*, the wake-up call and sacred text of a new wave of feminism, came out in 1963. It is not clear if King read that book at age nineteen and absorbed its message that women were entitled to full equality and unlimited choice in how they lived their lives, but a year later she made her big choice. With Larry's encouragement, she quit her desultory college education and accepted a three-month, all-expense-paid trip to Australia from a tennis patron named Bob Mitchell. She would get free lessons from Mervyn Rose, a former world-class player turned world-class coach. Only by total immersion, by dismantling her game and rebuilding it, would she ever have the chance to become the number one singles player in the world.

Today, it would be an obvious choice, but in those days it was every bit as bold a declaration of independence as Ali's "I'm free to be who I want," another key statement of 1964.

King credits Larry, whom she married in 1965 and later divorced, with "really waking me up to what it means to be a feminist." They were walking across campus one day when he suddenly said, "You're a second-class citizen." Larry pointed out that he, as the last man on a six-man tennis team, had gotten financial aid while she, with a world ranking, the best known athlete in the school, couldn't get any.

"That's the day I became a feminist," she says. It was soon afterward that she decided to go to Australia and commit herself to her game.

It was a good time to go for it. There was a vacuum in women's tennis—the American champions, Maureen Connolly and Althea Gibson, had retired—and the social ferment of the times would create a climate in which tennis players could finally become professionals instead of pampered guests.

By the sixties, the amateur ideal—playing for love instead of money—

had as long a history of perversion in tennis as it had in college football. There were a few pros like Jack Kramer, Pancho Gonzalez, and Bobby Riggs operating on the margins of the game, barnstorming and hustling, but they had little prestige and few big paydays. Meanwhile, most tennis players were considered amateurs—there was no other way to qualify for the major tournaments such as Wimbledon and Forest Hills. The players often stayed with wealthy patrons during tournaments and were expected to be grateful guests; it was how they were supposed to act as well to the officials who ran the tournaments and slipped them cash in brown envelopes. In 1967, when King was No. 1 in the world, she made about four thousand in under-the-table payments. And she hated it. She wanted to be independent, above board, free to be an equal.

King also sensed that tennis was on the cusp of change; the stodgy old amateur officials, those bush-league Brundages who lived for the control they exerted, would soon be swept aside in the new wave of agents, corporations, endorsements, and contracts that was sweeping through major sports.

The amateur officials had problems with Billie Jean, despite her crowd pleasing box office style. She talked about money and freedom too much, she acted too much like a man. She knew change was coming, and she wanted to be part of it and profit from it directly. She wanted to control her own destiny.

Between 1965, when King returned from Australia with new strokes and tactics, and 1968, when "Open" tennis—amateurs and pros playing together, the pros for cash, the amateurs for silverware—began as the first giant step toward today's all-embracing, big money professionalism, King established herself as the most important woman player of her time. She rose to No. 1 in the world in 1966, a ranking she held four other years (she was in the top ten for seventeen years), and she won the first three of her six Wimbledon singles titles in 1966, 1967, and 1968. She won the U.S. title in 1967 (she would win it three more times) and the Australian in 1968.

She also began to accumulate $1,966,487 in career prize money, an astonishing amount considering her late start as a pro and the relatively meager purses of her time. Nowadays, also-rans on the tour retire with more than she did.

King also began to court the press; she was accessible and outspoken, always good copy. "I'd like to get away from this sissified image of tennis," she would say. "I mean, after all, they stop the action because a player's got a blister. The fans have to laugh; they've seen hockey players get their teeth knocked out and keep playing."

And those fans should hoot and howl, she said, as at any other game. If someone was clinking jewelry in the stands, there would be glares from the court and ushers would rush over. Reporters at courtside were not allowed to type during a match lest the clicking of their little manuals upset the concentration of the pampered pets of sport.

Tennis has yet to achieve fan friendliness, but with the arrival of Open tennis, power shifted from the amateur officials with the legal rule book in one hand and their illegal brown envelopes in the other, to the players and the promoters who could now deal over the table.

But in the mad dash for the new money, the men simply shouldered the women aside, taking a bigger piece of tournament prize money and in some cases squeezing them out entirely. It was assumed that fans came to see the men play. For two years (1968 until 1970) the women lobbied, agitated, and complained.

The event that ultimately set them free was promoted by Jack Kramer, a former champion. In Kramer's tournament, men's prize money was $12,500, women's $1,500. Led by King, a group of women threatened to boycott unless the distribution was more equitable. Kramer refused and nine women signed $1 contracts with Gladys Heldman, publisher of *World Tennis* magazine, to start their own tennis tour. The move caused a great deal of wrangling at the time and threats of suits and countersuits between the new group and established tennis bodies. The press tended to cover Billie Jean as a "radical" leading a "breakaway" group. Her own analysis was that she was trying to create an opportunity for a group of desperate, determined women with few options for making a living at their chosen profession.

With the backing of Joseph Cullman, CEO of Philip Morris, Heldman promoted the first all-women's pro tournament at the Houston Racquet Club. It coincided with Philip Morris' marketing of a cigarette for women whose slogan was "You've come a long way, Baby." The Virginia Slims tournament was born.

For all of her candor on most issues, King tends to blow smoke on the debate over the seemliness of a cancer-causing agent sponsoring a supposedly healthful event, especially as the lung cancer rate of women rose along with the number of women in sports. As were most of the women pros, King was grateful for the sponsorship and quick to defend Philip Morris, then and now.

"Not one of the Virginia Slims players has ever been asked by those who work for Philip Morris to smoke, appear in cigarette advertising, or otherwise endorse smoking," wrote Billie Jean in an editorial-page letter to *The New York Times* in 1993. She went on to state that women's tennis might be a "mere footnote" to the men's game without "the bold stroke of corporate leadership provided by Philip Morris."

Bold stroke or devil's deal, without cigarettes, claim Billie Jean and other female pros, they would not have made a living. This is a touchy issue among some feminists because the soft porn Virginia Slims ads certainly offered a mixed message—those independent women smoking and stroking in the ads were clearly sex objects. How long a way had they come, baby?

On the other hand, didn't women have the same right as men to buy into the sometimes corrupted world of commercialized sport? Years later, as more and more women received college athletic scholarships, the argument raised its ugly head again: what's the point of gender equity if all it means is that women are going to become another talent pool for the gladiator shows of higher education?

King and other women athletes are not sure such a critique is fair; why should women be held to a different standard? What's equality about?

Money, for starters. In 1971, when King became the first woman athlete to earn $100,000 from prize money, President Nixon called to congratulate her. She hit six figures again in 1972. By 1973, the money was being spread around; the Slims tour reached twenty-two cities and distributed $775,000 in prize money. (The men's tour that year encompassed twenty-four cities and gave out $1.25 million.)

"There are three differences between the men's and the women's game in tennis," King said, in what seemed like one long, lively interview in those years. "Men hit harder, because they're stronger, but otherwise we're just as good. Men get more good business deals, because the game is run by men. And men tank more matches than women do. I guess we just have more pride."

Her relentless courting of the press in those years was critical; the media treated women athletes shabbily, if it noticed them at all. (There were very few women sportswriters in those days. An excellent football writer named Elinor Kaine was denied a seat in the Yale press box for a pro football exhibition game in the 1960s, forget about going into a locker room.) Women's sports were not covered on a regular basis, and only the controversy swirling around the first woman jockey, little league player, or minor league umpire got much play.

Meanwhile, Billie Jean was everywhere, playing in her crowd pleasing, flat-out style, posing for ads, giving interviews day and night. Her marriage to Larry was mostly a business partnership. Even when they were traveling through the same city, they stayed in different hotel rooms. She wanted a divorce, but there was simply no time for the meetings and paperwork. King says she came to realize that the two probably should never have married, but the times had required a kind of nod to "normalcy" which she had respected. It also didn't hurt to be "Mrs. King" while building up a sport, a lesson she might have learned from reading about Mrs. Zaharias, who received far more respect than Babe Didrikson.

Nevertheless, as she reported in 1970, "Almost every day for the last four years, someone comes up to me and says, 'Hey, when are you going to have children.' And I say, 'I'm not ready yet.'

"And they say, 'Why aren't you at home?'

"And I say, 'Why don't you go ask Rod Laver why he isn't at home?'"

In retrospect, King's protestations seem disingenuous. She would often allude to the "fantastic," albeit infrequent, sex she and Larry had during their years of a bicoastal marriage. Actually, insiders on the tour knew that Larry was seeing other women and that King seemed particularly intimate with her traveling companion/hairdresser/secretary, Marilyn Barnett.

The issue of lesbianism among female athletes, which had only begun to be discussed frankly during the ascendency of Martina Navratilova, was particularly complicated in the early seventies. Men and women threatened by feminism used the specter of lesbianism as a form of control, much the same way that cold warriors yelled "Commie!" to close a debate. It was a particularly effective tactic for those manning the barricades against gender equity.

Some of women's sports' most devoted fans were lesbians (the late Dinah Shore's annual golf tournament was known as a lesbian convention), and there is no doubt that many fine athletes were lesbians. Women tennis players have always maintained, however, that there were more gay men than women on the tour, and that the mostly male sportswriters would never question a male player's sexuality or write sly innuendo. But for all that, and despite the positive responses that "liberated" women were getting, female athletes did not feel secure enough to either "come out" or dismiss the discussion by saying it didn't matter. They also were not comfortable enough to align themselves with the feminist movement.

How could they, in a climate in which a respected sportswriter like Edwin Shrake of *Sports Illustrated* could write of the Slims players, "Nobody had a beard...not a lumberjack in the group."

Or, as the *L.A. Times*'s Pulitzer Prize–winning columnist Jim Murray would write, "King has never forgiven nature for the dirty trick it played on her in preventing her from being free safety for the Green Bay Packers."

Whispers about King's homosexuality, however, were temporarily silenced by reports of her abortion. Finding herself pregnant in early 1971, she wrote in her autobiography with Kim Chapin, she went ahead with an operation she found far less painful or traumatic than her knee operations or the yanking of her wisdom teeth. She did think the cost,

$580, was "ridiculous," and both she and Larry thought it was "wrong" that he had to sign permission papers. She told only a few friends.

A year later, Larry handed her a *MS.* magazine petition calling for the national legalization of abortions. King says she thought she was merely supporting the issue; when the petition was published, it was headlined "WE HAVE HAD ABORTIONS." Again, uncharacteristically, King hedged when asked directly in press conferences if she had had an abortion.

It would be many years later, again in the age of Martina, that Billie Jean's odd combination of boldness and shyness would make more sense. She was not entirely comfortable in her skin, she was certainly not easy in her sexuality, and she had a very fifties concern with privacy in matters she considered intimate or that might embarrass her parents. She both pushed for change and respected tradition.

Claiming she disdained "labels," King distanced herself from "card-carrying women's libbers"; yet like them, this spiritual daughter of Babe Didrikson recognized that SportsWorld was an important arena in which to push women's claims for equality. What other televised area of American twentieth-century life more publicly displayed male power, more openly boasted of male superiority, more exclusively defined separate and unequal roles for men and women, and more visibly symbolized a bastion of male entitlement?

So when it really counted, when it came to more public matters of performance, promotion, or quests for fairness, Billie Jean could—as she would say—"go for it."

She became a symbol of female possibility and a catalyst for social change. She was an inspirational force in the passage of the 1972 Educational Amendments Act whose Title IX declared that "no person on the basis of sex should be excluded from participation in any educational program or activity receiving federal financial assistance."

While this was aimed at the broad spectrum of college and university programs, it would have the most obvious impact on sports. Male athletic coaches and administrators dreaded the possibility that their programs would be cut to pay for legally mandated participation for women. They did their best to undermine this challenge to their power, this perceived threat to American manhood.

Title IX went into effect in 1978, yet well into the nineties, according to an NCAA report, while women represent more than half of all college students, they make up only 30 percent of varsity athletes. Men receive 70 percent of scholarship money and 83 percent of recruiting money. Ironically, even though men campaigned against women's sports and manned the barricades against gender equity, they have profited from it far more handsomely than women.

In 1972, more than 90 percent of coaches and administrators of women's collegiate athletic programs were women. By 1990, more than 50 percent of coaches and 80 percent of administrators were men.

But there have been enormous gains. Before Title IX, only 11 percent of college athletes were women, and there were hardly any scholarships. The effect of the law was dramatic: between 1970 and 1977, the number of young women participating in organized high school sports rose from 300,000 to 2 million. Gymnast Mary Lou Retton's successful 1984 gold medal campaign drew as much coverage as any other Olympic competition and put her face on a Wheaties box.

Although women are still struggling, in less than a quarter of a century sport has gone from a tainted "unfeminine" activity engaged in at one's personal risk to a respectable, sometimes highly lucrative activity.

It's a long way indeed from the supercharged atmosphere of sex, sport, feminism, and gender equality in which Bobby Riggs's 1973 "Mother's Day Massacre" of Margaret Court brought Billie Jean to the barricades.

That match captured the imagination of the country, particularly among women, and even among those who did not publicly identify themselves as supporters of women's liberation. Billie Jean became a heroine who was easy to love, a chunky, flat-chested, bespectacled, outgoing, friendly, married twenty-nine-year-old with no radical agenda ("It's not women's lib," she would crow, "it's women's lob").

She had a real sense of fairness and the ability to connect her life with everyone else's. "Being a girl was not the only thing I had to fight," she told Frank Deford of *Sports Illustrated*. "I was brought up to believe in the well-rounded concept, doing lotsa things a little, but not putting yourself on the line. It took me a while before I thought one day: who is it that says we have to be well-rounded? Who decided that? The people who aren't special at anything, that's who. When at last I understood that, I could really try to be special."

She was pitted against a villain so piggish he was making antifemale remarks just to jack the side bets. There were wagers in offices around the country. The match dominated the monologues of television comedians. The Saturday before, at halftime of a football game against Penn State, the Stanford band formed the letters BJK and played the feminist anthem "I Am Woman."

Two nights before the King-Riggs match, the author Grace Lichtenstein heard Riggs say of his opponent, "On the court, she's like greased lightning. She makes me look like I'm in slow motion. I haven't played three out of five sets since 1950; I'll be lucky to get through three."

As she recounted in her book on women's tennis, *A Long Way, Baby*, Lichtenstein then asked Riggs why he was the betting favorite to win. He replied: "This is my cup of tea, my dish, this pressure, this circus stuff. I don't believe that she's as stable as I am with the eyes of the world on us."

When ABC hired Jack Kramer to assist Howard Cosell in the broadcast booth, King told Roone Arledge that she would not step on the court if that old foe of women's tennis were broadcasting. It took Arledge a while to realize she was serious and substitute Gene Scott, an amateur player and tennis entrepreneur. King's friend on the tour, Rosemary Casals, would be the third voice.

By showtime, King was calm enough to breeze through an Astrodome cocktail party for her supporters, many of whom had bet on Riggs. "Thought I'd say hi. How are you doing?" The drinkers were shocked; with twenty minutes to go why wasn't she at least praying? She laughed. "I've done everything I can."

King was, as she likes to say, focused "in the now." She would let nothing shake her concentration. Or spoil the spectacle. She was carried out on the arena floor like Cleopatra, in a gold litter held aloft by four muscular athletes from nearby Rice University. Bobby was wheeled in on a rickshaw pulled by six professional models in tight red and gold outfits, "Bobby's Bosom Buddies." As spectators in the $100 courtside seats sipped champagne and a band blared brassy march music, Riggs presented Billie Jean with a large Sugar Daddy candy bar. He received, in return, a brown baby pig.

It took King two hours, four minutes, to beat Bobby, 6-4, 6-3, 6-3, a crushing rout before 30,492 spectators, the largest live crowd ever to see a tennis match.

In Neil Amdur's classic account of the match in *The New York Times*, he wrote: "Mrs. King squashed Riggs with tools synonymous with men's tennis, the serve and volley. She beat Bobby to the ball, dominated the net, and ran him around the baseline to the point of near exhaustion in the third set, when he suffered leg cramps and trailed, 2-4.

"Most important perhaps for women everywhere, she convinced skeptics that a female athlete can survive pressure-filled situations and that men are as susceptible to nerves as women."

The millions who watched the television broadcast received another less obvious lesson from this "battle of sexes." Along with the expected partisan squabbling between Scott and Casals ("Bobby walks like a duck") were the surprising comments of Cosell, who by this time was perceived as a "New York liberal," especially because of his support of Ali on constitutional grounds.

But here was Cosell, father of two grown daughters, opening the broadcast with "Some have said that there's not been anything like this since Minnesota Fats played Zsa Zsa Gabor in billiards" and later describing Billie Jean as "a very attractive young lady and sometimes you get the feeling that if she ever let her hair grow down to her shoulders, took her glasses off, you'd have somebody vying for a Hollywood screen test."

And, finally, "There's the velocity that Billie Jean can put on the ball, and walking back she's walking more like a male than a female."

Such comments, unspeakable a few years later, were worth raised eyebrows then; in 1973, the preeminent sports journalist of his time hadn't quite gotten it yet.

But the ad men got it. Besides the $100,000 winner's purse and the $75,000 each was guaranteed from the ancillary rights, King and Riggs both made far more, both directly and from endorsement deals.

King had the final summation: "This is the culmination of nineteen years of work. Since the time they wouldn't let me be in a picture because I didn't have on a tennis skirt, I've wanted to change the game around. Now it's here. But why should I want a rematch? Why any more sex tennis? Women have enough problems getting to compete against each other at the high school and college levels. Their programs are terribly weak. Why do we have to worry about men?"

A year later, she broadened the thought: "To me, women's liberation means that every woman ought to be able to pursue whatever career or personal lifestyle she chooses as a full and equal member of society without fear of sexual discrimination. That's a pretty basic and simple statement, but, golly, it sure is hard sometimes to get people to accept it. And because of the way other people think, it's even harder to reach the point in your own life where you can live by it."

As she found out. First, there was Chris Evert. Then there was Marilyn Barnett.

King and Evert appeared together on the cover of the February 3, 1975, issue of *People* under a headline that angered both of them. It read: "Bye Bye Billie Jean, Hello Chris."

The thrust of the story was that the Evert Era in tennis had begun now that Billie Jean, the "fiery feminist dynamo," had softened and Chrissie, once a "placid all-American teenager," was revving up, on and off the court, to be more like King. Chris's game was becoming more exciting, as was her social life (she had recently broken off her engagement to Jimmy Connors; Burt Reynolds was in the future) and her involvement with the Women's Tennis Association. She had supplanted King as No. 1 in the ranking's; more important, she would become No. 1 in America's heart.

"People like to put labels on people," said King in long-range retrospect. "It makes them comfortable. I think I make people uncomfortable. They don't know what to do with me. They like people who are safe, who are easy to understand on the outside. Chris Evert was a perfect example. People felt safe. The girl next door, ultra feminine and still could win. You know, she's probably the most competitive player I ever played against."

Evert, eleven years younger than King, was embraced as America's sweetheart—nonthreatening, heterosexual, a Daddy's girl. She wore makeup and jewelry on court and played a "ladylike" baseline game. She seemed ... vulnerable.

Evert laughs at that in 1994, a shrewd forty-year-old who had to grow up in the limelight. "I never felt vulnerable. I felt in control. Single-minded. Tunnel vision, that was me. Killer instinct."

King was among the first pros to reach out to the youngster (most were jealous of the early attention Evert got) and helped her through her breakup with Connors. King and Evert became—and still are—close friends. But the two were pitted against each other in the media, as were Chris and Martina when their oncourt rivalry flared a few years later. Part of it was plain old dramatic writing, and some of it had to do with supplanting King with a seemingly more malleable figure. But there was also the sense that Billie Jean—like Babe Ruth, Jackie Robinson, and Muhammad Ali—was too independent a spirit to be allowed any controlling interest in the game. In 1981 she found the limits of her freedom.

That year Marilyn Barnett, the secretary/hairdresser/traveling companion, sued Billie Jean for half of her income during the seven years in which she claimed they were lovers. Billie Jean at first denied the allegations, then began damage control. She went on television so Larry could tell Barbara Walters that his lack of attention had driven her into Barnett's arms. She wrote a new autobiography. None of it helped that much. While King won the case, she spent so much money on lawyers that she had to postpone her retirement from the tour for two years.

"It cost me millions of dollars overnight. Within twenty-four hours, every corporate sponsor dropped me. I was thirty-seven, finishing up my career, and it was devastating to think people made their decisions because of that."

The case may also have set back World Team Tennis, that wonderful early idea of how tennis should be played. Warm up with a friend, not an opponent. Four point games, one set matches. Total games won are as important as matches won. Gender is not devalued; women's and mixed doubles matches are important. And please cheer. Continuously.

By the mid-nineties, the professional side of WTT was a firefly season between Wimbledon and the U.S. Open in which teams of stars, including such old goldies as Martina and Jimmy Connors, played for various cities toward a championship.

The recreational side was a national network of men and women, seniors and kids, hackers and trophy hounds, breaking down the barrier between the ersatz classism of the game and the pure orgasmic fun of finding the racket's sweet spot. King gave clinics, gave advice, and hectored middle-aged fatties into overhead smashes they would carry in their dreams forever—all with her trademark missionary zeal.

Billie Jean is the greatest evangelist the game has ever known. Tennis may be too limited for her; she may need her own religion. Of course, she thinks she has it. It seems to be about tennis but it's really about being a full and equal member of the club. It suffuses anything she talks about, and King is ready to talk about anything. Movies, for example.

In a November 1982 interview with Susan K. Reed, she said: "I went to see *E.T.* the other night. I loved it…. There was only one thing really wrong with it…when those boys soar off into the sky on their bikes, not one girl gets to fly…. I kept thinking of all the little girls who were thinking, 'Hey, I want to go on the bike in the sky, too.'"

PART VI

POSTMODERN IDOLS

CHAPTER FOURTEEN

ARNOLD

SCHWARZENEGGER

EYES BULGE, TEETH GLEAM, OILED BODIES BULGE AND PULSE IN A SHOWER OF LIGHT
under a wave of orgiastic screams. Professional bodybuilding contests
are the closest thing to public masturbation this nation sanctions. And
like our other flesh-lust sport, boxing, it found a controversial, charismatic Moses in the late-twentieth century to lead it into our living
rooms. Ali was the "onliest fighter they ask questions like a senator."
Arnold Schwarzenegger may one day be the only senator they ask questions like an idol.

Arnold has always said that he could only have done what he did in
America. The ultimate immigrant, his voyage from the boondocks of
Western Europe to the golden coast of California was a kind of journey
home.

Unlike most idols, Schwarzenegger possessed perfect pitch for
the tenor of his times. He tapped into America's obsession for self-
improvement and its quest for the body beautiful and injected them with
hormones from his homeland—discipline and grandiosity. He became
the fulfillment of a century-old movement hatched in the turnvereines

of Midwestern German immigrants. Even while critics dismissed him as looking like a "condom stuffed with walnuts," derided his reactionary politics, and heckled his screen performances, Schwarzenegger smoothly stroked his own myth to cultural climax.

In the nineties, as American politics shifted to the right once more and his wooden acting style spawned an entire school of action heroes, his last laugh echoed over and over again, from Muscle Beach to Hyannisport.

But Schwarzenegger's story is really about American's obsession with strength, whether it was personified by Paul Bunyan and Babe, his Blue Ox; the Great John L. and lesser white hopes; or those colossi of clout, the Bambino and the Mick. It all came full circle in Arnold's time.

After so much tragedy and struggle, just as women and people of color were discovering their own history and successfully making claims to equality and opportunity, the call went out for a cultural icon who could signal it was time to close the gate and return power and control where it belonged—in the hands of white American males.

If there was no Sir Galahad to ride bearing the colors of the power elite, at least there was a Terminator.

Arnold Schwarzenegger was born July 30, 1947, the year Secretary of State George C. Marshall announced a plan for European recovery and Jackie Robinson joined the Brooklyn Dodgers.

Thal, in rural Styria, Austria, was filled with the brokenhearted in the wake of Hitler's fall. One of them belonged to Gustav Schwarzenegger, local police chief and leader of the department's marching band. Embittered by the loss of the national dream, he drank hard and drove his two sons, a year apart in age, even harder.

Meinhard was older, blond, and charming, and Gustav made his preference clear.

"Arnold is a bastard child!" he would bluster, and the terrified future Mr. Universe sometimes wet his pants.

Many weekends Gustav took his sons out for lessons in rivalry and domination, pitting Meinhard and Arnold against each other in sprints, boxing matches, and ski races. Umpired by Gustav, ties usually went to Meinhard, and Arnold learned to dread the final ritual. Bowing in defeat, the loser was forced to admit his own inferiority to the victor while Gustav would try to weave some lesson around the humiliation, some moral about discipline and dedication.

It was in the movie theater in nearby Graz that young Arnold first glimpsed possibilities for himself, drowning his pain in double features and discovering his hero in the Hercules movies starring bodybuilder Reg Park. Perhaps for him in later years the nexus between athletics and entertainment was less the epiphany of a jock already at center stage than the innate understanding of a frustrated thirteen-year-old. But before all of that came a more fundamental desire: the dream of strength.

"Weakness is a crime" sounds like Hitlerism, but it was in fact the mantra of Bernarr Macfadden, American fitness guru and flamboyant showman who elevated bodybuilding to spectacle through the use of lights and makeup. His rise from hardscrabble poverty in the Ozarks to international fame and fortune predated Schwarzenegger's by a hundred years, but both were self-made men who began by remaking their own bodies.

Macfadden, publisher of dozens of magazines that promoted the burgeoning "physical culture," was notable but not alone in his crusade.

The new technologies of western capitalism had created a class of "brain workers," clerks, secretaries, managers, and accountants whose flabby guts and frayed nerves would betray America as it geared up for imperialist adventurism and moral and economic supremacy. Exhorted onward by religious groups and temperance organizations, informed by techniques brought over by various immigrant groups, the fitness movement of the last century flowered into a lifestyle suitable for mass consumption.

You could not only eat Sylvester Graham's crackers but follow his ascetic program of calisthenics and vegetarianism. Or you could cleanse your soul and your colon simultaneously with Dr. Kellogg's regimen. Various schools, theories, beverages, and contraptions competed for attention in fitness magazine ad pages. Spring and pulley ancestors of the Nautilus machine could be delivered to your doorstep along with a few volumes to guide you on your path to health. Quacks and placebos dominated the market, not unlike today's cable television culture of body priests and powershakes.

The ideal craved by consumers—and promised by instructor and huckster alike—was that of the "muscular Christian," the mythical white "uberman" popular in serial books and cartoons. It was this ideal that got the credit for cleaning up the frontier by eradicating the "red savage," but unless good Christians did their duty and developed strength and stamina, they would be overrun by heathens of other hues—African-Americans and newly arriving immigrants. The SportsWorld of the next century would feed on this anxiety, and it is from this place of fear the call would go up for a white Christian muscular enough to tackle Jim Thorpe or knock out a "nigger" bad as Papa Jack Johnson, and, ultimately, ace Billie Jean King and the jockettes who were beginning to encroach on the sacred domains of masculinity, in and out of SportsWorld.

Bodybuilding, an offshoot of the fitness craze, was brought into vogue by Macfadden and others but was always rooted in antiquity's notion of the perfect physique. At different times in history, other cultures privileged the hairy endomorph or the lithe miler as ideal body types, but bodybuilding in the West from Macfadden to Charles Atlas to Schwarzenegger was an expanding cartoon from the classical Greek and Roman statues.

Bodybuilders are not as strong as the thick-bellied, neckless weightlifters with whom they share a mutual disdain—nor are they as fit as many seemingly less-developed athletes who exhibit no "cuts." But they inhabit a world where to appear powerful is to possess power, where pose is performance. Young Arnold may have already understood that as he sat in the movie theater in Graz watching Hercules/Reg Park toss styrofoam boulders across a cheesy soundstage.

The local Hercules, a former Mr. Austria, Kurt Marnul, was said to consider Meinhard, with his broad shoulders and slender hips, better championship material, but he invited both boys along to train at his gym in Graz. It was Arnold who proved a natural for the rigors of the gym.

The two brothers, once close, drifted apart. Arnold began to distance himself from his whole family. When his father died years later, Arnold shocked many by refusing to break training and attend the funeral.

Arnold found a new family with Marnul and the Graz bodybuilding community and a new patron named Alfred Gerstl, a Jewish business-man who invited Arnold into his home and laid out training table feasts for his promising investment.

Meanwhile, along with the muscles, a different Schwarzenegger began to emerge, confident and charming but still tinged with the bully streak he had developed as a defensive reaction in younger, more vulnerable days. When they were kids, Arnold and Meinhard used to terrorize the neighborhood children, and once they even beat up the milkman. Gustav, as chief of police, always kept them out of serious trouble.

Now Arnold found a different source of protection. As his physical transformation unleashed a newfound charisma, Schwarzenegger began to assemble an entourage of fellow-bodybuilders and hangers-on, people to laugh at his pranks and pump his ego.

Arnold's first years at the gym in Graz not only set him toward paths of muscular glory but allowed him the chance to study the art of the psych-out. One story has him prescribing a special diet to a worshipful neophyte that included increasing portions of salt. The young man went to the hospital, and Schwarzenegger continued to hone a brand of gamesmanship that bordered on dirty tricks and would someday make him nearly invincible on the posing platform, even on those rare occa-sions when his body betrayed him.

Arnold stayed in Graz for a few years, working as a bricklayer, often living at the gym, and a few times posing for the photograph collections of older men. This was a common source of income in those days, one of a number of secrets in the bodybuilding subculture and perhaps its most innocent; drugs and homosexuality are the true taboo subjects among bodybuilders.

He entered regional contests and did well, gradually learning the intri-cacies of competition, the interplay of tone and symmetry and definition along with more intangible qualities like presence, poses, and music.

Bodybuilding contests maintain, as do figure skating and beauty pageants, a veneer of empirical criteria that masks the outcome's largely subjective nature. One of Schwarzenegger's greatest skills was manipulating that outcome, which at times was as simple as having the backdrop color changed to better contrast his skin tone and blur the definition of a darker-skinned rival.

After he turned eighteen, Schwarzenegger began compulsory service in the Austrian army. He was stationed near Graz in a tank division. It was the fulfillment of a childhood fantasy and perhaps a good testing ground for his later incarnation as a Hollywood commando. He continued to train and packed away a lot of army food.

Meanwhile a buzz was building about him in the bodybuilding world, and some German muscle magazines dangled sponsorship offers if he went to the Junior Mr. Europe contest in Stuttgart. Schwarzenegger knew the army would never give permission for such a dalliance, but how could they understand the sacrifices he had made to get even this far? His decision to go AWOL was a defining moment in his life. He returned to base with the title and spent a week in a stockade cell, where even officers came by to congratulate him.

In the spring of 1966, his army service completed, Arnold went to live in Munich and train with a newfound soulmate, a bodybuilder and ex-boxing champion from Sardinia, Franco Columbu. They worked out in a gym owned by Rolf Putziger, who knew a meal ticket when he saw one. Arnold was mop boy and king of the gym at the same time, cleaning for his keep while out-training everyone.

Schwarzenegger made a lot of connections, but his best friend was pain. Pain would introduce him to size, and size would deliver him.

"I have no fear of fainting," he once said. "I do squats until I fall down and pass out. So what? It's not going to kill me. I wake up five minutes later and I'm okay. A lot of other athletes are afraid of this. So they don't pass out. They don't go on."

Like many athletes, the bodybuilder pays fanatical attention to the body's signals so that they can be disregarded.

When Schwarzenegger did an interview with Barbara Walters to promote *Pumping Iron* years later and admitted to past use of steroids, his candor was so disarming that no one blinked twice. This was, of course, before "roid rage" became the scandal of the day—before anabolic monsters rose up from the sports pages to devour everything in their path before succumbing to the auto-destruction of tumorous tissue. It was before the banning of sprinter Ben Johnson when his urine tested positive after he won the 100-meter dash at the 1988 Seoul Olympics, and before the lament of Lyle Alzado, the football player who blamed his brain cancer on steroids. But it was no revelation inside SportsWorld.

From the ancient Greek Olympians through nineteenth century French cyclists, to modern American ball players, athletes have used various chemicals—alcohol, cocaine, caffeine, opiates—to enhance performance. But nothing works like steroids, laboratory-manufactured derivatives of the male hormone testosterone.

During World War II the Nazis injected steroids into their stormtroopers before an attack. East German Olympians, women especially, became notorious for steroid use during their gold medal rush of the fifties and sixties, evoking outrage in the amateur athletic community while at the same time raising interesting questions about gender construction. The recent controversy surrounding Chinese swimmers and the use of human growth hormone has engendered similar protests and tensions on the international scene.

Steroids have never been a substitute for training; in fact, users tend to train harder because they tire less easily and their muscles repair faster after injury. Steroids simply "rev up" a biological function. The synthetic testosterone flows through the bloodstream and clings to muscles along the way, creating a chemical effect that increases size and stamina. Steroids certainly have something to do with the fact that nineteenth century strongmen look puny and undefined beside today's average male action movie star, or, for that matter, pumped-up yuppie lawyer.

The psychological effects of steroids have been well-documented. Steve Michalik, an ex-Mr. Universe who was expected to replace Schwarzenegger during the late 1970s, almost died from steroid use on several occasions and in a *Village Voice* article by Paul Solotaroff recalled his bouts with destructiveness and his absurd sense of jock entitlement and invincibility.

"Here I was, a church-going, gentle Catholic, and suddenly I was pulling people out of restaurant booths and threatening to kill them just because there weren't any tables open.... I was a nut, a psycho constantly out of control—and then, thank God, the contest came, and I won it and got off the juice and suddenly became human again."

During one episode, Michalik cut off a truck on the highway, ripped off its door, and smashed the driver's face with one punch. But for all his brushes with disaster, even Michalik escaped the fate of one colleague who, Michalik remembered, tried to stop a speeding Buick head-on with his bare hands.

In the shadowy world of bodybuilding in Munich in the 1960s, there were always rumors of violent incidents, some involving Schwarzenegger, but the authorities tended to treat these situations the way a father who happened to be police chief might. Besides, Schwarzenegger claims that bodybuilders of his era never approached the dosages of today's athletes.

After he left the army, Arnold conquered the junior circuit and went to London to compete in the Mr. Universe contest. Bodybuilding was still in its dark ages then, proffered the same respect as roller derby or pro wrestling by sportswriters and devoid of an Avery Brundage or Kenesaw Mountain Landis to goose it with sham moralism. The National Amateur Bodybuilding Association (NABBA) was the nominal governing body, but the promoters, magazine publishers, dumbbell hawkers, and power pill pushers ran the show. This shady confederation did know how to turn a profit, however, and the Mr. Universe contest became the Super Bowl of bodybuilding.

Schwarzenegger went mostly to "network" and pick up some training tips and posing techniques. Barely out of his teens and up against veterans, he did not expect to do that well. But as he swelled into his final poses, his body pumped and gleaming, his cocky good nature coming through his grin, the crowd went wild.

When Schwarzenegger lost on the scorecards to more proven

contenders, the audience booed the results. They had found their idol, as had one of the judges, a British promoter named Wag Bennet who felt he had glimpsed the future in Arnold. He took him home to plot world domination—but not before Hercules himself, Reg Park, gave Arnold the once-over and predicted greatness for his biggest fan. Little did he know.

By 1968, after winning his second straight Mr. Universe title, Schwarzenegger was the top bodybuilder in the world. He came to America.

He arrived in the so-called "hard year": King, Kennedy, and the Chicago Convention. If anyone bothered to ask Arnold what his political views were, his answers would not be much different from what they are now. That could easily be him doing his duty for his country in Vietnam, or his father the cop left with no alternative but to break Yippie heads in the streets of Chicago.

Life was no calmer in Europe. The British were in Northern Ireland, the Prague Spring in Czechoslovakia was due for an early frost, and the Situationists had finally forced a real situation on the French government as Parisian students and workers rioted.

It was Joe Weider, the godfather of the bodybuilding world, who first brought Schwarzenegger to America. Weider, raised poor and scrawny in New York, sculpted his own Horatio Alger myth that began with him hefting junked machine parts in empty city lots. He went on to publish the first bodybuilding magazine and was largely responsible for helping to move bodybuilding out of the freak tent. Now he headed the International Federation of Bodybuilding (IFBB), a rival to the NABBA, and he needed a Joe Namath, a golden boy, to carry the IFBB through its infant stages. He invited Schwarzenegger to Miami for the IFBB version of the Mr. Universe contest. Schwarzenegger packed a gym bag along with his homegrown arrogance.

"I'll eat them up, baby," he proclaimed.

Pasty and a little soft, not to mention jet lagged, Schwarzenegger lost to America's Frank Zane. He slinked back to his hotel room, humiliated and far from home, and cried himself to sleep. That was probably the worst it ever got for Arnold Schwarzenegger.

Soon after, he signed a contract with Weider that paid a salary plus training expenses in return for Schwarzenegger's promotion of Weider magazines, events, and products. His name appeared monthly over a ghostwritten column in which Schwarzenegger supposedly offered training techniques. There was no mention of the salt diet.

Schwarzenegger moved to Santa Monica, California, America's bastion of buff, and convinced Weider to sign on his buddy Columbu as training partner and play pal. Though he sweated and swung with gusto, Arnold never veered from his path to self-improvement, taking college courses to master both English and the intricacies of his own business deals. He took control of his career as precisely and methodically as he had his body. He knew that the victory stands of bodybuilding tournaments were merely platforms for the next step up.

California was a perfect place for Arnold in the sixties and seventies, brimming with beautiful bodies and sexual openness but still gripped by reactionary American politics. The popular Californian Ronald Reagan was governor. The soon-to-be-unpopular Californian Richard Nixon was president. Arnold supported them both, as he would later support George Bush.

As far as the struggle for racial equality and empowerment in America went, Schwarzenegger never shied away from expressing his opinions. "Black people are inferior," Wendy Leigh, in her unauthorized biography, claims Schwarzenegger once told black bodybuilder Dave DuPre. "They are stupid," he supposedly continued, proposing a genetic theory to explain inherent disadvantage among African-Americans.

It is not known whether this was a sincere belief or another psych job on a fellow competitor, but such statements rarely came back to haunt Schwarzenegger. Unfortunately, there is no reason to think they would. Only a half-century earlier, Americans had trumpeted hysterical fears of race dilution to restrict opportunities for African-Americans and to limit Asian and European immigration. The "science" of eugenics was promoted. Americans today still earnestly debate the merits of *The Bell Curve*, a 1994 book that argues that intelligence, in large measure, is hereditary, with blacks falling out at the bottom of the curve.

Schwarzenegger's racism, of course, might be viewed from another angle. The only man he feared, the only one who knew how to beat him, was black.

Originally from Cuba, Sergio Oliva was a respected champion with a magnificent physique and the rare ability to shake Arnold's confidence. Backstage at the IFBB's Mr. Olympia competition, when Oliva took off his trademark overalls and subtly flexed his lats in Schwarzenegger's direction, the Austrian felt all his power drain away. They carried on a war of tiny gestures for years—and built an epic rivalry along the lines of Frazier-Ali.

Both men peaked for the 1970 Mr. Olympia contest, and it was here that Schwarzenegger's gift for head games reached its full flowering. Already distracted while he was pumping up backstage by a rumor that Schwarzenegger had gone out for french fries, Oliva finally met his nemesis one-on-one in the last pose-down. The two of them fired their muscles at the crowd, popping and flexing and smiling, twisting into poses that sent volcanic ripples across their bodies and orgiastic shrieks through the crowd. After a while Schwarzenegger leaned toward Oliva and whispered, "I'm tired, let's stop now."

Oliva consented.

"You lead off," said Schwarzenegger, and they walked off together while the crowd screamed for more. Once Oliva had reached the wings Schwarzenegger turned around and made for the lip of the stage. He posed alone to ecstatic applause and victory.

It was this kind of hunger for glory, loyalty to the crowd, and showmanship over any sportsman's code that set Schwarzenegger apart and propelled him to the top. It also led George Butler, a freelance photographer, and his writing partner, Charles Gaines, to cast Arnold as the star of their book on the bodybuilding scene, *Pumping Iron*. The book would prove popular, but the subsequent movie would transform Schwarzenegger and the sport forever.

Around this time, Schwarzenegger has claimed, he studied the life of Ali. Ali was once said to be the most recognizable man on the planet. A similiar case could be made for Arnold through the eighties and early nineties, but the gulf between them, like the eras themselves, is vast.

If Ali came to symbolize the Oppressed's confrontation with the Oppressor in the struggle for human and civil rights, Schwarzenegger, as sociologist Harry Edwards suggests, embodied the ethos of self-gratification that reached its peak in the greed of the eighties.

Ali may have had nothing against them Viet Cong, but Schwarzenegger always would, and his style of gee-whiz patriotism was calibrated perfectly to suit changing times. He was no prude, but there was nothing subversive about him. Through his succession of box office smashes he filled a cultural void left vacant by John Wayne, the "Duke," and abandoned by more sensitive American-born actors of his generation. Somehow, punctuated by his cartoon presence and off-kilter delivery, Schwarzenegger's glib carnage and strong-arm tactics seemed acceptable once more. Only Sylvester Stallone did more for the Gulf War.

Schwarzenegger's tenure as President George Bush's fitness czar and his marriage to television journalist Maria Shriver, a member of the Kennedy family by birth, signaled his political ambitions. The nineties have seen him soften his image, a recent example his portrayal of a pregnant man in *Junior*, a flop that may have taught him a lesson—stay tough! He has become a successful business mogul as well, but it's too early to tell what his political plans might be, or precisely what platform he might embrace.

Ali meant different things to different people, but he was always a distillation of their hopes for change, for the idea of principled rebellion. What Schwarzenegger offered was permission to not give a damn about anything but your pecs and your portfolio. This spirit maintains its strongman's grip. Ali is a distant punchy memory to many a grown-up Reagan child who, glimpsing a photo of Tommie Smith and John Carlos, might wonder what those weird gloves were for and why someone had forgotten to emblazon the words "Just Do It" across the bottom of the picture.

Schwarzenegger's desires rested on the axis of pleasure and pain. He became a conduit for the submerged desires of more and more Americans coming back from the successes and failures of the civil rights, feminist, and antiwar movements who resolved to make money instead of history, to work on their bodies and their buzzes.

By 1977, when the movie *Pumping Iron* opened, Arnold had conquered all in his path. If Oliva was Schwarzenegger's Joe Frazier, then Lou Ferrigno was his young George Foreman. Ferrigno, television's future "Incredible Hulk," was not incredible enough. Schwarzenegger beat him out for the 1974 Mr. Olympia title at New York's Madison Square Garden. Once more the crowd worked itself into a ritual frenzy; Schwarzenegger, like Ali before him, was on the way to becoming a crossover idol, just like the one both men studied—Elvis Presley.

Three years later the rest of the world found out what all the excitement was about. *Pumping Iron*, billed as a documentary about the bodybuilding world, was really a paean to Schwarzenegger, who through the course of the film struts, preens, and intimidates his way to the 1975 Mr. Olympia title.

That the contest takes place in South Africa amidst a growing storm of boycotts and controversy over apartheid never seemed to bother Schwarzenegger. He seems focused on the belief that this film would make him a superstar; his performance, both in competition and during his "off-guard" moments, never wavers from this goal. Though people appear shocked at the end when he announces his retirement, it seems nothing more or less than the savvy resolution of an astute scriptwriter, namely Schwarzenegger.

Pumping Iron plugged into a rebirth of physical culture in America that began in the sixties. Everyone seemed to be jogging, and though they might smoke pot, they gave up cigarettes (or tried, anyway). Natural food stores and health clubs formed a powerful consumer complex as people took their vitamins and exercised on gleaming new machines that worked on principles not so different from the spring and pulley contraptions of a hundred years before. As they had a century ago, dozens of spiritual and physical culture movements competed for attention and money.

The American people's fascination with Schwarzenegger translated into fascination with themselves, which in turn fed their fascination back to him. People began to imagine possibilities for their own quads and lats, and they yearned to feel powerful.

Schwarzenegger tapped into male insecurities about masculinity. The women's movement had chipped away at unearned entitlements in the bedroom, boardroom, and ball field. If some people did not actually move into the gym, they still yearned for the sense of dominance Schwarzenegger seemed to exude with overmastering ease.

As the anthropologist Alan M. Klein wrote in *Little Big Men: Bodybuilding Subculture and Gender Construction*: "Though he may not realize it, every man—every accountant, science nerd, clergyman, and cop—is, or has been, engaged in a dialogue with muscles."

After *Pumping Iron*, Schwarzenegger became the mediary in this dialogue for millions of people. His crossover gender appeal brought women's bodybuilding out of the basement, too. Now there are as many gradations of pumped women as men, from hardcore professionals to ordinary working women, perhaps former high school or college jocks themselves, looking to keep toned and fit.

At the same time, the reactionary cultural politics Schwarzenegger often espoused onscreen and in interviews helped cement dominant gender constructions in American society at the very point it could be most effectively challenged. Instead of celebrating bodybuilding as a site for reimagining and recreating the body along new gender lines, most leading women bodybuilders try to compensate for their "manliness" with heavy makeup and traditionally feminine hair styles. Subject to gay baiting regardless of their sexual orientation and competing to survive in a limited market, they can't be blamed; as women become stronger and more visible, they become more vulnerable to attacks as "witches" or "bitches," not really women at all.

On any given day you can turn on a cable television sports channel and see men and women bodybuilders in action, thanks to Schwarzenegger.

In his book, *The Education of a Bodybuilder*, Schwarzenegger wrote: "I wanted every single person who touched a weight to equate the feeling of the barbell with my name."

That wish came true—and stayed true—as millions serve life sentences in gyms and health clubs across the country.

Weakness is still a crime.

CHAPTER FIFTEEN

MICHAEL JORDAN

BEFORE HIS DEFECTION TO THE FIELD OF DREAMS, BEFORE HIS CHAMPIONSHIP dominance with the Chicago Bulls, before his literal embodiment of corporate America and the true national pastime—consumerism, Michael Jordan stood for one thing: Michael Jordan.

And he defined that potent symbol with one shot.

The Georgetown Hoyas and North Carolina Tar Heels were counting down the seconds in an epic final game for the 1982 NCAA basketball championship. All tournament long these two teams had been barreling towards one another, each under the command of a revered, dynastic coach whose powerful teams and lip service to scholastic achievement made them college sports icons, Knute Rockne's of their time.

John Thompson of Georgetown was huge, intense, and stern, one of the few black coaches in the history of Division I. Now at the top of the heap, he was perhaps the first black coach given a real chance to build a solid program. His brave commentary on the exploitation of black college players had earned him respect, admiration, and enmity

throughout the college basketball fraternity, but what he really wanted was a title. His star center, Patrick Ewing, gave him his best chance in years.

Dean Smith of North Carolina was an institution in his own right, the most popular man in the state, lauded for his commitment to his players' education but haunted by the ghosts of tournaments past. His teams had lost in the finals before. Given the talent he had on the floor, especially future National Basketball Association stalwarts James Worthy and Sam Perkins, this could be as good a chance as he would ever have.

But the untested can rise to the occasion in a game like this, too. The last few minutes had belonged to one of Smith's freshmen, Michael Jordan, whose three quick baskets, a steal, and a rebound had brought the game to the brink. Smith called time-out and surveyed his team huddle at courtside.

There were seventeen seconds left in the game.

Georgetown was leading, 62-61.

There was time to set up one more shot. Win or lose. Who would take the shot? The obvious decision was a choice between Perkins or Worthy. But Smith knew that Thompson, like most good coaches, specialized in squelching the obvious. So Smith turned to Jordan.

"Make it, Michael," he supposedly said.

And Michael did, for all time.

Just imagine the moment. Sixty thousand screaming fans in the New Orleans Superdome, two Georgetown players bearing down on him as the ball snaps into his hands on a pass from the top of the key. Jordan rises, tongue out, and floats a rainbow to the basket, seventeen feet away. And the ball does what it always does in hoop daydreams—it swishes softly through the net before it drops to win the game and make the dreamer a legend.

People like to say that Michael Jordan transcended thorny issues like race and economic equality and so became the locus of universal adoration, of commercial monotheism: one shoe all could wear, one god all could love. Despite his stunning skills, athleticism, and knack for coming through in the clutch, Jordan did not transcend racial and social divisions in this country. Rather, his easy charm and corporate halo helped some to forget about them and gave others shallow justification for the status quo.

Before he made that famous shot, Jordan was another talented but lesser-known basketball player at a major college program, distinguished by the fact that unlike most everyone else competing at that level, he had once been cut from his high school varsity team.

After the shot he was on the path to becoming simply Michael, elevating the game and the resulting fortunes a player could reap from it. But Jordan worked hard to get to every place he got. His genious lay in arriving at the perfect time.

He was born on February 17, 1963, into a loving home with middle class aspirations, the fourth child and youngest boy of James and Deloris Jordan of rural Wallace, North Carolina. James, a sharecropper's son, had risen from forklift operator to supervisor at a General Electric plant. Deloris worked as a bank teller.

The Jordans instilled the spirit of hopeful integrationism into their children. "You just didn't judge people's color," Deloris remembers teaching her children. The Jordans's ethic of racial harmony, clung to in the turbulent, divisive sixties and passed on to their children as part wishful thinking and part survival instinct, seemed to take root in Jordan as he navigated the often tricky white waters of coaches, network suits, agents, and sponsors with confidence and aplomb.

Throughout his life Jordan honed his skills and fueled his desire by challenging everyone around him—friends, teammates, and family, too. Before there was Earvin "Magic" Johnson or Charles Barkley to push him to the limits of human capability there was his older brother Larry. Their epic one-on-one duels are Jordan driveway legend. Whether it was sports or cards or board games, Jordan played with an almost frightening will to win.

"Michael is a little bit of a shark," said Bulls coach Phil Jackson. "He's competitive to the extent that he'd like to beat you for your last cent and send you home without your clothes."

Tracing his evolution as an athlete and personality, some ironies reveal themselves only now. His first love was baseball, but unspoken racial lines were clearly drawn in Wallace. The white kids played baseball while the black kids were steered toward hoop. Jordan endured tension and the occasional epithet as a ninth grader en route to the Babe Ruth League's Most Valuable Player Award. This vindication remains his "favorite childhood memory."

Soon after, his passion for basketball began to emerge, even as his determination outstripped his ability. His sophomore year at Laney High School he was cut from the varsity squad, a humiliation that would end the aspirations of most high school athletes. But that summer Jordan practiced every day, hung around basketball clinics, and won the genetic lottery, shooting up to 6-feet, 3-inches. The next season he was a star.

Still, Jordan remembers typical moments of teen angst. He shared some memories with television's Diane Sawyer years later: "A lot of guys picked on me, and they would do it in front of the girls. They would joke about my haircut and the way I played with my tongue out and just different things."

That his tongue-lolling drives to the basket would someday connote control and power and sexy grace probably never occurred to the shy but driven high school kid who signed up for a home economics class because he felt he'd better learn to cook for himself. No girl would ever want him.

It certainly never occurred to Buzz Peterson, his best friend and rival guard at Laney High. "I mean, I knew he was pretty good, but I didn't think he was going to be that good," Peterson said later. No one else did either, and when the college recruiters came around it was for Peterson.

A few regional schools showed interest in Jordan. University of North Carolina coach Dean Smith's friendly home visits and avowed focus on education swayed Deloris Jordan, who convinced her son to sign the letter of intent. A player's first agent is often mom.

Peterson also became a Tar Heel, there to witness the first stage of Jordan's ascendancy. Within a year Jordan had made The Shot. Pop culture, basketball, and corporate strategy would never be the same. But how the ball came into the hands of the skinny freshman from North Carolina is another story.

It begins in 1891, during another hard winter in Springfield,

Massachusetts, where an energetic minister fretted over the physical and spiritual erosion of young men waiting for the snow to melt outside. Without a game of football or baseball, how could a muscular Christian keep his muscle tone, and more importantly, keep his Christianity?

When Dr. James Naismith nailed a peach basket ten feet up a wall, and with the help of his wife devised a set of rules that would insure a game anchored in methodical collective effort, he created something modeled on the engine of steady progress powering America toward industrial and imperial dominance.

Almost a hundred years later basketball is "showtime" to the nation's pastime, embraced and cultivated over the span of the century by virtually every ethnic group. The game has changed as much as its myriad faces, and like Jordan and his "Jordanaires," most pro teams boast a superstar and his uniformed livery, eschewing the plodding anonymity of the game's nascent years.

After several waves of immigrants, at the end of the nineteenth century, endured brave crossings to escape hopeless poverty and violence in Europe, only to be met by hopeful poverty and violence in America, the children of these immigrants—Irish, Italian, Polish, Jewish, and many more—found themselves in an alien world. While their parents toiled in sweatshops the children explored a loud and crowded maze of backlots and alleyways and tenement roofs. They discovered new games to play, like stickball or kick the can, improvised and ritualized in this new industrial landscape. And in the process they became Americans by participating in American games.

Basketball found a home here, too, at times resembling the fast and furious court games of older cultures, perhaps like the ones the Mixtec Indians used to play in the ancient cities of Oaxaca. Scholars debate the details of these games but agree that a losing team might risk sacrifice to the Mixtec gods. What Pete Axthelm later called the "city game" possessed its own stakes, like neighborhood respect and territorial violence, from the beginning.

Basketball was the city game because it was such a natural for the singularities of urban recreation. Simple and cheap, all you needed was a ball and a hole to drop it in. Immigrant white ethnic kids on Manhattan's lower east side dunked rolled-up socks into garbage cans.

"Its battlegrounds are strips of asphalt between tattered wire fences or crumbling buildings; its rhythms grow from the uneven thump of a ball against hard surfaces," Axthelm wrote. "Basketball is the game for young athletes without cars or allowances."

Even while it migrated to the cities, the game as played by Naismith-inspired teams popped up around the country, in schools and YMCA's and athletic clubs, bound in a rigid code of tactics and conduct, passed like holy scripture among coaches and players. Call it the "textbook" or "classroom" or "college" game.

Early "cagers," playing behind chicken wire screens, followed detailed game plans conceived around intricate passing sequences. Improvisation and individual style were frowned upon, and with no shot clock to spur the action, a team with a lead could stall its way to glory. Adherents of this game shared a geometry teacher's appreciation of angles and an industrialist's devotion to conveyor-belt Fordism.

Meanwhile the "city" game developed without the factory-like trappings of game clock, referee, and coach. The code of city ball was forged from experience, a delicate balance of teamwork and individual initiative. Call it the "schoolyard" or "playground" or "city" game.

Eventually, over the course of decades, the two games would more or less merge as players met and mixed in various school, college, amateur, and industrial leagues. As churches and settlement houses used basketball to reach teenagers, clutches of "schoolyard" players were molded into something like textbook teams. As schoolyard ball players were recruited by colleges around the country, the dazzle of city ball was integrated into formerly rigid patterns.

By the time Jordan was learning to play in the sixties and seventies in the rural South, the game he was watching on network television was a synthesis of those two types of play. But that synthesis took many years to spread and evolve.

Touring professional teams like the Original Celtics introduced the game to thousands more in the 1920s. The Celtics' "Big Man," 6-foot, 5-inch, Joe Lapchick, was an anomaly in his support and acknowledgment of the African-American game, which had its own rich tradition in black colleges, community centers, and school leagues. Later, as coach of the New York Knicks and St. John's University, he helped forge alliances between black and white teams who ran on parallel segregated tracks before the integration of the game and the predominance of African-Americans in basketball.

A precursor to that predominance was the Harlem Renaissance, named for the Manhattan ballroom where they played their home games, and a team most observers of the time agree was the best of the twenties. Formed by a Caribbean immigrant named Robert Douglas in 1923, the Rens coincided with a fertile age of black identity and culture in Harlem. The music of Duke Ellington, the poetry of Langston Hughes, and the flowering nationalism of Marcus Garvey made Harlem headquarters for the rising African-American elite of art and commerce.

Douglas assembled legends like Tarzan Cooper and Pops Gates to compose the nucleus of what for several seasons was an invincible team on the order of the 1980's Los Angeles Lakers or the early 1990's Chicago Bulls. Playing with a big laced ball under dance hall chandeliers, they reinvented the game night after night, thrilling the crowd with dazzling speed, tricky passing, and fierce defense.

A handful of white teams, like the Original Celtics, could sometimes keep pace, but the Rens were the unofficial champions of professional basketball until they made it official by beating the Osh-Kosh All-Stars in Chicago in 1939.

The Rens proved more than dominating, as Nelson George points out in his book *Elevating the Game*. They showed by power of example that African-Americans could thrive in all aspects of the game—playing and coaching as well as owning and operating teams and leagues. Despite the early lesson and a history of integrationist effort in schools, clubs, and professional leagues prior to World War II, the sport was not immune to the effects of Jim Crow laws in the South and custom in the rest of the country.

While the great black players of the time were systematically denied their opportunities to compete, there really wasn't much to go around; white pro basketball was a poorly paid gypsy life of draughty arenas reached after day-long car rides, not substantially better than black basketball.

The Harlem Globetrotters became a last resort, and their legacy still carries the burden of anger and resentment. Owned by a Jewish entrepreneur, Abe Saperstein, the Trotters toured the country and raked in cash with their goofy antics, all the while doing breathtaking things with the basketball. Critics view the Globetrotters as a sad example of black talent and skill exploited; the Jordans of that era, like Marques Haynes, were reduced to jokey routines in a SportsWorld minstrel show. Others, however, claim them to be innovators, their game of risk and flash clearing a path for superstars of later generations.

All the while, a new game, an ever-changing game, was rising from the playgrounds of the cities. After World War II, mammoth low-rent housing projects were erected, concrete islands built to contain the working poor, many of whom had come north during the great black migrations. Once again, as the children of these projects found themselves cut off from parks and other recreational options, the possibilities for play were reduced to one surface: asphalt. Basketball became the sport of necessity.

Nelson George and other writers have described the mirroring of basketball and jazz in the history of African-American self-expression. While Charlie Parker, John Coltrane and others created bebop and forever changed the way the world listened to music, the playgrounds spawned a new kind of soloist, judged by the magic created in midair, "above the rim." Like a jazz musician exploring a riff, stretching the envelope within a structure of notes, the great playground player expressed himself without compromising the game or losing control of the ball.

Before these days of the hip-hop soundtracked sneaker commercial, in which aesthetic decisions are made in the boardroom and rebellious fervor is just another product to download off the Internet, the new jazz and the new game both carried more than a hint of danger. Bebop revolted against the dictates of composer and conductor, claiming authorship and control in the performing moment. Playground ball provided autonomy to players, decisions made in the mix instead of the locker room, the antithesis of "classroom" ball. But there remains a symbiotic relationship between the two approaches. Much of bebop sprang from variations on established standards, and basketball also achieved its own kind of balance.

The playground game blossomed under the auspices of the community and through traditions like the famed Rucker tournament in New York, named for the playground worker who created it. The tournament often pitted college players home for the summer against local stars who never left, victims of the myth that basketball was a "ticket out of the ghetto." Legends were both created and debunked. Deities of the playground pantheon abound, but none embody its tragic trajectory like New York's Earl Manigault.

As a 6-foot, 1-inch, teenage guard in the 1960s, The Goat (because people had trouble pronouncing his last name) could pin a dime to the backboard, dunk over the seven-foot phenom Lew Alcindor (later to change his name to Kareem Abdul-Jabbar), and bring a normally blasé Harlem playground crowd to its feet in thundering adoration. Some claim witness to Manigault's "double-throwdown," or double dunk, in which he jammed the ball, caught it as it dropped through, then rose again above the rim for a second slam-dunk. Manigault has steadfastly called his double dunk apocryphal and says it is not possible. Still, it remains testament to the shape and magnitude of—and need for—playground myth.

By his twenties, though, Manigault had slipped into the netherworld of addiction and petty crime, his college career a washout, his NBA dreams in ruins. He was both hero and victim of the streets that raised him, and his fall from grace pointed to painful paradoxes in the development of city ball. It was supposed to be a way out, but so few ever made it that the names of those who did were whispered like charms across the blacktops of America, in tournaments and summer leagues often funded by the only role models left in the neighborhood—pimps and drug dealers.

"We all cannot make it," Manigault said years later, finally clean and working with kids on the very playgrounds he used to rule. "Somebody has to fail. For every Michael Jordan there is an Earl Manigault."

After World War II the most powerful pro league to emerge was the National Basketball Association, but as a spectator sport the game was small-time. Arena football comes to mind as a contemporary parallel, but it is difficult to make analogies without accounting for the difference television made for all sports. Basketball was a game many people played but fewer watched. The color line made it virtually impossible for a black player to earn a living at anything other than the clownball of the Globetrotters, but even white teams struggled to survive.

Then, three years after Jackie Robinson signed with the Dodgers, Chuck Cooper joined the Boston Celtics, the first African-American with an NBA contract. Soon after the Knicks signed ex-Globetrotter "Sweetwater" Clifton. But it was Earl Lloyd of the Washington Capitols who actually broke through the barrier, the first African-American to play in an NBA game. Within a decade integration began to transform basketball, pioneered by two clashing titans, Bill Russell and Wilt Chamberlain.

Russell, the great Boston Celtics center, practically invented modern defense while leading the University of San Francisco to two NCAA titles and an undefeated season. His prowess and technique under the boards was coupled with a moral and intellectual approach to the game and to issues of race and empowerment surrounding it. Later the first black head coach in the NBA, Russell was an innovator who often took the heat in his own time for what was later deemed noble defiance of sports hypocrisy.

Chamberlain, eventual self-styled playboy of the Western Conference during his L.A. Lakers years, grew up on tough Philadelphia streets, and his seven-foot height, bulk, and power shocked the league in the sixties far more than Shaquille O'Neal's did in the early nineties. He reveled in his size and sometimes scored at will, driving to the hole with a wild intensity that made his incredible body unstoppable.

Critics called Chamberlain selfish, undisciplined, and lazy on defense. But it is hard to imagine a white player of that era averaging fifty points a game being criticized for anything short of failing to walk on water. Threatened by his ability, sectors of white America—the sports media, especially—resorted to its trusty book of stereotypes. White athletes were "hard workers" who exhibited "mental toughness" to compete against the "natural athleticism" of African-American jocks. The same writers called Joe Louis a "jungle cat" and a "born killer." But Oscar Robertson, the third black superstar of the sixties, always left the media a little speechless. He outsmarted everyone on the court but could barely jump, let alone dunk.

Perhaps the first to really rattle perceptions of the black athlete in basketball and sweep the game into a new era of glamour was Kareem Abdul-Jabbar. Like Jordan he was no street kid. His father, from Trinidad, studied to be an orchestra conductor, his ambitions cut down by, among other things, racial presumptions in the music world. He became a New York City transit cop, and although he was bitter he tried to keep roads open for his shy, smart son. Unlike so many of his peers, Lew Alcindor grew up surrounded by books and music, encouragement and ideas.

He enrolled in UCLA in 1965 and played for the legendary John Wooden, a masterful coach in his own right who was wise enough to tailor his strategy to the strengths of this 7-foot, 2-inch, wunderkind. UCLA, already a dynasty, won three more NCAA basketball titles, and in retaliation for Alcindor's humiliating dominance, the NCAA banned the slam-dunk. Enter the skyhook.

Tucked away inside the lush UCLA campus, Alcindor submerged himself in the spiritual and intellectual pursuits that would lead him to a new life and career as Kareem Abdul-Jabbar. It was an era of self-assessment and outspokenness for the black athlete, and like Ali, Smith, Carlos, and Jim Brown, Jabbar played an important part in that process.

Though his path would be somewhat different, Jordan also enjoyed the campus cocoon during his first vulnerable years of celebrity. After the instant fame of The Shot, Jordan settled into the comfortable role of local superstar. The next year, with James Worthy off to the Lakers, the Tar Heels fell short of successfully defending their title; that summer he played in the Pan American Games in Caracas, Venezuela, where the American team won the gold medal.

Before Jordan's junior year, the Tar Heels were picked to go all the way. But disputes brewed over Dean Smith's basketball philosophy. Some felt his rigid game plans hampered Jordan. Others laid the blame on Jordan for failing to weave his skills into the fabric of the team. The criticism would trail Jordan into his early pro career, until the 1991 championship run of the Bulls laid the theory to waste. In the meantime, Indiana knocked North Carolina out of the 1983 tournament in the third round.

Soon after, Jordan announced his intention to enter the NBA draft and forgo his senior year. The decison to leave college early is de rigueur for today's "blue chip" player, but it was still infrequent in 1984. Deloris Jordan was not pleased, but the father, son, and holy coach all agreed the time was right. Smith had already gotten his money's worth in the last few minutes of the 1981–82 season, and both James and Michael knew that it would be foolish to risk a million dollar future for one more season of college ball.

Basketball was beginning to rival football and baseball in popularity, and as the craft of televising sports evolved, basketball benefited the most. Football was war waged by two armies on a faraway battlefield and baseball was an interminable chess match interrupted by infrequent spurts of action, but television showed basketball to be a fast, intimate, "in-your-face" experience. The casual fan could quickly comprehend the details of the game as ten men slam danced in their underwear on a glossy dance floor.

Like Russell and Chamberlain in the sixties, the eighties' rivalry between Magic Johnson and Larry Bird was a running sports soap opera which the NBA rode to mega-dollar eminence. They first met in the 1979 NCAA finals where Magic's Michigan State team beat Indiana State, led by the "Hick from French Lick"—Bird. Over the ensuing years, as Bird's Celtics and Magic's Lakers traded championships, ratings soared and advertisers thronged. The era of "showtime" was born.

The honest admiration Magic and Bird expressed for each other gave their competition all the trappings of fable. Bird resisted the racial symbolism some bigoted white fans and journalists tried to drape him with, but at times he was powerless; for some Bird was the last example of European-American athletic worthiness in a sport whose players were now mostly black, whose modern form was based mostly on black innovations, but whose owners, executives, coaches, boosters, scribes, and ticket holders remained predominately white. These fissures widened when Isaiah Thomas, the great Detroit Piston point guard and a bona fide peer of Bird and Magic, supported rookie teammates' assertions that SportsWorld tended to overrate Bird because of his color.

The media vilified Thomas for not denouncing the comment, but Thomas seemed to understand the complexities of the issue. The fact that Bird, who lived up to his billing, was the wrong example did not excuse the fact that historically white players were routinely overpaid and overhyped. The incident haunted Thomas throughout his playing days, but of the three it is Thomas, entrepreneur and part-owner of an NBA expansion franchise, the Toronto Raptors, who has taken his skills and determination off the hardwood and up into the management sky-box. The originator of the remarks came into his own, too, as the punk-coiffed, media-ready rebounding scourge, Dennis "Worm" Rodman.

During the 1980s the NBA underwent another sea-change in which the selling of the game and hawking of consumer products—sneakers, clothes, soft drinks, alcohol—merged into one mammoth enterprise. Bird and Magic brought the world into their playground and made it hungry for more—more basketball, more television, more Pepsi, more Bud. They pushed each other to new heights (with ample prodding from Thomas's two-time champion Pistons) and helped make the NBA the model for the rest of the corporate-athletic complex. Jordan would take things even further, but he would go it alone.

"It's what Michael Jordan is missing now," Magic said after he and Bird had retired. "He knows he has no one to measure himself against."

Against the past Jordan measured up well, even in his rookie year. He seemed to possess some of everything, from the hang time of Julius "Dr. J" Erving and the creativity of Magic, to the intensity of Bird and the peerless control of Jabbar. Basketball insiders sensed they were on a voyage of athletic discovery.

Jordan electrified Chicago fans, conditioned to the second-rate fumblings of the Bulls, and after several amazing performances word spread and crowds gathered to glimpse tomorrow's god today. There were moments, moves, explosions of power, and speed that stunned even the veterans, while fomenting jealousy, too. They saw the future and it was not them.

A few agents and executives also saw the future and proceeded to buy it. Jordan signed with ProServ, one of IMG's major rivals. They negotiated his contracts, handled his money, and arranged his endorsements. Nike was the first company to take a chance on him, and the rest is marketing and cultural history.

Jock endorsements are nothing new; idols since the Great John L. have pitched products. You can find Mickey Mantle beaming from the pages of old magazines, pledging allegiance to a brand of cigarettes, or cereal, or car. But most advertisers eschewed team athletes as spokespersons—certainly black athletes—and most products were endorsed by golfers, tennis stars, and auto racers—white performers associated with the middle class.

The unprecedented success of Air Jordans—Jordan's personalized brand of Nike basketball sneakers—was due to a combination of factors. Jordan's affable charisma was the main ingredient, and the public's demand for multicolored hightop sneakers was further whetted by a state-of-the-art campaign that included (the movie director) Spike Lee's television spots. Jordan's burgeoning popularity buried doubts about the marketing potential of a black player in a team sport, at least if his name was Michael Jordan. Later he signed with McDonald's and Coca-Cola and became the ubiquitous pitchman, synonymous with the cash and carry decade.

Air Jordans, one of many Nike designs, repeatedly outsold other sneaker companies all by itself. While suburban middle-class America mobbed the malls for them, poor kids discovered a serious drawback to looking cool. "Just Do It" translated to "just do him" as reports of kids shot dead in the streets for their brand new Air Jordans began to surface.

Many professed shock at this development, but it was no suprise to anyone familiar with the hot zones of American cities, where the bodies of young black men were already piling up. Kids had killed before for particular leather jackets and sunshades. The fury of the crack wars and the acquisitive nihilism it engendered in already impoverished neighborhoods was spilling over, and a call went up for Jordan and Nike to "act responsibly." What that meant no one was quite sure, but many looked instinctively to Jordan to somehow end the bloodshed with a word or gesture. To be a "role model."

Some African-American commentators and others expressed disappointment with Jordan for failing to reach out to the kids who idolized and identified with him. But Jordan was not a child of the streets. The comfort and security he had always known had more in common with the lives of the suburban kids who mowed the lawn in their Air Jordans without any fear of attack.

In an era when identity politics has come to the floor of public debate, the question of the African-American entertainer's accountability as role model is slippery at best. No one, it has been pointed out, ever urged Barbra Streisand to denounce the unethical practices of Jewish-American junk bond traders. Nevertheless, some point to the urgency of the cities, where the blood continues to flow in the streets, as evidence that the position of the African-American rap star or sports hero is a unique one. Styles and attitudes are readily adopted by kids who must make life or death choices at a ludicrously young age.

Pundits, politicians, and clergy have carved careers out of declaiming the evils of rap music as a cultural stumbling block to the uplifting of African-Americans. They fear that kids are getting a message to model themselves on Gangsta Rappers like Snoop Doggy Dogg or Tupac Shakur, who sell records by realizing their own mythology. If you can't rap your way to number one on the billboard charts like Snoop, at least you can emulate him by standing trial for murder.

Athletes are a different breed than rappers, generally more conservative.

But the melding of the two into the generic category of "role model" stems partly from the urgency of the situation, partly from the common bond of American music and American sports as expressions of black culture and also from the packaging of the two by advertisers. Consider it to be soundtrack and picture for the highlight reel of mass consciousness.

The veteran stars also exhibited strong feelings about Jordan's commercial stature. When Wilson Sporting Goods Company landed Jordan for a signature ball the company dropped its other stars, including Isaiah Thomas. Magic Johnson, a friend of Thomas, was resentful as well. The small galaxy of NBA stars feared a future scorched by the blaze of one obliterating sun. This led to the notorious "freeze-out" orchestrated by Thomas and the rest of Jordan's Eastern Conference teammates at the 1985 All-Star Game in Indianapolis. The rookie-of-the-year, abandoned and ignored by his teammates on the floor, was humiliated before a nationwide audience tuned in to see him up against the best.

A few nights later, Jordan got revenge when he racked up forty-nine points against Thomas and the Pistons, but the problem did not end there. Some of Jordan's fellow teammates were envious also, feeling irrelevant in his shadow, more retinue than team. They admired his intensity but resented his attitude, especially when he castigated them for mental lapses or questioned their desire to win. Unable to satiate his desire for a championship or sometimes even feed him the ball, they felt his scorn.

Early in his second season in Chicago, Jordan sat out with a foot fracture that did not heal properly. Doctors kept him out for months with stern warnings about the dangers of a premature return and the risk of never regaining his full capacity. Jordan went home to his family and brooded.

Meanwhile the Bulls stumbled through another dismal season, and when Jordan refused to join them on the road for moral support, radio call-in switchboards lit up with admonishments from Chicago fans. The truth was that he could not bear to watch his teammates' pathetic efforts. Finally, against all medical advice, Michael put himself back in the lineup for a few minutes a game. Chicago fell in love with him all over again. The gesture smacked of Hollywood, the wounded idol hobbling out into the lights of the arena to win the game and heal the city. After all the cheap shots and put-downs he had absorbed with nervy cool, Jordan suddenly belonged. He was voted an all-star and came to the game on crutches, welcomed by the NBA elite.

Through the latter half of the eighties the Bulls began to gel as an organization. New coach Phil Jackson, an ex–New York Knick, played the hippie zen master for the sake of lively copy but did little to hide his Vince Lombardi–like appetite for winning. A few trades and draft picks later the Bulls had juice. Scottie Pippen was young and prone to dumb mistakes, but the future all-star proved he could pick up any rare Jordan slack. Bill Cartwright, Horace Grant, B. J. Armstrong, and John Paxson, the three-point sniper, rounded out the squad.

Jordan kept remodeling himself. Like most top athletes his secret was relentless training. When he was not honoring an intense endorsement schedule, he was honing his game. Some experts predicted Jordan's star would fade as teams devised new strategies to contain him, but Jordan always came up with surprises. His shooting went from dangerous to deadly, and his rhythms began to flow through the team in powerful waves.

By 1990, the Bulls were more than ready to take on the Lakers in the finals, but nervous and tight, they gave away the first game. They then proceeded to dismantle the L.A. dynasty. The showdown was a culmination, a changing of the guard, but its poignancy would not fully unfold for several more months.

On November 7, 1991, Magic Johnson announced his retirement due to infection with the HIV virus that causes AIDS. SportsWorld heaved and shuddered at reality's intrusion, and while praise was heaped upon Magic for his honesty and courageous spirit, any thorough exploration of the issues was ignored.

The sympathy lavished on Magic never seemed to trickle down to the hundreds of women to whom he may have transmitted the virus, much less the millions of ordinary Americans who suffered from the same affliction. There was little moral discussion or public scorn, especially after Magic made it very clear, especially on late night variety shows, that he was not, repeat, no way, a homosexual; he had gotten the virus from one or another of the two thousand-plus women he had enjoyed.

Except for Martina Navratilova, who pointed out that any woman athlete who slept with, say, two hundred men would be called a "slut," and that if she herself had caught the virus people would say she deserved it because she was gay, few in the athletic community offered anything but sympathy. Even Navratilova said that her remarks were an attempt to emphasize the double standard; they were not an attack on Magic.

Far more than Michael, Magic had been a lovable sports hero; the unselfishness of his passing game, the passionate joy with which he played, had been a critical element in the selling of the NBA. Johnson's energy and personality, however, was never channeled, as promised, into AIDS education or fund-raising. And as far as corporate America was concerned, the infected Johnson became a disappearing act. Showtime was dead, long live showtime—now expanded to include all of the NBA, without the maestro.

The Bulls rolled through the 1991–92 season and faced the Portland Trailblazers in the finals. Some were eager to see Jordan eclipsed, and the Trailblazers's Clyde Drexler, at the peak of a career season, was often touted as Jordan's heir apparent. The coup proved short-lived, though, as the Bulls cut Portland down in six games.

That summer the U.S. "Dream Team" swaggered into Barcelona, Spain, for the 1992 Summer Olympics. They lived large, played ugly, and showed no mercy. Even some nationalistic American fans winced when Charles Barkley elbow-slammed a hapless Angolan defender without apology, then tossed off some bon mot about African teams wielding spears. The Dream Team carried out their policy of search and destroy with smug, brutish mastery, to the increasing disgust of the rest of the planet. When they stayed in four star hotels instead of the athletes' village, they merely confirmed the arrogance of Operation Olympic Scorn.

The scandal that ensued at the medal ceremony, in which Jordan and a few other Nike soldiers at first refused to wear the Reebok team jacket, then covered the logo with an American flag, was treated as a moment of clarity for those still drunk on the stale ambrosia of the amateur (sporting) spirit. It was, in fact, the Dream Team at its least hypocritical. After all, it was the Olympic officials—those supposed guardians of the sacred amateur ideal—who allowed professional basketball players to compete in the Olympics. With the collapse of the Soviet Union, the Games had lost their great East-West rivalry. They were just another sports spectacular on a crowded calendar, and they needed the best players in the world.

If only someone could have told Jim Thorpe that seventy years hence the story of his "disgrace" would make no sense at all.

The Dream Team's gambling spree in Monte Carlo while on a warm-up tour had made for some cute feature stories, but sportswriters went for the jugular when Jordan was spotted at Atlantic City gaming tables between playoff games against the New York Knicks the following season (1993).

James Jordan came to his son's defense and explained that gambling was a balm for Jordan's frayed nerves. Dropping ten grand at a blackjack table or on a putting green relaxed Jordan the same way that dollar-ante poker might help the average citizen unwind. The press backed off, still slightly ravenous.

Journalists, sports officials, and fans alike for over seventy years have made every effort to maintain ignorance about the true relationship between sports and gambling. Since the Black Sox scandal of 1919, through the point-shaving scandals of college basketball in the fifties, to the excommunication of Pete Rose in the eighties and the outrage directed at Jordan, gambling has been regarded as a monster child, born of the union of sport and society, howling from its cage in the basement, an ugly, terrible entity better left unacknowledged.

The fact is that sports and gambling are inextricably linked with varying degrees of visibility. Some sports, like horse racing or jai alai, exist solely for the wager, but every professional team game—basketball, football, baseball—has its own "line," whether betting is legal or not, and newspapers publish them. At every sporting event, there are fans who seem to be cheering inappropriately; they are gamblers less interested in who wins or loses than by the dictated margin or "spread." They have bet on how many points will separate the teams at the end of the game.

As far as the athletes themselves are concerned, they are bred for competition. That they might stake money on a contest is as natural as risking everything else people cling to, like pride or self-esteem. Like most athletes at his level, Jordan has been a pathological competitor since childhood. If it was not basketball it was cards, video games, or anything where he could stake what he had against what you had. If he was losing at Monopoly, friends remembered, he would flip over the board.

More than money was at stake for Jordan after the Bulls clobbered the Knicks and faced off against the Phoenix Suns for the 1993 title. Self-proclaimed "Nineties Nigga" Charles Barkley was making a run to supplant Jordan in the popular mind and on the airwaves. Barkley, thoughtful and outspoken, allowed himself to be packaged as an intimidator. He was halted by Jordan's astonishing but reassuringly familiar clutch heroics and a last-minute bomb from John Paxson as Jordan's Bulls prevailed in six games.

"Three-peat," the word that had entered the lexicon of sports lore like a holy grail—became a solid fact—and for Jordan, yesterday's headline. Maybe four-peat did not have the same ring. Who knows? In any case, Jordan had graver matters to attend to when the body of his murdered father was fished out of a South Carolina creek in August 1993. Jordan announced his retirement. "I have nothing more to prove in basketball," he said.

Though he denied it, many saw Jordan's departure as a response to his overwhelming grief at the loss of his father, who had also been his best friend, closest counsel, and biggest fan. Many also assumed this mourning period would end with Jordan's triumphant return to the hardwood. Soon after came another announcement. The greatest basketball player of all time was seeking greener pastures. He would play again, but it would be the game of baseball. Jordan arranged a deal with Bulls owner Jerry Reinsdorf to play for the Chicago White Sox organization. Different world, same boss.

Even as major sports magazine covers urged Jordan to "Bag It" he persisted in his dream of playing in the major leagues. Jordan told Ira Berkow of *The New York Times* that it had been his father's idea; as they watched Bo Jackson and Deion Sanders excel at two different sports, James encouraged his son to test the limits of his own athletic gifts.

By most accounts Jordan's baserunning was the only facet of his game remotely major league. His fielding skills were light years away from most minor league AAA players. He lacked bat speed.

Though many baseball insiders resented Jordan's intrusion into their sanctified sect and likened his presence to midget Eddie Gaedel's gag appearances in the batter's box for the St. Louis Browns in 1951, others saw something brave and moving in Jordan's dubious quest.

"My father used to say that you never know what you can accomplish until you try," said Jordan, a sentiment as American as basketball, hip-hop, and apple pie from McDonald's.

It is just that ambiguity about Jordan that makes him so intriguing. He was the best in the world at what he did, quite possibly the greatest player ever, and he did it with passion, and he became rich and famous. Not only did he live the daydream of The Shot, he fulfilled its wildest promises.

And then, at the height of his powers, he gave it all up—at least momentarily—to risk playing the fool at what many consider the most difficult game of all.

Was it hubris, did he want too much?

Was he willing to take on a challenge at which he could fail because he needed the challenge?

Didn't he have an obligation to his fans?

But then, wasn't watching Jordan try and fail more inspiring than watching him succeed yet again?

Of course, there was also the bottom line. No matter what he did, he still made more money than any other athlete. Not surprisingly, McDonald's heralded his return to the Chicago Bulls in March 1995 with a new round of Big Mac television commercials featuring M. J. and a host of other NBA stars.

Jordan may have given up his dream to play in baseball's big leagues, but there was plenty of room for him in SportsWorld's endorsement field of dreams. In 1994, he had a three-peat of his very own—it was the third year in a row that he topped *Forbes* magazine's list of top-earning athletes. In 1994, his income was listed as $30.01 million. Since he earned about $1,200 a month with the minor-league Birmingham Barons that year, almost all the money came from Gatorade, Wilson, McDonald's, Sara Lee, Wheaties, Upper Deck, and Nike, the real Olympic teams of the nineties, the modern major league franchises.

Our present-day commodified idols whom Jordan personifies are merely merchandized extensions of the Sultan of Swat. The main difference today is that we are all more open about sports as a business and the mad scramble between players, owners, and other capitalists for their share of the buck. If the twenties were indeed golden, then the nineties are platinum—Babe Ruth and his agent, Christy Walsh, as the forebears of Michael Jordan and IMG.

In a time of moral confusion, when the phrase "do the right thing" was a sardonic trick, Jordan seemed to have risen above the rim and stayed there, untouchable.

CHAPTER SIXTEEN

MARTINA NAVRATILOVA

AND BEYOND

"I HONESTLY BELIEVE I WAS BORN TO BE AN AMERICAN. THIS COUNTRY WAS WAIT-ing for me. It would give me friends and the space and the freedom and the courts and the sneakers and the weight machines and the right food to let me become a tennis champion, to play the best tennis any woman ever played."

This ringing endorsement of the American Century in sports was written by Martina Navratilova in her 1985 autobiography. She had defected from Communist Czechoslovakia twelve years earlier for the freedom to swing free; the Statue of Liberty was raising a racket for her as well as a torch.

Navratilova was not quite thirty years old at the time she wrote her memoir, a champion playing the best tennis any woman ever played, presumably already a multimillionaire. She was on her way to becoming, as had Arnold before her and as Michael would be, a one-name sports celebrity. As they had, she dominated and energized her sport.

War horse champion and symbol, Navratilova was the quintessential

postmodern sports performer. Her career embodied the rub between love and money that fired the late-twentieth-century athlete, and her life can be viewed as a prism of that age-old struggle to define what is masculine and what is feminine. Sport will no doubt wrestle with it into the twenty-first century.

By the time she retired in 1994 at age thirty-eight, she had earned an estimated $20 million in prize money over twenty-two years of tournament tennis. Navratilova's statistics were amazing. She played 1,653 singles matches and lost only 210 for a winning percentage of .873. She won 18 Grand Slam singles titles (including a record 9 Wimbledons and 4 United States Opens) and 31 Grand Slam doubles titles.

But her influence went far beyond numbers. As a lesbian, Navratilova expanded the dialogue on issues of gender and sexuality in sports. In the years that she and Chris Evert were locked in their fierce rivalry to be Number One, sports fans saw it was possible for two very different women, different physically and emotionally, different in lifestyle and playing style, to both be great champions—and friends.

Navratilova was also the first—and among the most visible—of a new wave of Eastern European athletes who may well transform North American sports.

"She goes from arrogance to panic with nothing in between," the late tennis couturier and commentator Ted Tinling once wrote about her. Navratilova's game and her life were always in an uproar, a reflection of tumultuous times when the pressure of the matches and rewards of victory became truly fabulous and often disruptive. Depth and subtlety may never have been her strengths off the court, but her gift for timing was remarkable; in fact, Navratilova's life is a kind of time line of the second half of the American century and a window into the future.

She was born in Prague, on October 18, 1956. That autumn, Soviet tanks rolled into Hungary. Five years later the Berlin Wall would go up, and in 1968, more tanks would rumble into Prague. Navratilova felt almost viscerally the tightening of the Iron Curtain around Eastern Europe, especially as sports, including women's sports, became a cold war arena. In America, a new Golden Age of sport was dawning; coach

Lombardi's football, Mickey Mantle's baseball, Arnold Palmer's golf and, most important for Navratilova, Billie Jean King's tennis. "Chris did it her way, I did it mine, but Billie Jean did it first," she wrote.

Skinny, quick, "boyish-looking" with jug ears and big feet, Martina grew up in rural Revnice, outside Prague. Her parents divorced when she was three, but her mother remarried; this time to a warm and jolly man who encouraged Martina to play sports flat out, to be an aggressive tennis player "like a boy." They lived in a room of the cement house that had once been part of Martina's mother's family estate. When the Communists took control of Czechoslovakia in 1948, the family's land was seized and redistributed. The room they lived in overlooked a red clay tennis court.

Navratilova has said that one advantage of growing up in a Communist nation was the equal treatment afforded to women in sports; she received good coaching early and the chance to play in international tournaments. She also grew up attracted to America by movies and music that seemed to give the lie to the Communist line on America as a land of oppression and poverty.

After the so-called Prague Spring when "socialism with a human face" was crushed and Russian soldiers occupied her country, that yearning for Western freedom became a magnet. Thousands of Czechs defected in the late sixties and Navratilova decided she would get out, too. In 1972 she won the Czech championship. A year later, the government allowed her to play the winter pro circuit in America. She was age sixteen. It would be good propaganda for the Party if she did well, and hard currency for the government.

In 1973, a peak year for women's tennis in America, Billie Jean King beat Bobby Riggs and there were two women's pro tours—the U.S. Tennis Association's and Virginia Slims. Evert was age eighteen, a rising superstar. The women's movement and women's sports, thanks to Title IX, were nurturing each other's growth.

Martina's English was limited, but her serve-and-volley game was a spectacular universal language. She was tabbed a future star. And she loved America—the freedom, the bright colors of its clothes, the availability of cheap and tasty food. She Big Mac'ed around the country. During her second year on the tour in 1974, she began seriously considering seeking political asylum. The Czech tennis federation, perhaps sensing this or, according to her, afraid she was putting herself ahead of the Party, began to curtail her trips.

In 1975, with the help of American friends and the FBI (who were, of course, always eager to embarrass the Evil Empire), she asked to remain in America. Within a month she had her green card.

Although at least one journalist referred to her as "the bisexual defector," neither Navratilova's sexual relationships with women nor her leap over the Iron Curtain was an issue that would capture the imagination of a country that considered tennis players something less than hard-core athletes. Within tennis, it was her attacking style that amazed everyone. Outside the game, both her lesbianism and defection were a kind of confirmation of traditional cold war values; of course, a great woman athlete is something less than a woman, and, of course, anyone would want to get out of the Evil Empire. Even the Russians were coming!

Twenty years later, on the eve of the twenty-first century, America's SportsWorld looms as a "new frontier," not only for invading Eastern Europeans in search of their own material dreams, but for enterprising American sports capitalists in search of international talent and markets. So far, Eastern Europeans have changed the face of professional hockey, revamped world tennis rankings, and threatened to turn basketball, that truly American invention, into an international, commercial playground where Russians and Croats body up and back door with the best that the United States has to offer.

Navratilova set the pace in tennis, along with fellow Czech Ivan Lendl, and was joined later by others, including Monica Seles, who was born in what was then Yugoslavia. At seventeen, Seles was the youngest player ever to hold the No. 1 ranking on the pro tour. (Two years later, in 1993, her career was sidetracked by a deranged German tennis fanatic who stabbed her in the back while she was seated during a courtside changeover.)

Today, many young hockey players in Canada and the United States hang their puck dreams on high-scoring Pavel Bure, the "Russian Rocket," who led the Vancouver Canucks in 1994 to their second Stanley Cup final, where they lost to a New York Rangers team with several Russians on its roster. In 1993, the first two players chosen in the National Hockey League draft were a Czech and a Russian—11 of the first 24 were Europeans as were 92 of the 284 players chosen overall in that draft.

Immigration is never without its problems. It was bad enough when burly American college boys began to horn in on Canadian ice time, but now swift-skating, sharp-passing Russians and Czechs threaten to change the tough, hard-hitting Canadian style of play even as they take jobs away from homegrown fringe players. The tough-guy network of muckers-and-grinders who came up via the thuggish Canadian junior hockey system have not taken kindly to the "snow-blowing" of the Eastern Europeans, who generally skate better, have star quality, and do not think that smashing an opponent's face into the Plexiglas is finesse hockey.

The Eastern Europeans have so far made less of an immediate impact on the NBA, although white, American fringe players are already taking cover in the face of high-priced Croatian talent actively pursued by team scouts in search of new blood and by league officials with their own agenda for international expansion: first beam games overseas, then export merchandise, then eventually sell foreign expansion franchises.

Aggressive efforts by the NBA to find new, international outlets encourage young Europeans to embrace the Chicago Bulls and buy league sanctioned merchandise. Thanks to the efforts of league commissioner David Stern, the NBA already sells its wares in forty countries and has television agreements in seventy-five. In 1988, Converse, which features NBA-licensed shoes, sold over 50 million pairs outside of the United States—some 25 percent of its total sales—in large part due to the increasing worldwide visibility of the NBA. That same year Nike sold over 40 million shoes internationally, and in no small numbers to thousands of youngsters from Yugoslavia to Spain who want to "be like Mike."

Talented European players are critical to this growth. Drazen

Petrovic, the "Dalmatian Sensation" who died in a 1993 car accident while leading the Croatian national team in the European championships, was the hub of a revitalized New Jersey Nets club. Vladi Divac hardly makes Lakers fans forget Magic Johnson and Kareem Abdul-Jabbar and Toni Kukoc will never replace Michael Jordan in the hearts and minds of Chicago Bulls fans—but who could? But along with the likes of the Celtics's Dino Radja and Lithuanian Sarunas Marciulionis of the Golden State Warriors who, in 1989, became the first Soviet player to sign an NBA contract, Eastern Europeans are making their presence felt.

Nor are they exploited immigrant labor. Represented by IMG, Marciulionis set the tone by signing a three-year, $3.8 million deal with the Warriors. Four years later, Kukoc inked a seven-year, $17.6 million contract with the Bulls.

Unlike their immigrant counterparts of a century ago, present-day Eastern European athletes come as individual performers rather than members of a mass migration. Unlike a Benny Leonard or Joe Louis, they did not grow up in this country and do not necessarily serve as beacons of possibility and hope for ghetto youngsters. More like "brain drain" engineers and physicians, they arrive as adults to practice a profession. And they have not always been welcomed by their coworkers.

Some of them, like Petrovic and Marciulionis, are idols in their own countries, even if their flight to America has enabled most of them to avoid the turmoil and trouble sparked by Soviet collapse and ethnic wars. Ignoring the tragic battles between Croatians and Serbs in her native land, Monica Seles told one reporter, "I am an individual, I play for Monica."

The tennis world, especially in the seventies and eighties, was no in-your-face macho-land. While the Jimmy Connorses and Ilie Nastases trash-talked and postured, most players, and almost all of the women, performed with a certain degree of civility. Even Navratilova and Evert, fierce rivals, could eventually find bonding connections on the tour.

Evert arrived first, reaching the semifinals of the U.S. Open at age sixteen, in 1971. She was blond, cute, demure in public, the Daddy's girl of respected teaching pro Jimmy Evert.

"I went out of my way to appear feminine," she recalled in 1994. "I didn't really want to be considered a woman athlete the way that women athletes were in those days, because they were masculine and that was a bad word, twenty to twenty-five years ago. You know, masculinity for a woman meant muscles and strength and that just wasn't feminine and I was afraid of it."

Evert's game was a calculating chess match she controlled from the baseline. America's sweetheart was also known as the Ice Maiden, although her tempestuous love affair with first love and fiancé Jimmy Connors should have given the lie to that.

But it was Navratilova, a few years younger, who was always seen as the passionate one. Her affairs with the author Rita Mae Brown, Judy Nelson, and others were marked by turbulence, lawsuits, and even violence, and her aggressive style on court was punctuated by histrionics.

Her off-court style was marked by indulgence and generosity. After famously fattening up on junk food, Navratilova bought a silver Mercedes (license plate X-CZECH) and shopped till she dropped a bundle on Rodeo Drive. She bought houses on a whim as easily as she bought dogs. She eventually brought her family to America.

Navratilova's game became more powerful and consistent with the help of the so-called Team Navratilova, a rotating group of coaches and consultants that included the golfer Sandra Haynie, the basketball player Nancy Lieberman, the nutritionist Robert Haas, and the transsexual tennis player and ophthalmologist Renee Richards.

Lieberman, a fierce competitor frustrated by the failure of the women's pro leagues, was critical to Navratilova's physical transformation from a chunky powerhouse relying on strength and talent to a lean and tireless dynamo whose stamina gave her more options on court. Navratilova became a model for the more rigorous, athletic training regimens of today's players.

Navratilova's comfort with her sexuality—she once told Barbara Walters on television that she enjoyed going to bed with both men and women but preferred waking up with a woman—was as remarkable in women's sports as any aspect of her game. As a superstar in an individual sport with few corporate endorsements, she could get away with it, but it was hardly a trend. Lesbian-bashing is alive and well in sports; in fact, female and male college basketball coaches routinely use it as a recruiting tactic, warning prospects away from rival teams by implying that their coaches are gay.

And the LPGA tour employs an "image lady" to offer tour pros the hair, jewelry, clothing, and cosmetics tips that will feminize them for fans and corporate sponsors.

For those who were not threatened by it, Navratilova's lesbianism allowed people to feel good about their degree of tolerance. It might even, as Bob Costas suggested, make a difference in their levels of tolerance.

"How are you going to look at Martina Navratilova and say, 'I admire her, but the other lesbians, they must be awful'?" Costas said in 1994. "People in public positions who are different than what the mainstream is generally comfortable with, as long as they embody the values that really matter, the other universal values of behavior and integrity, little by little they chip away at those things."

The closets of SportsWorld tend be very deep ones. Despite major events like the Gay Games, and gay and lesbian conferences and publications, gay athletes have been reluctant to come out, especially if it might affect their commercial possibilities. The lack of open discussion has made it difficult to acknowledge the historical importance of gay athletes and coaches, particularly lesbians in such sports as golf, basketball, softball, and track and field, much less to assess the gay and lesbian population in sports today. It has made it easy to use the fear of being "outed," or even of being erroneously labeled gay, as a club to maintain the routinely homophobic, misogynist perspective of the locker room, primarily to maintain the power of coaches and owners.

There were other athletes during the era besides Navratilova who contributed to what little public dialogue there has been. Olympic diving gold medalist Greg Louganis not only came out publicly during the 1994 Gay Games in New York but soon published a bestseller, *Breaking the*

Surface, in which his homosexuality was revealed as perhaps the least of his problems—he had also faced racism, dyslexia, and physical abuse. He now had AIDS. His near perfect dive moments after splitting open his head on the board during the Seoul Olympics in 1988 was an act of courage. ("Toughest sissy on the planet," later cracked the coauthor of his autobigraphy, Eric Marcus.)

Louganis's revelations about his homosexuality were no surprise within sports, and coming from a diver, no threat to traditional SportsWorld; the more artistic individual sports have never been considered bastions of masculinity.

But denial has always existed about homosexuality in the "manly" sports. The revelation in 1977 that former NFL football player David Kopay was gay was greeted with one of the great silences in sports journalism. There were few follow-ups to that story. And the announcement in 1991 that Magic Johnson had AIDS included his assurances, in press conferences and talk shows, that it came from unprotected heterosexual contact. Navratilova had her own spin on that tale.

"There have been other athletes who died from AIDS, and they were pushed aside because they either got it from drugs or they were gay," she said.

The standard is supported by the male sports fans' traditional need for trickle-down testosterone. As Knute Rockne knew when he told his Bickerdash story to roaring boosters, or when Mariah Burton Nelson wrote *The Stronger Women Get, the More Men Love Football*, that odd-shaped pigskin ball is a symbol of the kind of masculinity that shaped the country, not always to the country's advantage.

"Football represents a world where men are strong, men are violent, men are worshipped," Nelson told Jennifer Frey of *The New York Times* in a 1994 interview. "And women are absent or sex objects—the only women are those on the sidelines, showing off their underwear.

"From this, little boys get the message that the most prominent, most revered men in this culture are men who beat each other up…men who would talk about women with contempt in the locker room."

Myriam Miedzian, in *Boys Will Be Boys: Breaking the Link Between*

Masculinity and Violence, argues that in the testosterone-high worlds of football and national security, men are rarely demoted or even chastised for mistakes that emerge from overzealousness. In an interview she was even more specific about football players.

"They are taught to hurt people," said Dr. Miedzian. "Empathy has been knocked out of them. If they don't see the guy across the line as a human being, how can they see a woman as a human being? As long as you rear boys to be tough, dominant, in charge, they simply won't be prepared for contemporary women."

Although there has been real resistance among fans and sportswriters to make the link, this is clearly the subculture that helped produce O. J. Simpson. Long before a jury ever got the chance to decide whether or not he killed his wife and her friend, many people knew he slapped her around. That O. J. beat his wife, that one of the greatest running backs in football history, powerful as well as elusive, plus handsome and charming, was physically abusive to a much smaller person, calls into question not only his character but the character of all those who determinedly avoided dealing with the truth.

Remember that much of Simpson's success was based on his ability to make the dominant culture comfortable; funny and self-deprecating, he could make the soft white men who clustered around him in bars, television studios, and advertising agencies—call them "sycofans"—actually feel "studly." Typically, Navratilova had something to say about this: "We have to keep the husband and human being totally apart from sports," she said on the eve of her last Wimbledon singles campaign. "Just because you are a star or run a rental car agency doesn't mean you're a wonderful human being."

The male sports fan is still hung up on the romance of a SportsWorld that never quite existed, a psychic theme park of courage and tragedy, revenge and redemption that is rolled out every season by sportswriters who are willing to be treated with contempt by athletes in return for limited access to that male clubhouse. Few write the truth because it would deny them that access, as well as cost them readers; sports fans want to wallow in a sweaty Oz where a man can avoid his family in a socially acceptable way, quaff his Macho Lite, and pretend to care deeply about something that makes few real demands beyond lip-service. If that was the end of it, if it was no more than watching an Arnold Schwarzenegger cartoon movie, it might not be worth reforming. But the system being perpetuated is a dangerous one.

A psychologist who tests professional baseball and football prospects, Dr. J. Morrow of SportSense Consulting, Inc., has found a higher level of aggressive, even antisocial conduct among athletes than among the general public. And a Boston-based researcher, Jeffrey R. Benedict, is formulating a thesis that sports actually may condition male athletes to antisocial behavior. He is one of several people mining the police and court records for what seems to be a disproportionate number of sexual assaults by individual high school, college, and pro athletes, and group rapes by team members.

"There's a real make-it-while-you-can, sex and money attitude in sports, and it's not so different in music, acting, maybe some aspects of politics," Benedict said. "But there's a special factor here; some of our best athletes are trained in violence and deception, and they just can't turn it on and off when we want them to. And given the money involved, coaches and owners might not want to risk them losing their edge for the game."

Perhaps this is why there was such a positive response to David Williams of the Houston Oilers, who in 1993 missed a game so he could be with his wife for the birth of their first child. The outpouring of acclaim for Williams seemed very progressive at first, very nineties, the best of political correctness and modern parenting. For any one accusation that this was a demasculinization of football, there were dozens of testimonials that it was really a humanization. His teammates thought he did the right thing (the Oilers weren't Super Bowl–bound anyway), and although one of his coaches likened it to dodging combat in World War II, William's father said, "He's proved to me he is a real man." Many women's groups were ready to make him Dad of the Decade before he even changed his first diaper.

But many male fans were justifiably confused by Williams's daddy track. Some even felt betrayed. Wasn't the allure of football—supposedly even its original purpose—the confirmation of the importance of men in groups, a symbolic reconstitution of the platoon, the posse, the work gang, the factory line, where real guys knew they could count on each other to cover their backs? It was all preparation for war, remember. Did anyone slip out of the Alamo on paternity leave?

The confusion will be with us for as long as American boys are primarily reared not to be girls. The sports anecdotes supporting this are clichés: from the Little League coaches exhorting nine-year-old boys to be "men out there" to Coach Bob Knight leaving Kotex napkins in the lockers of his Indiana University players to make them more aggressive.

Despite all this fake manliness—perhaps because of it—there has been a sudden new interest in women's sports, particularly college basketball, among men as well as women. The game is played not only with an exuberant, almost giddy joy, but its reliance on finesse and teamwork evokes memories of the male game before it became a storm of dunk and howl. Is this the sportsMANship we miss from the major male collegians and the pros, those erratic sneaker salesmen who talk trash to cover the insecurities caused by their illiteracy, looming felony raps, and psychological battering of coaches who assemble and juggle all-male dysfunctional families just so they can win games? Now that more and more male coaches are taking over women's teams, one wonders how tomorrow's Bob Knights will deal with these hardworking, appealing young women.

Should we even care?

Isn't this the gender equity that will help create a level playing field throughout American society?

Or is this just a chance for colleges to make women the accomplices/victims of a system which is already morally bankrupt as far as men are concerned?

Or both.

Consider these and other confusing symptoms of postmodern sports we suffered in the waning days of Navratilova's career.

While young female athletes were burning out and copping out, that perfect symbol of the acceptably nonthreatening "feminine" athlete, the figure skater, was in the thick of a plot to maim a rival. Tonya Harding's husband and bodyguard were implicated in the clubbing of rival skater Nancy Kerrigan before the 1994 Lillehammer Winter Olympics.

The century-old struggle between player and owner shut down the National Pastime in the middle of the 1994 season. The baseball strike didn't end in time for the scheduled opening of the 1995 season, and when it did open there was no promise it wouldn't happen again. Charles Comiskey and Shoeless Joe Jackson might have been astounded by today's television revenues, salaries, and the price of a hot dog, but they would have understood the underlying issues. As former Yankee pitcher and *Ball Four* author, Jim Bouton, put it, "The owners screwed us for one hundred years and we've been screwing them for twenty. As I see it, we have eighty to go."

Hockey, which had suffered a 1994 lockout, seemed dominated by a superstar who was a marketing idol—the Mighty Duck. The Walt Disney company's new Anaheim team, the first major franchise in any sport named for a children's movie, became an enormous success—if not in the standings, at least where it really counted in postmodern sports, as the leading team logo in the sports merchandise game. Their home ice arena was named, appropriately enough, The Pond.

Mike Tyson came out of jail in the spring of 1995 after serving three years for rape. He immediately became the hottest boxer in the world and the object of a bidding war won by his old promoter, Don King, whose own jail time had been served for manslaughter.

An America's Cup challenger sent an all-woman crew to the cup trials, and it quickly squelched predictions that women didn't have the muscle to win. What women didn't have was the experience; eventually a male tactician was added to the crew, and they lost.

If that was a setback, it was balanced neatly by Nike's announcement of the Air Swoopes, the first athletic shoe named for a woman. Sheryl Swoopes had led Texas Tech to the NCAA title in 1993. Two years later, the University of Connecticut's rally to preserve an unbeaten season and win the NCAA title may have had the largest TV audience in the history of women's basketball.

Nevertheless, continuing court cases indicated that Title IX was not being observed in many colleges. In a decision expected to have implications for years, a federal judge ruled that Brown University had discriminated against women by eliminating the volleyball and gymnastics teams.

And our present-day idols? What do they represent? Charles Barkley of the NBA's Phoenix Suns has it right. In this postmodern world, he has no business being a role model unless it's good business to be one. And the fact is, when athletes attempt to step outside those parameters—witness Earvin Johnson's efforts on behalf of AIDS (which only came about because of behavior as an NBA superstar, behavior that hopefully most parents would not want their sons to emulate), or Martina Navratilova's activism on behalf of gay and lesbian rights—they disappear from the public scene, cut from commercials and endorsements.

Our new idol, the packaged television product, is the ultimate athlete created by commercial forces—the cutting edge of new technology and marketing that arcs back to Sport's first Golden Age and the culture of abundance, to Grantland Rice as the "Evangelist of Fun." And in a post–Cold War age where American leaders applaud themselves for the collapse of Communism, blithely ignoring real problems and inequities that exist in a democratic, capitalist American world, they encourage us to ignore those problems, too: instead to enjoy, consume, to become, perhaps, our own idols, narcissistic clones of the sculptured flesh that Arnold Schwarzenegger made famous but that now is hawked by everyone from Cher to Dr. Pete—an ESPN chiropractor with a Charles Atlas body who leads his daily watchers through "Bodyshaping," along with a sexy cast of sweaty weight pullers known appropriately as the Bodyshapers—poster available by toll-free number!

Where does this leave us? Does the future hold another search for a new frontier at the turn of another century—some nostalgic, simplistic, marketable wish for a world where men are men and women are women—all profitably marketed via satellite dish, television tube, and interactive video that will finally give us the chance to go head to head with Wayne Gretzky and Michael Jordan, and maybe even terminate the Terminator in our own virtual reality pose down?

Even as we contemplate such grim prospects, it's important to remember what else is possible. Our idols, even as they allow themselves to be manipulated by the dominant culture's ideology du jour, to be commodified for profit, also serve themselves. In their own determined quest for success, they provided hope, celebration, empowerment, and pride to immigrants, African-Americans, and women. In searching for their own identity, they helped others find theirs.

And more. Beneath the hype and the money and the demand to "be like Mike," they made real the beauty and transcendent essence of sport for each of us, the sense of pride and achievement that our idols could share with all of us.

It is an old story. Think of John L. Sullivan, "like the clapper of some great bell that... boomed the brazen message of America's glory as a fighting nation from one end of the earth to the other," and think of Babe Didrikson encouraging young women to just "loosen your girdle and let it fly."

Think of Joe Louis, sent by "God... from the black race to represent the human race," and Muhammad Ali crying, "Float like a butterfly, sting like a bee!"

And think of Navratilova in 1994, having just lost in the singles final of her last Wimbledon, stopping to pluck a pinch of grass to drop into the pages of her memory book.

The grass would wither and turn brown, but as a symbol of the energy, the hope, the spiritual sustenance that sport can bring, it would never die.

NOTES

LIPSYTE'S CAREER AS A SPORTS JOURNALIST AND LEVINE'S WORK AS A SOCIAL HIS-
torian of American sport are the basis of *Idols of the Game*. The authors
make use of published primary materials, especially newspapers and
magazines, and draw heavily on the work of sportswriters, historians,
social critics, and athletes. Quotations come from either the original
sources as noted in the text or from the work of those writers cited in
these notes. Citations of Bobkat Production refer to original interviews
for the Turner Broadcasting System's television documentary, also called
Idols of the Game.

CHAPTER ONE: JOHN L. SULLIVAN
Michael T. Isenberg's *John L. Sullivan and His America* (Urbana, 1988)
describes Sullivan's life and career. Elliott J. Gorn's *The Manly Art: Bare-
Knuckle Prize Fighting in America* (Ithaca, 1986) also provides details
on Sullivan's career and is especially important for understanding
Irish working-class saloon culture and the role of men like Richard
Kyle Fox in promoting boxing. Also useful is Sullivan's own *Life and*

Reminiscences of a 19th-Century Gladiator (1892). Several works provide the documentation and help explain the sense of crisis that pervaded the United States at the turn of the century and the ways in which sport was promoted as antidote. They include Harvey Green's *Fit for America: Health, Fitness, Sport and American Society* (New York, 1986), Peter Levine's *A. G. Spalding and the Rise of Baseball: The Promise of American Sport* (New York, 1985), Donald Mrozek's *Sport and American Mentality, 1880–1910* (Knoxville, 1983), and Gerald Roberts's "The Strenuous Life: The Cult of Manliness in the Era of Theodore Roosevelt" (Ph.D. dissertation, Department of History, Michigan State University, 1970). And Richard White's wonderful *'It's Your Misfortune and None of My Own,' A New History of the American West* (Norman, 1991) gives us Frederic Remington. For discussions of sport in early 19th-century America, see Melvin Adelman, *A Sporting Time: New York City and the Rise of Modern Athletics, 1820–1870* (Urbana, 1986) and Jennie Holliman, *American Sports, 1785–1835* (Durham, 1931).

CHAPTER TWO: JACK JOHNSON
Randy Roberts's *Papa Jack: Jack Johnson and the Era of White Hopes* (New York, 1983), a full and rich interpretation of Johnson's life, provides much of the detail for this chapter. Equally important is Al-Tony Gilmore's *Bad Nigger! The National Impact of Jack Johnson* (Port Washington, New York, 1975), which, along with William H. Wiggins's "Jack Johnson as Bad Nigger: The Folklore of His Life" (*Black Scholar*, January, 1971, pp.4–19) and Lawrence Levine's *Black Culture and Black Consciousness: Afro-American Folk Thought from Slavery to Freedom* (New York, 1977), provide rich documentation of Johnson's importance to African-Americans. Jeffrey Sammons's *Beyond the Ring: The Role of Boxing in American Society* (Urbana, 1988) also provides a useful account of Johnson's career. Johnson's own *In the Ring and Out* (London's Proteus reprinted the book in 1977) offers the fighter's own version of his life. Also helpful were Lipsyte's interviews with Muhammad Ali and Nelson George.

CHAPTER THREE: JIM THORPE

Jack Newcombe's *The Best of the Athletic Boys* (New York, 1975) is the best biography of Thorpe and contains good detail of his years at Carlisle as well as of Pop Warner's career. Also helpful are Robert Wheeler, *Pathway to Glory* (New York, 1975); Brad Steiger and Charlotte Thorpe, *Thorpe's Gold* (New York, 1984); and Peter Nabokov, *Indian Running* (Santa Barbara, 1981). For an understanding of Native American history and culture see Dee Brown, *Bury My Heart at Wounded Knee* (New York, 1970); Vine Deloria Jr., *Custer Died for Your Sins* (New York, 1969); Oren Lyons and John Mohawk, et al, *Exiled in the Land of the Free* (Santa Fe, 1992); and Peter Nabokov, *Native American Testimony* (New York, 1991). Donald Mrozek's *Sport and American Mentality*, 1880–1910 (Knoxville, 1983) provides good backdrop for understanding the popularity of sport and the role played by people like Teddy Roosevelt. The definitive history of college football is yet to be written but useful on the early years of the game is Ronald Smith's *Sports and Freedom: The Rise of Big-Time College Athletics* (New York, 1988). Also see Michael Oriard's *Reading Football: Sport, Popular Journalism, and American Culture, 1876–1913* (Chapel Hill, 1993). There are many standard accounts of Olympic history, but one that deals specifically with Avery Brundage is Allen Guttmann's *The Games Must Go On: Avery Brundage and the Olympic Movement* (New York, 1984). Also important for this chapter were Bobkat Production's interviews with Dagmar and Jack Thorpe.

CHAPTER FOUR: KNUTE ROCKNE

There are a number of books and biographies about Rockne and Notre Dame football. Most useful were Murray Sperber's *Shake Down the Thunder: The Creation of Notre Dame Football* (New York, 1993); Michael Steele, *Knute Rockne, A Bio-Bibliography* (Westport, Conn., 1983); and Francis Wallace, *Knute Rockne* (New York, 1960), which, among other things, contains all the quotations about Rockne's funeral. Also helpful is Coles Phinzey, "We Know of Knute, Yet Know Him Not," and "Win One for the Gipper" (*Sports Illustrated*, September

10–17, 1979). There is also a ghostwritten autobiography called *The Autobiography of Knute Rockne* (Indianapolis, 1930). Unpublished but very helpful is William Baker's *For God, the Gipper and the Green: The Making of the Notre Dame Mystique*. The Carnegie Report on the corruption of intercollegiate sport is still an interesting read. It appears as Howard Savage, American College Athletics, Bulletin #23, Carnegie Foundation for the Advancement of Teaching (New York, 1929). On the problems of intercollegiate sport, see also Murray Sperber, *College Sports Inc., The Athletic Department v. the University* (New York, 1990). Grantland Rice's career and the influence of sportswriters generally is covered in Charles Fountain, *Sportswriter: The Life and Times of Grantland Rice* (New York, 1993). Also see Robert Lipsyte, *SportsWorld: An American Dreamland* (New York, 1975) and Grantland Rice's *The Tumult and the Shouting* (New York, 1954). Of interest is Jerome Holtzman's oral history of Golden Age sportswriting, *No Cheering in the Pressbox* (New York, 1973) and Paul Gallico's *Farewell to Sport* (New York, 1938).

CHAPTER FIVE: BABE RUTH

The two best biographies of Babe Ruth are Robert Creamer's *Babe: The Legend Comes to Life* (New York, 1974) and Ken Sobol's *Babe Ruth and the American Dream* (1974). Also see Babe Ruth and Bob Considine, *The Babe Ruth Story* (1969) and *Babe Ruth's Own Book of Baseball* (New York, 1928). Our analysis of the 1920s and 1930s is informed by Warren Susman's essays that appear in his *Culture as History* (New York, 1984). Especially important is his "Culture Heroes: Ford, Barton, and Ruth." Richard Crepeau's *Baseball's Diamond Mind* (Orlando, Fla., 1980) and Leverett T. Smith Jr.'s *The American Dream and the National Game* (Bowling Green, Ohio, 1975) also provide provocative analyses of Ruth's importance to baseball and American culture. G. H. Fleming's *Murderer's Row: The 1927 New York Yankees* (New York, 1985) is the source for many of the contemporary newspaper references to Ruth. Eliot Asinof's *Eight Men Out* (New York, 1963) offers chapter and verse about the Black Sox scandal, and Peter Levine's

Ellis Island to Ebbets Field: Sport and the American Jewish Experience (New York, 1992) tells the story of Jewish immigrants Andy Cohen and Babe Ruth. Donn Rogosin's *Invisible Men: Life in Baseball's Negro Leagues* (New York, 1983) is useful for the links between Ruth and black baseball players.

CHAPTER SIX: BABE DIDRIKSON

Based on interviews with many people who knew Babe Didrikson, William O. Johnson and Nancy P. Williamson's *"Whatta-Gal!," The Babe Didrikson Story* (Boston, 1977) is a critical source for this chapter. Also important for details about Babe's life is Babe Didrikson as told to Harry Paxton, *This Life I've Led* (New York, 1955), and Gene Schoor's *Babe Didrikson, The World's Greatest Athlete* (Garden City, New York, 1978). Paul Gallico's musings about Didrikson can be found in his columns and also in his *Farewell to Sport* (New York, 1938). Charles Fountain's *Sportswriter* (New York, 1993) provides similar material for Grantland Rice. Susan Cahn's *Coming On Strong: Gender and Sexuality in Twentieth-Century Women's Sport* (New York, 1994) offers important ideas about women and sport as well as a useful interpretation of both the Babe and the All-American Girls Baseball League. Donald Mrozek's *Sport and American Mentality, 1880–1910* (Knoxville, 1983) contains an important chapter on women and sport, and Lois Brown's *The Girls of Summer* (New York, 1992) adds to our knowledge of women and baseball. An important collection of documents relating to women and sport is Stephanie Twin's *Out of the Bleachers: Writings on Women and Sport* (Old Westbury, N.Y., 1979). Also see Allen Guttmann's *Women's Sports: A History* (New York, 1991). The literature on women, gender, and culture is vast and ever expanding. Ellen Dubois's *Feminism and Suffrage* (Ithaca, 1978) and William Chafe's *American Woman, Her Changing Roles, 1920–1970* (New York, 1974), are useful for understanding the changing nature of feminist arguments. Chafe also provides a solid understanding of the situation of women during and after World War II, as does Elaine Tyler May's *Homeward Bound: American Families in the Cold War Era* (New York, 1988).

Also important is Susan Hartmann's *The Homefront and Beyond: American Women in the 1940s* (Boston, 1992). The extensive ruminations of Betty Hicks come from her articles in the November and December, 1975, issues of *womenSports* magazine. Other reminiscences are from Bobkat interviews. See also Mariah Burton Nelson's *Are We Winning Yet? How Women Are Changing Sports* (New York, 1991) and *The Stronger Women Get, the More Men Love Football* (New York, 1994).

CHAPTER SEVEN: JOE LOUIS

Chris Mead's *Champion: Joe Louis, Black Hero in White America* (New York, 1985) provides the details of Louis's life and many of the anecdotes included in this chapter. Also useful here is *Joe Louis, Fifty Years an American Hero* by Joe Louis Barrow Jr. and Barbara Munder (New York, 1988); Louis's autobiography, coauthored with Edna and Art Rust Jr., *Joe Louis: My Life* (New York, 1978); and John D. McCallum's *The World Heavyweight Boxing Championship, A History* (Radnor, Pennsylvania, 1974). Lawrence Levine's *Black Culture and Black Consciousness: Afro-American Folk Thought From Slavery to Freedom* (New York, 1978) and essays in two collections by Gerald Early—*Tuxedo Junction* (New York, 1989) and *The Culture of Bruising* (New York, 1994)—provide important insights into the meaning and importance of Joe Louis to African-Americans. Black reaction to Louis's fights are well-recorded in Jeffrey Sammons's *Beyond the Ring: The Role of Boxing in American Society* (Urbana, 1988). Steven Reiss's "A Fighting Chance: The Jewish-American Boxing Experience, 1890–1940" (*American Jewish History*, 74, March, 1985) offers insights into the career of Mike Jacobs. Peter Levine's *Ellis Island to Ebbets Field: Sport and the American Jewish Experience* (New York, 1992) describes Jewish reaction to the Schmeling-Louis fights. William Baker's *Jesse Owens, An American Life* (New York, 1986) is the best source for Owens and the 1936 Olympics. Howard Sitkoff's *A New Deal For Blacks: The Emergence of Civil Rights as a National Issue* (New York, 1978) discusses Richard Wright's reactions to Joe Louis. Wright's views appeared in the *Daily Worker*, June 24, 1938 and in *New Masses*, July, 1938. Maya Angelou's reminiscences appear in *I Know Why the Caged Bird Sings* (New York, 1969). Malcolm X's *The Autobiography of Malcolm X* (New York, 1964), Dr. Martin Luther King Jr.'s *Why We Can't Wait* (New York, 1964), and Jackie Robinson's *I Never Had It Made* (New York, 1973) contain their words on the Brown Bomber.

CHAPTER 8: JACKIE ROBINSON

Rachel Robinson shared her thoughts about her husband in a 1994 interview with Lipsyte. Jules Tygiel's *Baseball's Great Experiment: Jackie Robinson and His Legacy* (New York, 1983) is the best account of Robinson's life and his impact on American race relations. Also important for the details of Robinson's life are Jackie Robinson's *Baseball Has Done It* (New York, 1964) and *I Never Had It Made* (New York, 1972). Robinson's years with the Dodgers are movingly detailed in Roger Kahn's *The Boys of Summer* (New York, 1971). The story of black baseball and the Negro Leagues is well told in Robert Peterson's *Only the Ball Was White* (Englewood Cliffs, New Jersey, 1970), Donn Rogosin's *Invisible Men: Life in Baseball's Negro Leagues* (New York, 1983), and Rob Ruck's *Sandlot Seasons: Sport in Black Pittsburgh* (Urbana and Chicago, 1987). Also important is Joseph Moore's *Pride Against Prejudice: The Biography of Larry Doby* (New York, 1978). Race relations in the United States in the 1940s are well-discussed in Harvard Sitkoff's *A New Deal for Blacks: The Emergence of Civil Rights as a National Issue* (New York, 1978). Martin Duberman's *Paul Robeson, A Biography* (New York, 1989) provides the story of McCarthyism, Paul Robeson, and Jackie Robinson. Robert Curvin's reminiscences about Jackie Robinson appear in "Remembering Jackie Robinson" (*New York Times Magazine*, April 4, 1982). Hank Aaron spoke to Lipsyte about Robinson and also offers his feelings about the man in Hank Aaron and Lonnie Wheeler's *I Had a Hammer, The Hank Aaron Story* (New York, 1989). Also important were Bobkat's interviews with Jesse Jackson and Harry Edwards.

CHAPTER NINE: MICKEY MANTLE

Lipsyte's interviews with Mantle from 1960 on informed this chapter as did Mantle's and Herb Gluck's *The Mick, An American Hero: The Legend and the Glory* (New York, 1985), which provides the details of Mantle's life in his own voice. There are a number of books that provide the history of the New York Yankees in Mantle's time, the best of which is Peter Golenbock's *Dynasty* (Englewood Cliffs, 1975). Jim Bouton's *Ball Four* (New York,1971) is invaluable for any inside understanding of baseball. For the impact of television on sport see Benjamin G. Rader, *In Its Own Image: How Television Has Transformed Sports* (New York, 1984); and William O. Johnson Jr., *The Super Spectator and the Electric Lilliputians* (Boston, 1971). Also important were Bobkat's interviews with Bob Costas and Jim Bouton.

CHAPTER TEN: ARNOLD PALMER

Mark McCormack's *Arnie, The Evolution of a Legend* (New York, 1967) and Thomas Hauser's *Arnold Palmer: A Personal Journey* (San Francisco, 1994) provide many of the details of Palmer's life and career that appear in this chapter. Also useful was Larry Guest's *Arnie: Inside the Legend* (Orlando, 1993). Herbert Warren Wind's "The Great Finish" (*New Yorker*, June 9, 1968) captures Palmer's style and flair on the course. Benjamin G. Rader's *In Its Own Image: How Television Has Transformed Sports* (New York, 1984) and William O. Johnson Jr.'s *The Super Spectator and the Electric Lilliputians* (Boston, 1971) describe the connections between sport and television. Susan Cahn's *Coming on Strong: Gender and Sexuality in Twentieth-Century Women's Sport* (New York, 1994) chronicles the media's treatment of African-American and Eastern European Olympic women athletes. Books that provided insights into our understanding of the 1950s include Kenneth T. Jackson's *Crabgrass Frontier: The Suburbanization of America* (New York, 1985), Taylor Branch's *Parting the Waters: America in the King Years, 1954–1963* (New York, 1988), Elaine Tyler May's *Homeward Bound: American Families in the Cold War Era* (New York, 1988), and David

Halberstam's *The Fifties* (New York, 1993). Bobkat interviews with George Plimpton, Tom Hauser, Nancy Lopez, and Jim Thorpe are the sources for their comments.

CHAPTER ELEVEN: VINCE LOMBARDI

Michael O' Brien's *Vince, A Personal Biography* (New York, 1987) provides much of the detail about Lombardi's life and coaching career. Also important are Tom Dowling's *Coach, A Season With Lombardi* (New York, 1970) and Jerry Kramer's *Instant Replay* (New York, 1968). Stanley Cohen, *The Game They Played* (New York, 1977); Charles Rosen, *The Scandals of '51* (New York, 1978); and Peter Levine, *Ellis Island to Ebbets Field: Sport and the American Jewish Experience*, provide detail and analysis of the 1950–51 college basketball scandals. Ben Rader's *American Sports, From the Age of Folk Games to the Age of Spectators* (Englewood Cliffs, New Jersey, 1983) provides a brief history of the National Football League, and his *In Its Own Image: How Television Transformed Sports* (New York, 1984) explains the ties between the tube and the NFL. The political and cultural meanings of football are discussed in Micheal Oriard's *Reading Football: Sport, Popular Journalism, and American Culture* (Chapel Hill, 1993), Mariah Burton Nelson's *The Stronger Women Get, the More Men Love Football* (New York, 1994), and Paul Hoch's *Rip Off the Big Game: The Exploitation of Sport by the Power Elite* (New York, 1972), which also contains George Sauer's views on the sport. David Klein's *The Game of Their Lives* (New York, 1967) recreates the 1958 NFL Championship Game between the Colts and the Giants. Max Rafferty's remarks appear in Jack Scott's *The Athletic Revolution* (New York, 1971). Some of the ideas about Namath and Lombardi first appeared in Robert Lipsyte's *SportsWorld: An American Dreamland* (New York, 1975). On Howard Cosell, see his autobiography *Cosell* (New York, 1973), and with Peter Bonventre, *I Never Played the Game* (New York, 1985). Roone Arledge provided his own thoughts on Cosell and *Monday Night Football* in an interview with Lipsyte. Also helpful was Joe Namath with Dick Schaap, *I Can't Wait Until Tomorrow... 'Cause

I Get Better Looking Every Day (New York, 1969) and interviews by Lipsyte and Bobkat with Joe Namath.

CHAPTER TWELVE: MUHAMMAD ALI

Much of this chapter is based on Lipsyte's many interviews with Ali, conducted over the course of thirty years. Lipsyte's *Sports World: An American Dreamland* (New York, 1975) and his *Free to Be, Muhammad Ali* (New York, 1977) are also important. So, too, is Ali's autobiography, coauthored with Richard Durham, *The Greatest* (New York, 1976). There are many other biographies and books about Ali. Full of wonderful anecdotes and reminiscences is Thomas Hauser's *Muhammad Ali, His Life and Times* (New York, 1991). Also helpful are Wilfrid Sheed's *Muhammad Ali* (New York, 1975), Jeffrey Sammons' *Beyond The Ring: The Role of Boxing in American Society* (Urbana, 1988), and Gerald Early's *The Culture of Bruising* (Hopewell, New Jersey, 1994). For Malcolm X see Malcolm X with Alex Haley, *The Autobiography of Malcolm X* (New York, 1965). On the Athletic Revolution, see Jack Scott, *The Athletic Revolution* (New York, 1971); Harry Edwards, *The Revolt of the Black Athlete* (New York, 1969); Paul Hoch, *Rip Off the Big Game: The Exploitation of Sport by the Power Elite* (New York, 1972); and Dave Meggysey, *Out of Their League* (Berkeley, 1970). For Arthur Ashe, see Arthur Ashe with Arnold Rampersad, *Days of Grace: A Memoir* (New York, 1993). Also important were Lipsyte interviews with Rocky Marciano, Nelson George, George Foreman, and Roone Arledge, and the Bobkat interview with Jesse Jackson.

CHAPTER THIRTEEN: BILLIE JEAN KING

Lipsyte's many interviews with Billie Jean King are an important source for her views and details about her life. Also important are her two autobiographies, Billie Jean King with Kim Chapin, *Billie Jean* (New York, 1974); and Billie Jean King with Frank Deford, *Billie Jean* (New York, 1982). For a history of tennis see Parke Cummings, *American Tennis: The Story of a Game and Its People* (Boston, 1957); and Larry Engelmann, *The Goddess and the American Girl* (New York, 1988). On the contemporary women's professional tennis scene, most important are Grace Lichtenstein's *A Long Way Baby: Behind the Scenes in Women's Pro Tennis* (New York, 1974); Karen Stabiner, *Courting Fame: The Perilous Road to Women's Tennis Stardom* (New York, 1986); and an unpublished Ph.D. dissertation completed at the University of North Carolina in 1993 by Mary Jo Festle called "Politics and Apologies: Women's Sports in the U.S., 1950–1985." The growing literature on women and sport in contemporary society also informed our views. Most important are Helen Lenskyj, *Out of Bounds: Women, Sport, and Sexuality* (Toronto, 1986); Stephanie Twin, *Out of the Bleachers: Writings on Women and Sport* (Old Westbury, New York, 1979); Carol Ogelsby, ed., *Women and Sport: From Myth to Reality* (Philadelphia, 1978); Susan Cahn, *Coming on Strong: Gender and Sexuality in Twentieth-Century Women's Sport* (New York, 1994); Michael Messner and Don Sabo, *Sport, Men and the Gender Order: Critical Feminist Perspectives* (Champaign, Ill., 1990); and Mariah Burton Nelson, *Are We Winning Yet? How Women Are Changing Sports* (New York, 1991) and *The Stronger Women Get, the More Men Love Football* (New York, 1994). Also important is Chris Evert with Neil Amdur, *Chrissie: My Own Story* (New York, 1982); Martina Navratilova and George Vecsey, *Martina* (New York, 1985); Bobby Riggs with George McGann, *Court Hustler* (Philadelphia, 1973); and Helen Wills, *Fifty-Thirty: The Story of a Tennis Player* (New York, 1937).

CHAPTER FOURTEEN: ARNOLD SCHWARZENEGGER
The details of Schwarzenegger's life are contained in George Butler, *Arnold Schwarzenegger, A Portrait* (New York, 1990); Charles Gaines and Charles Butler, *Pumping Iron* (New York, 1991); Wendy Leigh, *Arnold, An Unauthorized Biography* (Chicago, 1989); and Arnold Schwarzenegger and Douglas Kent Hall, *Arnold: The Education of a BodyBuilder* (New York, 1977). Harvey Green's *Fit for America: Health, Fitness, Sport and American Society* (Baltimore, 1988) and Robert Ernst's *Weakness Is a Crime* (Syracuse, New York, 1991)

provide useful material on the history of bodybuilding and Bernarr MacFadden. Also helpful is David Chapman, *Sandow the Magnificent: Eugen Sandow and the Beginnings of Bodybuilding* (New York, 1993). On muscular Christianity, see James Whorton, *Crusaders for Fitness: The History of American Health Reformers* (Princeton, 1982). Lipsyte's interview with Harry Edwards provides his views.

CHAPTER FIFTEEN: MICHAEL JORDAN

Michael Jordan's *Rare Air* (San Francisco, 1993) and Jim Naughton's *Taking to the Air: The Rise of Michael Jordan* (New York, 1992) provide much information on Jordan's life and career, as does Sam Smith's *The Jordan Rules* (New York, 1992). The story of the early history of professional basketball is well told in Robert Peterson's *Cages to Jump Shots: Pro Basketball's Early Years* (New York, 1990). On the history and meaning of black basketball, most important is Nelson George's *Elevating the Game, Black Men and Basketball* (New York, 1992). Also important are various autobiographies of professional basketball players, especially Kareem Abdul-Jabbar and Peter Knobler, *Giant Steps: The Autobiography of Kareem Abdul-Jabbar* (New York, 1983); Bill Bradley, *Life on the Run* (New York, 1976); Bill Russell and Taylor Branch, *Second Wind: The Memoirs of an Opinionated Man* (New York, 1979); and David Wolf, *Foul! The Connie Hawkins Story* (New York, 1972). Peter Axthelm's *The City Game* (New York, 1970) and Rick Telander's *Heaven is a Playground* (New York, 1976) set the stage for the 1994 documentary *Hoop Dreams* and Darcy Frey's *The Last Shot: City Streets, Basketball Dreams* (Boston, 1994), all of which deal with basketball and its relationship to African-American culture and youth. For the game's impact on another minority group see Peter Levine's *Ellis Island to Ebbets Field: Sport and the American Jewish Experience* (New York, 1992). Also important were Lipsyte's interviews with Nelson George and Earl Manigault.

CHAPTER SIXTEEN: MARTINA NAVRATILOVA AND BEYOND

The single best source for this chapter was Martina Navratilova with George Vecsey, *Martina* (New York, 1985), an unusually candid and well-written sports autobiography. Also helpful were Nancy Lieberman-Cline with Debby Jennings, *Lady Magic* (Champaign, Ill. 1992); Grace Lichtenstein, *A Long Way Baby: Behind the Scenes in Women's Pro Tennis* (New York, 1974); and Chris Evert with Neil Amdur, *Chrissie: My Own Story* (New York, 1982); as well as Susan Cahn's *Coming On Strong: Gender and Sexuality in Twentieth-Century Women's Sport* (New York, 1994), Mariah Burton Nelson's *Are We Winning Yet? How Women Are Changing Sports* (New York, 1991) and *The Stronger Women Get, the More Men Love Football* (New York, 1994); and Myriam Miedzian's *Boys Will Be Boys: Breaking the Link Between Masculinity and Violence* (New York, 1991). David Kopay and Perry Deane Young, *The David Kopay Story* (New York, 1977) and Greg Louganis with Eric Marcus, *Breaking the Surface* (New York 1995) were important; as were the Bobkat interview with Chris Evert and Lipsyte's interviews with Greg Louganis, J. Morrow, and Jeffrey R. Benedict.

ACKNOWLEDGMENTS

THE PEOPLE IN OUR CORNER KNOW HOW IMPORTANT
THEY WERE TO US: ERIC FRETZ, WAYNE KABAK, SAM LIPSYTE,
TROY PAINO, RICHARD WHITE, AND KATHY SULKES,
PRESIDENT OF BOBKAT PRODUCTIONS, INC., WHICH PRODUCED
THE SIX-HOUR TV DOCUMENTARY, *IDOLS OF THE GAME*,
FOR TURNER ORIGINAL PRODUCTIONS.